ONE MAN'S SAN FRANCISCO

☆☆☆☆☆☆☆☆☆☆☆☆☆☆☆☆☆☆☆☆☆☆☆☆☆☆☆☆

ONE MAN'S SAN FRANCISCO

☆☆☆☆☆☆☆☆☆☆☆☆☆☆☆☆☆☆☆☆☆☆☆☆☆☆☆☆

By Herb Caen

DOUBLEDAY & COMPANY, INC.
GARDEN CITY, NEW YORK
1976

☆☆☆☆☆☆☆☆☆☆☆☆☆☆☆☆☆☆☆☆☆☆☆☆☆☆☆☆

Library of Congress Cataloging in Publication Data

Caen, Herbert Eugene, 1916–
  One man's San Francisco.

  1. San Francisco—Description. 2. Caen, Herbert Eugene, 1916–
I. Title.
F869.S3C1268   917.94'61'0450924
ISBN 0-385-01427-9
Library of Congress Catalog Card Number 75–14808

To San Francisco on her 200th birthday,
this modest gift of bouquets and brickbats

ONE MAN'S SAN FRANCISCO

The Misty City

"SAN FRANCISCO, the gateway to the Orient, was a city of good food and cheap prices; the first to introduce me to frog's legs à la Provençale, strawberry shortcake and avocado pears. Everything was new and bright, including my small hotel. Los Angeles, on the other hand, was an ugly city, hot and oppressive, and the people looked sallow and anemic. Nature has endowed the North of California with resources that will endure and flourish when Hollywood has disappeared into the prehistoric tarpits of Wilshire Boulevard . . ."

In his autobiography, Charlie Chaplin thus recalls his first visit to California, in 1910. His observations are unremarkable, to be sure, but how eagerly we who are fascinated by San Francisco read these words, as we read everything we can lay hands on about the mysterious City That Was. We keep trying to solve the riddle that haunts us all our lives: what *was* there about Old San Francisco that made it so special in the eyes of the world? Why did this small city, pulsating at continent's end under a cocoon of fog, capture and fire the imagination of sophisticates who had been everywhere? If there was real magic, where did it go, or is it still in the air; and if it has vanished indeed, how responsible are we who came in the wake of the myth-makers?

Will Irwin, a respected observer who knew the pre-firequake city as well as anybody, insisted to his death that something intangible, some mystical quality, vanished in the flames of 1906. "There was only one San Francisco," he

1

often said. "The city that arose after the quake was quite another thing." To him and a few others, the new city looked, felt and even smelled different, but he must have been judging too harshly, for generations of San Francisco lovers were yet to come, Charlie Chaplin among them. In the sea gulls' scream, chunk-chunk of ferryboat paddles, naughty giggles in upstairs rooms at the St. Germaine and Blanco's and slap of cable on what Gelett Burgess called "The Hyde Street Grip"—in these things and more, the magic seems to have endured long after '06.

The city has many lives but few golden ages and most of us suspect, not without hard evidence, that this is not one of them. We stare at the ancient, flyspecked, yellowing photos of cobbled streets long gone, we gaze at the almost foreign faces of yesterday's San Franciscans, looking for the key. In their photos, they look solid, stolid, not particularly dashing. Yet they must have had style in profusion; one has only to read the lavish menus of circa 1910, the accounts of glittering balls, the stories of escapade and scandal to know they were a rare, crazy lot. Pampered, poised forever on an earthquake fault—no wonder the San Franciscan had a reputation for living fast to die young and beautiful.

Golden ages. They came in waves, inundating the young city, spreading its fables. Abandoned sailing ships in a Gold Rush harbor whose boundaries long since have been filled in. Gaslights and lamplights, fleas and sand, cobbles, cables, cobwebs and the clatter of carriages in and out of imposing courtyards. Golden ages of garish mansions on Nob Hill (how nouveaux the rich and how rich the nouveaux) and the old Palace Hotel, with one thousand items on the menu daily and ten thousand bottles of the finest French wine gathering dust in the cellars. Golden age of snobbish Gertrude Atherton, Jack (London) and George (Sterling) and a Bohemia of candlelight and Dago red (you could say Dago then) on Nannygoat Hill, the free souls wearing hand-loomed clothes and Indian turquoise jewelry, singing their way to Marin each weekend on the gingerbread ferries, the beautiful boats of extravagant proportion . . .

From the testimony, there was still magic in the twenties, described so warmly by Charles Caldwell Dobie, illustrated

2

by the filigree etchings of E. H. Suydam. Still a smallish town, maybe six hundred thousand people, but hardly any of them commuting, all of them very much involved with the life of the place, ruled indulgently by a Sunny Jim of loose rein and looser reign, a few tall buildings going up here and there, but always, more by accident than design, in the right places. "The Quality City" was one of San Francisco's least inspired slogans, but the quality was very much there. You still get the sense of it in the Flood Building lobby, at the Merchants Exchange, in the solid, built-for-the-ages exteriors of the old St. Francis and Fairmont.

The Saroyan-Sam Spade city—perhaps that was the last of it, as far as storybooks are concerned, but there is no way to give up on San Francisco, once you have fallen under its spell. You keep looking for the magic, and now and then, when the wind and the light are right, and the air smells ocean-clean, and a white ship is emerging from the Golden Gate mist into the Bay, and the towers are reflecting the sun's last rays—at moments like that you turn to the ghosts and ask, "Was this the way it was?" and there is never an answer . . .

So It Goes

I WAS LOITERING in the St. Francis lobby one day, drinking in the ceaseless ebb and flow of metropolitan life (well, actually, I was leg-watching, as usual), when it dawned on me that the old place looked different. Black boards covered the entrance to the Mural Room, where so many of us geriatric cases had danced away our youth. By pressing a beady eye to a crack in the boards, I could see that the dance floor had been ripped out and the famous murals by Albert Herter removed from the cold stone walls. The room has vanished, to become the carriage entrance to the new St. Francis Tower.

Well, as the saying goes, nostalgia isn't what it used to be, and nobody has really cared about the Mural Room, one way or another, for a number of years. Still, before the joint vanished, you'd think there'd have been one last night of what used to be called "dinner dancing," maybe with Freddy Martin's orchestra and the other forgettable accouterments of that peculiar genre: limp salads, cold creamed chicken, stale peas, runny ice cream, haughty "maitre dees," waiter captains with their hands out, and waiters whose uniforms smelled of perspiration. Dan London would be seated ringside in black tie, Dave and Marge Falk would dance every dance, and toasts would be drunk to the late E. Pym Jones, a man who took cafe society with commendable seriousness.

It's easy to make light of it all now, but those nights in the Mural Room (and the other "dinner dancing" places) were the end of our generation's F. Scott Fitzgerald era—silver slippers, rustle of taffeta, Cape jasmine gardenias and dancing cheek-to-cheek to "What's New," long before it became a KSFO news flash signature. For the memories-that-bless-and-burn dept.: Betty Grable singing with Ted Fiorito's band, Perry Como sounding like Bing Crosby with Ted Weems's orchestra, Merv Griffin playing a meek second piano to Jack Fina (or somebody) with Freddy Martin. Opening nights were jammed and *de rigueur*. If you didn't show up, it's because you were at death's or debt's door.

It was all part of the unbelievable innocence of those times—when bandleaders were actually Celebrities, and places like the Mural Room contained all the world's glamour (in truth, it was a hot, stuffy and boring room with lousy acoustics). Nevertheless, it meant something large to play there. When Dick Jurgens' young band came down from Sacramento for its first engagement, we back home all crowded around the radio nightly to listen and enthuse. One of Our Boys was Making It! When Griff Williams left the Mark to play at the St. Regis in NEW YORK, the whole city was proud. Today nobody even cares that the Grateful Dead are world famous, which may be a healthier attitude but isn't half as much fun.

Hotel St. Francis was the "Frantic" in those days—the

4

quaint nickname is long dead, too—and the Mural Room was the Muriel Room. Next to it was Dan London's $500,000 pride and joy, a vast bar with a lucite ceiling, acres of orchids and black patent leather walls. Unfortunately, it was as joyless as a mortuary lobby, which it resembled. It soon became known as "Coffin Corner" or "The Bar Sinister," but it was handy for sneaking into the Mural Room for a free dance, hoping that waiter captain Bobby Nielsen didn't catch you and slap on a cover charge. If it was the last dance, he'd look the other way while you snuggled with your girl to "I'll See You in My Dreams," and then drove up to Coit Tower to neck.

By day, the Mural Room, still hot and airless and with lousy acoustics, served as a luncheon spot for our finest ladies. I won't bore you with yet another account of the famous "Monday Lunches," which were stifling beyond belief. It is dear to my heart only because of the time Mrs. George T. Cameron swept regally in past Mrs. A. B. Spreckels' table, ignoring her completely. "Is it possible," Mrs. Spreckels was asked, "that you and Mrs. Cameron don't know each other?" "Well, dear," replied Mrs. Spreckels, "she has been very cool to me ever since my husband shot her daddy."

While I was mulling these deep purple thoughts, the news came in that Ted Lewis had died. The obituaries were strictly so-what, but not to those who remember his opening nights at the Bal Tabarin. The full flower of what passed for cafe society was there to hear him recite "I'm Stepping Out with a Memory Tonight," and when he came to the part about "I'll ride with you in a hansom through Golden Gate Park," there wasn't a dry eye in the house. Hookers sniffled, gamblers honked into silk hankies and even the washroom attendants came out to applaud. Corny as Kansas, man, but there was some sort of magic, too, and now it's all gone. Anybody care?

A Moment in Time

"LEMME BUY YOU a drink," Richard Palladian said to me in the bar of Il Trovatore. Around there, they call him "The Vegetable Man": he drives a beat-up truck around town, peddling vegetables to places like Ernie's. Once I let him buy the Campari, he owned me. "I know who you are," he said, peering into his bourbon without ice. "You write garbage. How does it feel to write garbage?" "Not too good," I admitted. The tough-looking guy behind the plank —Charlie "Baby Doll" Puccinelli—looked sternly at Palladian. "If you can't act like a gentleman, get outta here," said Charlie. "He not only writes garbage," said The Vegetable Man, "he's a prostitute." "Look, I'm warning you," said Charlie to Richard. "You're being insulting to this gentleman, and I don't like it." "Charlie," I said, "you can't insult a prostitute. Cool it—we're getting along fine." "We're not getting along at all," said The Vegetable Man, a kind of good-looking man with a ravaged face. Suddenly he arose and ran out of the place, leaving his unfinished drink. "Whaddya gonna do?" shrugged Charlie.

Il Trovatore is that kind of place. A lot of cops and characters hang out there. It's at the corner of Bryant and Gilbert, an alley masquerading as a street, right across from the Hall of Justice. Upstairs is a restaurant done in Early Marina Moderne and downstairs there's a coffee shop and this bar, with the Naugahyde armrest slashed and repaired with Scotch tape. "I don't know what's going on any more," admitted Charlie, who has lived at the same address (432 Vallejo) for fifty-eight years. "People have a drink and the next thing they're digging a knife into the furniture. Whaddya gonna do?" He and his brother, bail bondsman Boyd Puccinelli, own Il Trovatore. From it's name, you'd guess it used to be in North Beach and you'd be right.

"How old are you, Boyd?" a reporter asked. "Well," he

6

answered. "I was sixty-seven yesterday—today I'm ninety-seven." His honest North Beach face (he moved over to Bryant when the Hall of Justice moved from Kearny) was whiter than his mock turtleneck sweater. The night before, "something awful" had happened at Il Trovatore. A twenty-four-year-old black named Miles Beaver had been shot to death, right outside the door in Gilbert Street, by Officer Eugene Larsen of the Tac Squad. According to witnesses, Beaver had become enraged in the bar when Boyd referred to him as "boy." "Don't call me a goddamned boy," Beaver is reported to have said in a rage. Then he went to his car, parked in front of the Hall of Justice, and reappeared with a .45. "I thought I'd had it," shuddered Boyd. "That's a big gun. I figured he was going to kill me and maybe half a dozen others. That Tac Squadder—he saved our lives."

There were reporters and photographers around, and Boyd sat at the bar, drinking "a pale Bloody Mary"—that's the way he ordered it—and shaking his head. The phone kept ringing: radio stations wanted a statement from him. "I tell 'em all the truth," Boyd said. "When I saw he was sore, I apologized. I apologized three times. How can a guy get so sore about being called 'boy'? Somebody calls me a Dago, it doesn't bother me."

"There's no Italian problem in this country," said a black reporter in a trench coat. "You call a black man 'boy,' the trouble begins. It turns 'em off. I mean, it turns ME off."

"Is THAT right?" said Boyd. He looked honestly bewildered. "I've been a bail bondsman for forty-eight years and I never knew that. I've done a lot of business with those people, too. Can't call 'em 'boy.' Well, how should I talk to 'em?"

"The same way you talk to anybody else," suggested a reporter.

"Uh-huh," said Boyd. "Anyway, I know I'm not prejudiced. Why, my wife is very active in Youth for Service —I give a free dinner for 'em once a month in my banquet room on the third floor. You know who ate up there at the last meeting? Miles Beaver, the same kid who was killed. Hard to believe."

7

Charlie "Baby Doll" Puccinelli, behind the bar, looked at the black reporter. "Would the gentleman care for a drink?" he asked carefully.

Boyd's son-in-law, Dean Woods, a burly dark-haired young man, arrived with a copy of the *Examiner*. He was so angry his hand was shaking. "Look at this headline on the front page," he stormed. "'Hall of Justice Tiff—Tac Officer Kills Black Gunman.' What tiff? There wasn't any tiff. You ask him to leave and he comes back with a gun. And did you read the story? Man, talk about slanted! That's the most slanted story I ever read."

"Forget it," advised Boyd glumly. "All I know is I'm too old to get shot." "It's all those guns," cut in Baby Doll. "I'm no angel. Hell, I was raised in North Beach and I got in as many fights as anybody but we didn't have any guns. Say, didja know that kid who got shot—he belted me one. Look." He pointed to a bruise on his right cheek. Still, there wasn't any tiff.

"Hey, Boyd," said a waiter. "Nick Daphne is waiting to see you. You know, the undertaker. And KFRC is on the phone." Boyd sighed. "Maybe I shoulda stayed home today," he mumbled. "I never had any trouble before."

Time, Life and So Forth

THE YEARS PLAY tricks, most of them dirty. You reread the book you loved twenty-five years ago, and wonder why you bothered. You get out the old records of songs you danced to in school and shake your head over their banality (and yours). Nostalgia City: it may have been a nice place to live but I wouldn't want to visit there. And so it was with some trepidation that I went, sometime back, to see ACT's revival of William Saroyan's *The Time of Your Life* at the Geary Theater.

It was almost thirty years ago to that night that Bill's play had had its premiere—next door at the Curran—in a San Francisco that was quite different from today's. It was a smaller city then, warmer, more sentimental, and Saroyan captured its flavor with great precision. All of us, having drunk too much, as was the style, laughed and wept a little through the opening performance, and then proceeded to forget about it. After all, young Bill had a million of 'em.

I think we tended to underestimate the play, and Saroyan because he was so familiar a figure. (Bufano suffered the same fate. By being too visible, he came to be regarded as a "character," not an artist. Hemingway's stature grew less as he revealed himself more. It's something Norman Mailer should think about.)

The San Francisco of the late thirties was Saroyan's town. He was buoyantly everywhere: prowling the waterfront with the young Bridges, darting into Opera Alley (off Third and Mission) to bet at his favorite bookmaker's, drinking champagne in Sally Stanford's parlor, being lionized by lush Nob Hill society ladies, philosophizing loudly and often brilliantly over the grappa at Izzy Gomez's or the steaks at John's Rendezvous.

But miraculously, books, short stories and plays kept bubbling out of his typewriter with dazzling speed. He wrote *The Time of Your Life* in one incredible six-day burst, holed up in a hotel room. The play established him, although he was already famous among the cultists. Not only was it a Broadway hit, he was awarded the Pulitzer Prize, which, characteristically, he turned down. "Now if it had been the Nobel," he said, "I'd have taken it—that's worth money."

It turns out Saroyan was way ahead of us, and the time of his life. We failed to grasp it on that opening night here in March 1941. We thought it was funny, but just fairly: the waterfront saloon setting (not really very much like Izzy Gomez's bar), the kid playing the pinball machine throughout the play, the character repeating "No foundation, all the way down the line," the hookers ("We wuz formerly models at Magnin's"), the sadistic Vice Squad cop, the Nob Hill slummers, Kit Carson with his tall tales ("Did you ever fall in love with a midget weighing thirty-nine pounds?") and the mysteriously rich Joe, drinking champagne at his table

9

stage front and philosophizing ("I believe in dreams sooner than statistics").

Saroyan's play is mournful, moody and undated, despite the slummers and the nickel jukebox. The characters created by "that character Saroyan," as he was known, turn out to have real character. "That crazy Saroyan" turns out to have had a sane message: peace is better than war, love is better than hate and the world is infinitely sad and mad.

Armenians, midgets, playwrights—maybe there is something left of the Saroyan city . . . The same day Saroyan's play opened, Mrs. Alta Burns was walking on Market when along came this hippie girl pushing a baby buggy and begging for money "to feed my little one." Mrs. Burns gave her a quarter, and then peered under the buggy's hood. There, grinning up at her from under the blankets, was a midget. Not the kind of thirty-nine-pound midget you'd fall in love with, however. This one sported a beard.

Also that day, playwright Lillian Hellman, who wrote *The Little Foxes* among other classics, walked into Speedy's old grocery on Telegraph Hill, another timeless landmark on the Saroyan map. She had just moved into a nearby penthouse (she was lecturing at UC-Berkeley at that time) and wanted to establish credit.

"You'll have to fill out the usual form," said George Atashkarian, the Armenian who owns Speedy's. "But I'm Lillian Hellman," protested the playwright. "That doesn't mean too much to me," said George. "Look, I'm George Atashkarian—does that mean anything to you?" "No," said Miss Hellman, "I see what you mean."

She trudged back to her digs and returned with a clipping of a newspaper interview, with her picture. She got the credit. And the clipping is now tacked to the wall of Speedy's. "I get some famous customers, you know what I mean?" says George Atashkarian.

☆ ☆ ☆

IT SEEMS to have escaped the record books, but the Golden Gate Bridge is now firmly established as the world's No. 1 jumping-off platform for suicides—by default. For a long time, we were running neck-and-neck in this depart-

10

ment with Paris's Eiffel Tower, but then a peculiar phenomenon occurred: the French began counting their Eiffel suicides backwards! A peculiar race indeed.

When the Gate Bridge achieved No. 410, I phoned the French Consulate to check on the Eiffel's record and got such evasive answers you'd think I was asking for Giscard d'Estaing's home phone number. So I put our man in Paris, Ferris Hartman, on the job and he came up with surprising information.

The Eiffel's top figure, he found, was 352, scored in April 1968—at which time the Gate Bridge's suicide figure was also 352! Apparently the French sensed defeat, for when, on June 27, 1968, one Jean Tapie Carraze jumped to his death from the Eiffel Tower because he had lost his driver's license (how Gallic), he too was listed as No. 352. The next suicide was numbered 351 and the numbers have been decreasing ever since.

"What is the latest figure?" Mr. Hartman asked the police chief of the Seventh Arrondissement, where the Eiffel is located. "Around 300," he was told. "Since we put up barriers, no more suicides." Conclusion: in this melancholy category, the Gate Bridge now has an insurmountable lead. Unless they put up barriers and start counting backwards, too.

FOOTNOTE: "This is my last selfish act." Of all the suicide notes left on the Gate Bridge, that strikes me as the most unforgettable. It was written by twenty-three-year-old Robert Dickinson, moments before he become No. 407—on Christmas Eve. His closest friend, Ling, a Thai waiter at Enrico's, brooded over that for the next few days. "I dream of Bob every night. He is in the water. He is drowning. I reach out to help him. I wake up screaming." On New Year's Eve, Ling became No. 408 off the Gate Bridge. He left the same note: "This is my last selfish act." Or perhaps his first unselfish one?

☆ ☆ ☆

I WALK down Market toward the Palace Hotel. The night before, a young Women's Lib lawyer had said in self-pitying tones: "I'm going to have to do it. I'm going to have

11

to sue the Pied Piper bar for discriminating against women. I went in there for a drink and they wouldn't serve me." I tried to point out that there were at least three other rooms in the Palace, a few yards away, where women are served. "What's the use?" she snapped, rolling her eyes. "You just don't understand."

For-men-only eating places don't interest me much, but, inspired by her wrath, I lunched at the Pied Piper for the first time in years. The room is definitely clubby, a paneled anachronism. Maxfield Parrish's great painting, which gives the room its name, glows over the bar where Elmer Brown, in proper barman whites, has presided since Lucius Beebe was a lad. The Sotomayer caricatures on the walls added their definitely dated touch: Lunt and Fontanne, Edward Stettinius, Einstein, Salvador Dali.

The place was crowded with men from another age, enjoying each other's company. Hair: short. Suits: three-piece. Ties: narrow. Shoes: shined. Now and then, women scuttle through on their way to Blum's without drawing a glance. (This must unnerve them.) At the bar, an old party in banker's gray drank a highball while reading the *Wall Street Journal*. Nearby, a younger man was nursing a martini and a cigarette, slowly dying by his own hand.

What I believe, dear Women's Lib lawyer, is that you should forget about the Pied Piper. It is one of the last traces of earlier civilization. Let it fade away as so many other San Francisco institutions have disappeared—slowly, gracefully, naturally, to a distant drum roll of dice and ice cubes.

Laugh, Clown, Laugh

"EVEN THOUGH" your heart is breaking," right? Well, all the world loves a lover and everybody loves a clown and it all came together in the kind of show that can only happen in San Francisco. Raggedy Robin, the young clown, married

Raggedy Jane, the only girl ever to graduate from Ringling Bros.' clown school, and there has never been a wedding like it, nor could it ever happen again. It took a special day in this special place.

Naturally, the scene was St. Relevant's, better known as Glide Memorial Church in the heart of the Tenderloin. As early as noon, they were streaming through the tacky old streets, frightening the tarts and the tourists: straights and freaks, heads and tails, graybeards and children, dogs, monkeys, snakes, drum majors wearing shakos and drag queens with lipsticked faces over chest hair curling out of silks and satins.

By 1 P.M., St. Relevant's was jammed and people were being turned away. "Seize Joy!" proclaimed the banner alongside the pulpit, and joy there was in this living church, a full seizure of it. A circus trapeze dangled from the balcony, bouquets of balloons blossomed from the pews, a stout and mustachioed ringmaster presided at the pulpit, blowing his whistle for the show to begin, this Painted Wedding on a May Day in the Arabian Nights city of Baghdad-by-the-Bay.

For two hours, the spectacle unfolded. You sat there and marveled at the textured richness of this strange and wonderful place: where do they all come from, what spirit moved them to perform at this wedding of two young clowns most of them barely knew? One hesitates to ascribe magical, mystical virtues to the very atmosphere of San Francisco, but, having been invited by Raggedy Robin, down the aisle they came in a pageant beyond the dreams of a Ziegfeld:

Bagpipers in solemn step, wailing and drumming behind their dignified major. Romeos and Juliets in velvet raiment, pirouetting and kissing. A dozen belly dancers writhing to the tinkle of golden cymbals, carrying swords and snakes. A singing dog that stopped the show, dancing bears that started it again. Walt and Magana Baptiste in all their Hindu finery. A lithe-limbed young lady who sprang onto the trapeze and did her circus turns. A wild oompah band, each member in a different costume, that scrambled onto the stage to play, inexplicably, "Yes, We Have No Bananas!" And through it all, the Cockettes in a corner, screaming, dancing, camping . . .

13

After a final mad procession of all hands, Raggedy Robin and Raggedy Jane did get married, by a bishop of some obscure order, and with a llama standing in attendance (a beastly two-l llama, not a priestly one-l lama). A three-l lama is a fire, of course, and a fire marshal kept worrying about the crowds in the aisles. But the police, bless 'em, stayed far away, and joy raged unrefined in this otherwise wicked world.

"Laugh, clown, laugh" . . . When it was all over, Raggedy Robin looked exhausted under his make-up, Jane was dazed. They and the rest of the crowd streamed out of St. Relevant's and headed for Polk Street, closed to traffic, open to life. Here the vibes were less happy. Heckling drunks stood outside saloons, glasses in hand. The Cockettes, mocked, bravely stuck out their tongues at their tormentors. But the street musicians were hard at it, and at the corner of Polk and California, a fine fresh-from-San Jose rock band called the Doobie Brothers brought back memories of the old Be-Ins at Golden Gate Park.

Robin and Jane had an organic wedding cake at the Shandygaff and finally dragged their weary young bones home to their honeymoon house near the Haight-Ashbury. "Wasn't it wonderful?" he said. "It all seems like a dream, as though it had never happened." Jane looked blanked out.

Next day, still in their clown make-up, they were at Enrico's Coffee House, Robin cranking away on his street organ and Jane doing a limp-jointed Raggedy Ann dance. In a quiet corner, he confided: "You know, Jane has amnesia. She didn't even remember that she had promised to marry me. She doesn't remember going to clown school. Her memory is slowly coming back, but"—and a tear trickled down his painted cheek.

Jane stood there in her baggy old dress and her striped stockings, eyes staring out from under the wig of orange yarn. She ran a finger across her grease paint and asked softly: "Why am I made up like a clown?"

Back on Shrader St., Raggedy Robin wrestled the street organ out of the car as the neighborhood children gathered to watch. He and a friend dressed in a white bear's costume carried it up the stairs, three flights, to the honeymoon nest at the top of the old house, an apartment with a shaggy dog, a parrot, a monkey, a rabbit and chicks. Robin and Jane joined gloved hands and smiled through tears at each other. "We're going to make it," said Robin. "We're going to be all right."

The infinite sadness of clowns, when the frolicking is over, the costumes come off, and the painted smiles are washed away . . .

Peace and War

FREAKY OLD San Francisco. At Post and Grant, an ethereal, long-haired blonde in blue jeans was plucking a homemade harp, making lovely sounds. Hurrying pedestrians slowed down to listen, their faces growing dreamy. Then suddenly, the air was made hideous by the siren screams of fire engines and police cars, drowning out the tinkling harp, and the mood grew hard again. It seemed a paradigm of the times. I never thought the time would come when I'd use a word like paradigm.

I turned into Maiden Lane. A hooker wearing a little sign reading "Available" braced me for a nooner. I turned her down while toying with the idea of asking whether the President had frozen her assets. Still, a hooker in Maiden Lane seemed pleasantly Old Francisco. Before jeweler Albert Samuels changed its name, Maiden Lane was Morton Street, alive with *filles de joie*. Or maybe it was Leslie Street. Anyway, something salty.

☆ ☆ ☆

NORTH SIDE of Market, with all those men's shoe stores, tongue by cheek. Dozens of them. Maybe hundreds. Black dudes gazing hungrily into the windows. Who buys all these shoes? Broadway, the street of broken dreams; Market,

15

boulevard of fallen arches, heels and soul brothers. "Got any spare change?" supplicated the hippie. "Yes," I said without slackening my pace. Screwm. I'm good for a quarter most of the time, but suddenly I'd had it. I thought of the Real Depression and Real Beggars, who had built a railroad and made it run (to the sun, yet), and all THEY wanted was a dime, brother. "Ever build a railroad?" I asked the next hippie, who looked at me as though I'd gone bananas and split. In front of Woolworth's, the Hare Krishna chanters—known in our set as the Harvey Krishman Singers—were laying down that same old boring beat. Couldn't they play a waltz once in a while? Or even "Only a Shanti in Old Shanti Town"? On Fifth, I chucked a quarter at the legless old guy who sells pencils. Maybe he'd built a railroad.

☆ ☆ ☆

SEVENTH AND MISSION, smell of beer and poverty, the old hotels with names redolent of a more romantic era— the Grand Southern, the Atlanta. In the nearby Greyhound depot, the atmosphere was even more Southern, black shoeshine "boys" snapping their rags, much drawly talk, tired GIs staring at coin-in-slot TV sets. I dropped a quarter in a game called "Jet Rocket." Indochinese hooches came and went in my gunsight. Squinting, I squeezed the trigger. Take that, you anti-Thieu Commie rats. Straw villages blew up in flashes of red. And that and that, enemies of the free world. Ten for ten! The villages stopped flashing past and I reached under the slot to see if I'd won an Air Medal. Nothing. I walked out, sneering at the damn civilians. What do they know about war?

The blood lust on me, I boarded a Mission bus that said "Ferry" (just as though the Ferry Building were still alive) and it started up so suddenly I was hurled against a post and into the lap of a dear woman who said, "Oh dear." The glasses in my breast pocket broke. The driver, smoking away under the "No Smoking" sign, didn't look around. He already knew he's scored ten points off me.

At the Transbay Terminal, I found another "Jet Rocket"

and destroyed another ten Vietnamese villages, or maybe they were Cambodian. Then I walked across the street to the Fun Terminal, where there's a fantastic game called "Sea Raider." Periscope and everything! Tiny ships floated across my field of vision. Every time you sink one, the ship explodes with a roar that shakes the whole building. For the Fatherland, I sank a hundred thousand tons of enemy shipping and reached down for the Navy Cross. Or the Iron.

Like Erich von Stroheim, I marched out past the Terminal Drugs at the corner. What's a terminal drug? Heroin? Strychnine? They really should change that name.

Suddenly I felt the need for the sweet smell of wet eucalyptus, the healing sight of ocean fog nestling in trees. I drove out to the zoo and rode the merry-go-round three times, strangely soothed by the tinny old waltzes as I whirled round and round into the past . . .

A Sort of a Day

I'M A POLE-BANGER. Not a wallbanger, Harvey—a pole-banger. By that, I don't mean I go around assaulting people from Warsaw. It's a game city boys play: you walk down the street, banging your open hand against light standards and signal poles, and if you get a nice, round satisfying "Thwonk!," you give yourself a point. Only hollow poles go "Thwonk!" On solid poles, all you get are a sore hand and a dull thud and that counts one point against you. This is similar to other games city nuts play, like flipping a cigarette butt at a sewer grating. Five points for sinking it well and truly and clean, Ernest. If it causes a great underground explosion in Amchitka, you win all the marbles.

We older screwballs start the day by betting on ourselves to beat the odds as published in the Irish sports section. That's the obituary page. After reading the headlines, you compound the depression by seeing who died yesterday. If most of them were older than you, you win and may be around for another twenty-four hours. If a majority is younger, you have lost and the end is close at hand. The honorable way out is to turn on the garbage disposal and throw yourself fingers first into the kitchen sink.

On this particular morning, I had lost badly—nine younger, three older—but decided to carry on anyway, mainly because it was a beautiful day. Fall was rising and the market was falling. Trees shedding leaves like strip-teasers, limbs as bare as topless dancers (I may be in a rut). Yellow school busses careened around the streets, scattering dear young ladies, in white middies and saddle shoes, on their way to Sacred Heart, and brave boys wearing their Town School sweaters or Cathedral neckties. Fairest flowers of our finest families, future leaders of San Francisco—hail! I reflected bitterly that they could turn to the obituary page and win ten-zip every morning, for thousands of mornings to come. Ah well.

I stashed the car at the Pickwick and walked toward Market. The Fifth Street Follies were in full cry. A stout lady with hairy legs and a coat that had been slept in was yelling obscenities. Who listens? Beautiful copper-toned Chicana chicks got off the bus from the Deep Mission and flashed their fine legs and teeth. East Indian ladies sulked around in their filthy saris, wearing caste marks or soot. That old black mammy who wears a bandanna was asleep in a doorway of Penney's, closed and gathering debris. She was snoring and the neat little lady at the corner was selling *Awake!* and it was beautiful.

I passed the Humboldt Bank building, where there's a permanent bronze plaque, highly polished, reading "Offices to Rent." That plaque has been there as long as I've been there. Haven't they ever filled that building? At Powell and Market, convention delegates were killing themselves in a mad rush to board the cables and the pickpockets were having a feel day. At Stockton near O'Farrell, a hippie stood outside a bakery, asking, "Got any bread, man?" Like, some crust. The trouble with the world, somebody once said, is that there are too many sneezers and not enough "Gesundheiters," but at that very moment a Little Old Lady

18

let out a mighty sneeze, and the hippie said, "Bless you." She stopped dead in her tracks and gave him a radiant smile. He grinned back. A nice scene. I gave him some bread, man, and he walked into the bakery, having passed the test with frying crullers.

The afternoon was waning. The sun sinks faster when you reach November and it's not such a long time till December, either. I popped into Jack's for a cup of coffee. Good coffee. It didn't taste, as Pat Buttram once said, like something you sit in to remove a tattoo. The lords of creation were having their late executive-type lunches, drinking martinis and gobbling up the great sour dough bread while waiting for their rich men's diet plates, "a New York steak and trim the fat." I walked over to Chinatown and ran into Charlie Leong. "Watch out for the hoodlums," he said, grinning. Hoodlum, the strange word that was born on the old Barbary Coast and is still alive, just a few blocks away. Grant Avenue was crowded with chrysanthemum children and Hong Kong emigrant ladies in their black padded high-collared uniforms. Chinatown is becoming more like Hong Kong every day, with a Barbary dash.

Dusk at Victorian Park, the gas lights glowing peacefully. A great place to unwind. The dying sun caught the old white walking-beam ferryboat, bringing it to life for a few seconds. Out in the lagoon, an old guy in a rubber cap was swimming strongly, leaving a wake. In the stillness, it was good to be alive, come what may on the morrow's obituary page.

☆ ☆ ☆

KOOKVILLE WEST: Bachelor Matthew Kelly returned to his Stockton Street town house late one night to discover that his digs had been burglarized of only two items—a huge white bearskin rug, complete with head, and a gold-handled cane. When the police arrived, Matthew observed: "Shouldn't be too hard to find a person wearing a bearskin rug and carrying a gold-handled cane." "Well," replied one of the officers, "in any other town, maybe, but in San Francisco, who'd look twice?"

☆ ☆ ☆

GAMES PEOPLE PLAY: Shirley Temple Black attended a United Nations Conference on Human Environment in Geneva—where, during one session, a member of the Russian delegation suddenly turned to her and remarked, "My two favorite film stars are Lana Turner and Shirley Temple." "Why, thank you," said Shirley, smiling, at which the Russian asked, "Where is Lana Turner?" "She keeps busy," replied Shirley, "doing movies and television." "And," continued the Russian, "whatever happened to Shirley Temple?"

☆ ☆ ☆

INTERNATIONAL GAFFE: John A. Vietor, publisher of *San Francisco* magazine, on a flying trip around the world, was met in Casablanca by a royal Moroccan limousine that rushed him to Fez, where he found himself surrounded by Berber horsemen firing their rifles, natives dancing and singing, and Moroccan nobles feasting in a richly caparisoned tent. Still suffering from jet lag and exhaustion, Vietor asked groggily: "What's going on?" "We are celebrating the circumcision of the Prince," replied a woman, at which our hero struggled for an appropriate comment and finally found it. "Uh," he said, "is it an annual event?"

☆ ☆ ☆

CLASSIFIED AD in the San Carlos *Enquirer:* "For sale. Nice dog. May be heard a 240 Club Dr. between 1 A.M.–5 A.M. Inquire next door."

☆ ☆ ☆

POET GARY SNYDER has been living near Nevada City, where there's a new ordinance against swimming naked which "they have been enforcing with almost prurient zeal." Gary's reaction was to write a poem, titled "Swimming Naked in the Yuba River," which we are privileged to republish here.

20

White, shining boulders in the sun. Light and water gather
in the gorge,
The world in every grain of sand. To step into this flowing
with a suit on
Would be a sin.

☆　☆　☆

LIFE IN THE CITY: He looked like just any other
shaggy-haired nondescript hitchhiker, standing there on Van
Ness Avenue, except that he was carrying an expensive
Mark Cross attaché case and inside the case was $55,000
cash, mainly in hundred-dollar bills.

How would anybody know this? Well, a few minutes
earlier, he had gone to a nearby bank to change three of the
hundred-dollar bills into smaller denominations, carelessly
allowing the teller to see what the case contained. Bug-eyed,
the teller immediately called the police. The police called in
the Feds. The kid was detained on a vague charge: "Under
investigation for possible possession of counterfeit money."

The $55,000 may have originated in narcotics sales, be-
cause the young man immediately summoned Attorney
Michael Stepanian, one of San Francisco's famous "dope
lawyers." "There is no way you can hold this boy *or* the
money," argued Stepanian, and shortly after, the young man
was released. A few minutes later, he was back on Van Ness,
again hitchhiking—but this time the load in his Mark Cross
attaché case was considerably lighter.

The Feds had taken out $16,000 for income tax. And of
course there was Stepanian's fee.

Later, the lawyer met the young man's father, the vice
president of a large corporation, and asked, "How do you
feel about all this?" "Well," replied the father dryly, "he
began smoking pot when he was fifteen and now he's twenty
three. I hardly expected that he might become a claims ad-
juster."

☆　☆　☆

THE NOTED RESTAURATEUR Victor Jules Bergeron,
better known as "Trader Vic," retained an old friend, author
Barnaby Conrad, to ghost-write his memoirs for a major

publisher. After spending long hours on the job and wearying of it, ghost writer Conrad in turn hired a ghost writer, the veteran newspaperman Robert Patterson, to "jazz it up a bit."

Well, what Barnaby didn't know is that if there is one man in the world Trader Vic can't abide—and there are several —it's Patterson. That's because when Patterson was writing a gossip column in the late 1940s, under the pseudonym of Freddie Francisco, he printed some very nasty insinuendoes about the Trader.

Naturally, Old Pro Patterson took on the job with gusto. It appealed to his baroque sense of humor to be secretly writing a book, in the first person, for a man who can't stand his very sight. He even had Vic saying such things as "There are some decent newspapermen in this town, but Patterson isn't one of them. He is a disgrace to journalism—a predatory menace who preys on innocent people."

When ghost Conrad read that, he asked subghost Patterson: "Why have Vic say that about you?" to which Patterson replied: "Vic doesn't know I'm doing this job, does he?" Conrad shook his head. "Then don't you see?" chortled Patterson with manic glee, "When this book is published, I'll sue Trader Vic for libel!"

After Many a Deadline

IF YOU LIVE long enough in this racket, you could spend half your time writing the obituaries of fallen comrades. The invisible sniper, firing at random, picks them off one by one—not that old newspaper guys are a difficult target. They're a dying breed even in the best of health, burning themselves out against the deadlines, drinking themselves out between editions. Some die in the gutter, others are found face down at their typewriters, still others suddenly pitch forward at their desks . . .

I stood on the Powell Street curb, across from the Sir

22

Francis Drake, and lagged a penny toward the cable car slot. It hit metal with a tiny "chinnng" and disappeared to join whatever pennies might still be down there, under the tracks. A ridiculous gesture but it was the only tribute I could think of to Larry Fanning, dead at fifty-six up there in Anchorage. If our roles had been reversed, he might have done the same for me, for the hell of it, for Auld Lang Syne, for bittersweet memories. Larry went the way we all go if we stay in this racket, down and out, at the desk and the deadline he had faced that once too often. The presses keep rolling but the ticker gives out—a heart that gets old in a hurry, hurry, hurry.

Before World War II, when the city was still young (a time that now appears to have been enchanted), Larry Fanning, a genius of a copyreader named Bob Ritchie, and I would close up the *Chronicle* at 3 A.M. We'd take final editions, the ink still wet, over to Tiny's, an all-night coffee shop on Powell (Sears' Restaurant occupies that spot now, an entirely different matter). There, we'd pick up a rival *Examiner* and sit till dawn, comparing, arguing, criticizing. We loved the *Chron,* we hated the *Ex,* we were excited about the business. And as the sun started to come out of the East Bay, we'd stand on the Powell curb and lag pennies at the cable car slot. I no longer remember how the game started or why, or even what the point was, since the "winner" was the one who lost his penny down the slot. It simply appealed to the child in us, the child that lives in every newspaperman of whatever age.

It was a great time to be young, in a city that hadn't quite grown up yet, in a world on the brink of disaster but still poised for the plunge. We were living in the twilight of a golden, or at least gold-plated, age of journalism: four dailies at each other's throat, and good newspapermen on all of them. Paul Smith, the boy editor of the *Chronicle.* Lindner and Wren at the *Ex,* with Hyer, Hyman and McQuade at the front typewriters. Benny Horne, who coined "Cow Palace," tough Tom Laird and Art Caylor at the *News.* A mob of tabloid terrors on the *Call-Bulletin,* and Larry Fanning, the kid managing editor of the *Chronicle*— lean, mean, talented and giving the paper the kind of devotion money can't buy. We were all like that, living and breathing the newspaper business. At the old Press Club at Powell and Sutter—open all night, with slot machines in the bar—we'd take on anybody who dared to denigrate the *Chron*. It was Jim Kieldsen of the *Ex* who called our staff "a bunch of young punks." And it was Larry Fanning who smashed him to the floor, where his head lolled between the cuspidors.

My God we were young and indestructible. We'd work all afternoon and run up to the Mark's Lower Bar for a drink (it was The Place, then) and down to the old Bay City Grill on Turk for dinner and then back to work till the final edition was off the presses, and then on to coffee and coin-lagging at Tiny's and sometimes instead of going to bed we'd drive straight out to Julius Kahn Playground to play tennis by the dawn's early light. Sometimes we'd go without sleep two days, without fatigue. We worked too hard, drank too much, married and divorced too often, blew our health and our home lives, loved our newspaper, dug each other and, in most cases, died too young. It never occurred to us to put in for overtime. We were having too good a time all the time.

Sunday was brunch day at editor Paul Smith's. It wasn't enough that we worked together six days a week, almost twenty-four hours a day, we had to be together on Sunday, too, there on the deck of Smith's Telegraph Hill digs, looking out over a city that was still softly pleasant, out toward Treasure Island, where there was still time for World's Fairs, out toward the bridges that were more than big enough to handle the traffic (we even worried that the Golden Gate Bridge might never make it, business was so slow). We'd drink and eat and sneer at the *Ex* and glow over the *Chron*. Paul called us "The Clan" and we were, closer than most families. There on Telegraph Hill, with the lights of Treasure Island coming on at dusk, we felt on top of the world, in the glow of youth and good scotch.

Now Paul Smith, after a series of strokes, languishes in a rest home down the Peninsula. Larry Fanning is dead. So are Horne and Caylor, Bob Ritchie, Kieldsen, Lindner, Wren, McQuade, Laird, the *News,* the *Call,* the old Press Club and Tiny's. Sometimes I feel like the survivor of a Last

Man Club. Throw another penny at the slot and remember the good times. Oh hell.

☆ ☆ ☆

THE VERY RICH are not like you and me. That's how they became very rich. To illustrate, the Auxiliary to the Little Children's Aid Society was having a rummage sale at Hall of Flowers, and Mrs. Edwin Gallagher, in charge of the millinery section, had a splendid idea: she wrote to Mrs. Rose Kennedy at Hyannis Port and asked her to contribute a hat to be auctioned. Soon, it arrived—a box from Mrs. Kennedy, containing a fine old Givenchy hat. Plus a note from Mrs. K.'s secretary, asking Mrs. Gallagher to have the hat appraised and the figure sent to her for tax-deduction purposes.

☆ ☆ ☆

FIRST NAME BASIS: Fresh from her triumph in *Il Trovatore* at the opera house, soprano Leontyne Price was at Trader Vic's for a midnight snack when up to her table walked a man who said, "You were great tonight, Leontyne, just terrific." "And what's your name?" asked Miss Price. "I'm Dr. Weitz, Leontyne," beamed the man. "No," went on the diva, "I mean your first name." "Uh—Ernie," he replied. With a bleak little smile, Miss Price said icily, "Good night, Ernie."

Life and Death

IT WAS A TYPICAL August day in New San Francisco. As the radio had promised that morning, "mild breezes." I mean, toupees were flying off, hats were skittering down the streets, and the seersuckered tourists were standing in purple knots, singing "I Wish I Wuz in Peoria." The radio had also predicted "Slight overcast near the ocean," and that's where we are, all right. Near the ocean. The overcast was so slight you could almost see across Fifth Street, but that's not such a bargain, either.

Inhaling and exhaling regularly, I walked over to Sixth Street, which has replaced Third as the Street of Broken Dreams. You can smell failure in every block. That and disinfectant. I stepped into a bar populated by crones and faceless men wearing wide-brimmed gray fedoras. I ordered a beer, served in a glass that promised several diseases for which no cure was immediately available. A chubby blond hooker with dark roots and a shy smile asked, "You busy this afternoon?" "Some," I replied in the classic manner of Willie McCovey the baseball star (a newspaperman who had phoned Willie early one morning asked, "Did I wake you up?" and Willie replied, "Some").

"Care for a drink?" I asked her, and she shouted at the bartender, "Straight shot with a water back" and then to me, demurely, "Thank you, sir." A lady, no doubt of that. "Well, happy days," I said, lifting my glass. "They used to be," she said lugubriously, looking like she might cry. Boy, the dialogue was terrible. Bowing gravely, I walked outside, wondering if any of the many shots I've taken cover hepatitis. Oh well. It's an "in" bug.

Sixth Street, phantasmagoria West. Odor of poverty and despair, anonymous rooming houses for anonymous people, hockshops filled with guitars pawned by kids who didn't make it, a Volunteers of America mission with empty chairs, hopeless streetwalkers who know you'll say, "No," panhandlers who pocket your quarters without a word, pinballs and stale doughnuts, little grocery stores with a few tired oranges in the window, a barber college with a sign: "Keep Americans Beautiful! Get a Haircut Today." There was nobody beautiful inside or out. I stepped into a lunch counter to test my theory that the crummiest places serve the best chili. Liberally doused with catsup, it wasn't half bad, but the cracked bowl worried me. Maybe you can't even *get* a shot for hepatitis.

Burping delicately—"You were expecting chimes?" I said

aloud, wondering if anybody remembered Monty Woolley—
I got into my car and headed for the other side of the
trackless. Grant Avenue in North Beach was deserted, and
here it was the shank of the evening. I stood at the site of the
long-gone Coexistence Bagel Shop as the shades of Ginsberg, Kerouac and Corso rustled along in the dark and
empty street. The beatniks who once made this the liveliest
stretch in town were as gone and forgotten as the Pelopon-
nesians. A hippie on a bad trip came screaming out of the
Coffee Gallery and ran up the middle of the street, almost
running head-on into a cab. A good American got out and
threatened to belt him one. The hippie ran on, still screaming, weaving back and forth like a rabbit trapped by head-
lights.

Considerably depressed, I headed for home. At Green and
Polk, a young, terribly pale man lay sprawled on the slanty
sidewalk, blood streaming into the gutter. Stabbed and
robbed. His broken glasses lay nearby. A police car pulled
up, its red light swimming madly under glass, radio chattering. Then an ambulance, whose attendants picked him up.
One went back and fetched his glasses. I found out later he
had died but there wasn't a line in the papers. Do you realize
you can live on Sixth Street or die on Green Street and
nobody gives a damn?

☆ ☆ ☆

SIGNAL: Mr. R., handsome and well born, moved here
from New York a few years ago—and his Hillsborough
friend, Mr. M., said, "You should belong to the Pacific-
Union Club." "No, thanks," replied R. "That's not my style,
and anyway, it costs too much." "Let me put your name in
anyway," suggested M. "There's a five-year waiting list, and
you may change your mind." Mr. R. shrugged, nodded and
forgot about it.

Some four years later, Mr. M. phoned R. and asked:
"How do you go to work in the morning?" Mystified, R. replied: "Well, I take my daughter to school and then I drive
down California Street to my office—why?" "That's perfect," said M. "The next time you drive past the Pacific-
Union Club and the flag is at half-staff, you're in!"

☆ ☆ ☆

CAST: Down on Beach Street, a cartoonist named Linus Maurer draws a comic strip called "Abracadabra," but now and then his thoughts must go back to Minneapolis in the early 1950s, when he was an art instructor there. Teaching at the same school were one Charles Schulz, a girl named Frieda Rich who had naturally curly hair, and a Charles Brown, a young man with round and innocent eyes. Now you know where Schulz found the names for his "Peanuts" strip, which at last count was syndicated to 1296 papers in fifty-six countries. His old friend Linus, whom he seldom sees, isn't doing quite as well. His strip is in forty papers.

Good Cop

ACTUALLY, things haven't changed much around Fifth and Mission in the past quarter of a century. The Old Mint is still standing there, doing whatever Old Mints do (they don't make money, that's one thing they do). The Old Chron, as the San Francisco *Chronicle* is known affectionately, is still across the street, putting out the best morning paper in town. Catercorner: the venerable Pickwick Hotel, where the walls talk back to you of pleasures past and hangovers present. The only major "improvement" is that big brute of a multilevel parking garage, on the site of the Original Hanno's Saloon for Artists, Writers and Newspaper Hacks.

But then came another major change. Honest John Gehring, the traffic cop who ran the show at Fifth and Mission since 1939 (with occasional strolls to Fifth and Market), quit after thirty-one years on the force. Good old Fifth and Mish' without Good Old John the Cop is like Powell without a cable, but there you are.

"I've had it," he said. "I can't take it any more. Winter's coming on and it gets dark early. There I am standing in the rain, with the traffic backed up all the way to Howard, and I'm telling the drivers to go thataway and they're telling me they want to go thisaway and I know that any minute some nut is going to come around the corner and hit me because he can't see me—well, anyway, I'm quitting. My nerves are shot. My uniform is worn out and so am I."

John and I have grown old together. When he first chewed me out for making a U-turn, his mustache was black and I had enough hair to stuff a mattress. Now his mustache is white, but he still has his hair (also white) so he's ahead of me there. In all those years, I've only seen him in his civvies once and he looked distinguished, like a retired banker or a maître d'hôtel in a good restaurant. But he has no regrets that he is neither.

"I guess I've been a pretty good cop," he says. "Nah, I don't mind people calling me a cop. That's what I am. A cop. The only term I can't stand is 'copper.' A woman driver called me a 'copper' the other day and I really let her have it. That's no lady, calling a cop a 'copper.' But I'll tell you one thing—I wouldn't want any kid of mine to be a cop. It's a lousy job. Too much night work, long hours, low pay. And no respect. Why, when I was a kid . . ."

Like all old-timers, cops or otherwise, John has a bad case of when-I-was-a-kiditis. "I was born in the Mission," he says. "My father was German, a sausage maker. When a cop told us to go *that* way, we went *that* way. Today everybody wants to give you an argument. The old Mission was great. Do you know we never even locked the front door? Never. Every day some bum would come around for a handout, and my mother would invite him right into the kitchen and cook him something. And my old man would sit down and have a conversation with him. When the bum would leave, my father would say, 'Mighty interesting fellow.'

"Imagine anybody doing that today? Everybody is suspicious of everybody else. Why, my wife won't even take the chain off the front door till she looks through the peekhole."

John Gehring, plain San Franciscan, good cop, quitting

29

The Force after thirty-one years with a perfect record. Never a promotion, never a reprimand. He has never fired a shot in anger. "I only pulled my gun once, about thirty years ago, but that was the first and last time." The legend around Fifth and Mission is that he still has his original book of tags. Not quite true, "but I don't believe in giving tags. I bawl 'em out instead. They remember that longer."

I don't know about you, but I feel sorry for cops. Most of them, anyway, and especially the old ones walking their beats, sensing the distrust and suspicion on all sides. Even when they're right, they're wrong—no wonder so many of them become firemen.

"You do something wrong now," says John, "and you're on your own. Nobody backs you up. The brass, the City Hall, the public, they're all against you. It wasn't like that in the old days."

The old days: for better or worse, the cops ran the town and nobody ran the cops. Even in Sacramento, where I broke into newspapering as a police reporter (prostitutes are turned out, presstitutes are broken in). I hung out with the cops for four solid years—the good ones and the crooked ones, the sadistic ones and the gutsy ones. But even then, I could see they were a closed corporation. It was us, the police, against them, the civilians, and neither particularly trusted or liked the other. The cops had more respect for a good criminal than they had for the Square John Public, maybe because they had more in common.

Now, when I hear people deriding the police as the "fuzz," or "pigs," I think about the good cops I knew—like Mike Strazzo, Sergeant Eddie Cox and Buck Lincecum in Sacramento, and Snooky Nelder and Tom Cahill here. And Honest John Gehring. They have one thing in common: a streak of sympathy that persists in spite of the brutalizing aspects of their job.

If the police have a theme song, it's "The public has no respect for us," but respect is a two-way street, and you may have noticed there are more one-way streets than there used to be. The good cops, though, like John Gehring, get all the respect they can handle. By the way, he's retiring because he has hypertension. They didn't have that in the old days, ei-

30

ther. When cophood was in flower, they called it "nerves" and said, "Go somewhere and relax," and that's what Honest John is going to do. Grit his teeth and relax.

A Native's Farewell

WELL, IF YOU were a native San Franciscan moving permanently to another city, far away, what would *you* do on your last day in town? Please, don't all raise your hands at once.

Instead, let us follow Tommy Moreland on his final rounds before leaving for Parkersburg, West Virginia, his new home: "I left my cottage on Fifth Avenue in the Richmond"—his use of the archaic word, "cottage," stamps him immediately as a native—"dropped my luggage off at the Tenderloin Terminal and proceeded down O'Farrell to the Hof Brau for a midmorning screwdriver. Thus fortified, I took the Mason Street cable to the end"—only latecomers say the Powell cable—"and had my last fresh crab cocktail at Hogan's on the Wharf. Thence to my private resort at Aquatic Park.

"As usual, the Red Mountain gallon jugs of Burgundy, Pink Chablis and Vin Rosé dotted the landscape. I mingled with high society, downing numerous libations laced with a few takes of the weed of forgetfulness. Floating over to the Buena Vista, where they pour the best booze at the best price, I partook of three Gibsons and bade farewell to Lucy, Lee, Emma, Barbara and the inscrutable Charlie.

"Aboard the Hyde Street car, I asked the gripman if he would wait for me at Union while I procured a butterscotch cone at Swensen's. Accomplishing this, I continued down Hyde, eating my butterscotch amidst the envious stares of Iowans and other guests in the city that used to know how.

"I debarked at Ellis, stopped in at Day's for a shot-and-beer, and bade farewell to Marvin, informing him that I

31

would not be there to share the annual dissipation on the Saturday before Christmas. Considerably saddened, I caught the limousine to the airport, where I proceeded to drown my woes in two more martinis and a scotch over. I then felt ready to face the Beefeaters on the United jet to Pittsburgh.

"It is a wrench, leaving San Francisco. I shall miss the Richmond, Sunset, Marina, Inner and Outer Mission, Breen's, Gray's, O'Doul's, Pier Seven, Dolph's, the J&B, best lunch in town for $1.50 at Twentieth and York, Enrico's, the Both/And, the Bay Guardian, Hoppe, Caen, McCabe and Gleason . . . I won't miss BART and Market Street, our so-called 'dynamic' mayor, the atrocious new buildings, the Giants, 49ers, Warriors, S.F. society, Candlestick Park and freeways—but I will say that the good things more than balance the corruption that increases in the onetime Jewel of the West."

Well, there you have it—the farewell address of a native San Franciscan, Tommy Moreland. The places he will miss seem mainly to be saloons, and, true to his code, he drank himself out of town (how did that ice cream cone get in there?). He is sentimental but not a slob about it: no final toast to the sunset from the Top o' the Mark, a place he probably wrote off long ago as strictly for tourists. A real San Franciscan in the time-honored style: resentful of outsiders and change, and sturdily anti-Establishment. Good luck in Parkersburg, West Virginia, kid. I hope they have at least one decent saloon; I think you'll need it, especially on those nights when you wake up suddenly out of a deep sleep, hearing foghorns that aren't there.

Tommy Moreland's words grabbed me for a variety of reasons. I don't know him but I've met a lot of native San Franciscans like him. They're a vanishing breed, disappearing in the facelessness of the New City. You see them in the older bars, drinking quietly and playing old tunes on the jukebox. They always seem to know the bartender, who produces the dice boxes as soon as they appear. No girls are around to disturb the sanctity of the ritual; they're generally alone and prefer it that way.

There used to be a lot of Tommy Morelands around, and they gave San Francisco a good part of its reputation for booziness and a kind of earthy sophistication. They knew the score and the way around: quiet men with quiet eyes, but not to be conned.

It wasn't till after they'd left that you realized they'd bought drinks for the house, or had picked up the check. And best of all, they had (and some still have) a fine toleration for the foibles of their fellow San Franciscans. The phrase "up-tight," which says so much in so little, applied to them not at all.

A lot of us get fed up now and then with the city, even as Tommy the Native did, but leaving it for keeps is something else again. What would you do on your last day? Unlike Tommy Moreland, I think I would have to go to Coit Tower at dusk, to look out on the Bay and the hills and the lights coming on. Then, like Tommy, I would get drunk as hell.

Every time I hear one of those chatty TV commercials (two or more people allegedly ad-libbing about a product), I wrinkle my considerable nose and say, "Phew, does that sound phony—real people just don't *talk* like that."

Well, I have been proved wrong by Rita Myers, who takes expert shorthand and has a fine ear for overheard conversation. During a coffee break at a Foster's, she was seated near two stenographer types who spoke, according to Rita's transcribed notes, exactly as follows:

"I just discovered it recently, but it's just *perfect* for my hair. It's called 'Just Wonderful' and [giggle] it really is just wonderful!"

"But strong hairsprays leave my hair too oily."

"Oh no, this one won't. My sister uses it, too, and she has oily hair. She loves it!"

"Yeah—well, maybe I'll try it."

"What I really like is, it's so *cheap*. You can buy it at Woolworth's."

Then, at a coffee counter near Montgomery and California, she heard these two men talking.

"What I like about PSA is that it flies so often."

"Yeah, it's great."

"I mean, if you miss a plane, you just go to the next gate and grab the next one."

"Yeah—beautiful."

"And as for the service and the planes . . ."

"Nothing wrong with 'em, nothing."

"That's right. They're really great."

Pretty scary, isn't it? It's bad enough that TV is gnawing at the intellect and morals of our country; now it's brainwashing people into talking like commercials. Why, I'd throw my set right out the window if I hadn't just bought a new one. It's great. The picture is so clear you think you're right *there*. Natural color, too—not too bright, just right. And in its handsome cabinet, it makes a darn fine piece of furniture . . .

☆ ☆ ☆

HILLSBOROUGH is different from your neighborhood and mine, and not just because there aren't any sidewalks. Late in the afternoon of Christmas Day, a resident of that gilt-edged community, accompanied by his wife and children, set out to sing carols for the neighbors. As they were tuning up outside their first stop, the lady of the house came to the door, looking distraught. "Look fella," she said. "I'm just a little busy. Plumbing's on the blink, can't get anybody to fix it, there's a mob coming for dinner—it's a real mess. If you really feel like singing carols, come back about nine o'clock, okay?" "Yes, ma'am," replied Bing Crosby, tugging respectfully at his forelock and herding his troupe elsewhere.

Purely Personal

ONE JULY DAY in 1966 it dawned on me that I had become a San Franciscan exactly thirty years ago, to the dot. As George remarked in *Who's Afraid of Virginia Woolf?*, that's a lot of blood under the bridge. Soon I would be able to palm myself off as a native and forget that I spent my first twenty years as a Sacramento boy—although I doubt that the readers will let me forget it. During my break-in period on the *Chronicle,* when I committed even more gaffes than I do now, every other letter-writer observed snidely that "You can take the boy out of the country but you can't take the country out of the boy." A cleverly turned phrase, I thought upon first reading it, but it soon palled.

At the time I was summoned to bigger and better things, I was working for the Sacramento *Union* as a police reporter. The *Union* is the oldest daily west of the Rockies, and in those days it looked it (oddly enough, it began flourishing shortly after I left). It was such a small operation, in fact, that late one night, when the police chief of North Sacramento was shot to death, an old Chicago hand named H. Lee Watson and I put out an "extra" all by ourselves. We were so proud of our feat that we stayed up all night and got drunk—not an easy thing to do in Sacramento at that time —but the publisher almost fired us the next day for squandering money. "Who cares about *North* Sacramento?" he kept saying. Nevertheless, when the *Chronicle* offered me a job at fifty dollars a week, he countered with an offer of thirty-five, a ten-dollar raise. I was touched, but not enough.

For my attack on the Big City, I bought my very first (and last) hat, which I wore with the brim turned up in front, like Front Page Farrell. On the ferry crossing the Bay, I stood at the rail, shook my fist at the approaching, frightening skyline, and vowed, "I'll lick you, San Francisco!" At which point the Bay breeze, understandably offended, plucked the hat off my head and flung it into the water, for the sea gulls to peck at. A bad omen, at least for the hatmakers. In those days, I had about eighteen pounds of hair, and by the time I arrived at the Chronicle Building, it was standing out in all directions, as though I had just been electrocuted. The then editor's secretary, a salty redhead named Dorothy McCarthy, took one look at me, slapped her forehead and croaked, "Migawd, now we're hiring people with fright wigs!" It's thirty years later, and I still haven't thought of a riposte.

My first job on the *Chronicle* was as radio editor (there was no TV in those days, children, honest there wasn't) because, to kill time on the police beat in Sacramento, I had been writing a radio column—without, I should add, ever listening to the radio. I just made it up. And anyway, as it turned out, the only reason the *Chronicle*'s then editor hired me was because he wanted somebody on the staff younger than he (he was twenty-seven).

The man I was replacing was the eminent J. E. "Dinty" Doyle, who was about to leave for what was then considered the pinnacle of journalism: New York. He was a hard-drinking, wisecracking old-time newsman who hated me on sight because I preferred Jack Benny to his favorite, Fred Allen. Besides, he'd wanted his job to go to a friend in Oakland. "The boss says I'm supposed to break you in," he said disgustedly, spitting into the wastebasket. "Well, let me give you some advice. The important thing about being a columnist—even a lousy radio columnist—is not the column. The important thing is to be *seen,* to become a character. That's what I've done, that's why I made it. I go to the fights, I go to ball games, I go to opening nights and people say, 'Look, there's Dinty Doyle—man, he really gets around.' That makes 'em want to read the column. No matter how rotten the column is, they're gonna read it because you're a *celebrity.* See?"

I didn't see, but I nodded. He put on his coat and said, "So come on. I'm gonna show you the town. We'll have dinner at the Palace for starters. I'll introduce you to headwaiters and bandleaders and other celebrities. We'll go to every joint in town, see everything. I don't think you can cut the job, but at least you'll get the feel."

Night was falling over the enchanted city as we stood at the corner of Fifth and Mission. "Where first?" I asked excitedly. "Hanno's," said Dinty. At that time, Hanno's was a clubby little bar on the opposite corner, and a true hangout for newspapermen. A great chorus of "Hiya, Dinty!"s rang out as we walked in. I was impressed and cowed and sat in a corner, nursing a drink, as Doyle shook hands and began downing straight shots in a very businesslike manner.

Doyle was a great raconteur, and he was soon regaling the customers with long and sometimes funny tales. The hours went by, and at 11 P.M., we still hadn't got any farther than Fifth and Mission. "Hey, Dinty," I kept asking, more and more feebly, "I thought you were going to show me the town." "Relax, kid," he advised, his eyes now as red as his face. At midnight, he looked at his watch and said, "Holy cow, kid, I got a column to write! C'mon, back to the office."

Once there, he put his head in the wastebasket and made awful noises for a few minutes. Then he looked up miserably and said, "You write the column, kid." In a panic, I pounded out a thousand words about something and laid the copy before him. He reached for a pencil and scribbled at the top, "By J. E. (Dinty) Doyle" just before he passed out for keeps. The next morning, everybody agreed it was certainly one of Doyle's worst columns, and I had to agree. "Not that I could do any better," I added modestly, and thirty years later, that still goes.

☆ ☆ ☆

SOME TIME BACK, before leaving on a world tour, Peter Paine, the Squaw Valley ski instructor, dropped in at the Pierce Street Annex saloon in the Marina and bought a sweat shirt, emblazoned "Pierce St. Annex," from co-owner Marty Davis.

On a side street in Cairo, Peter ran into a little man, clad only in turban and towel, leading a donkey laden with goods to trade. The little man traded a knife and scabbard for Peter's sweat shirt and sunglasses. That night, Peter dashed off a postcard to Marty, telling him about this bizarre incident.

Some six weeks later, a TWA stewardess dropped in at the Pierce Street Annex and exclaimed to Marty, "Hey, you'll never guess what I saw in Cairo, never, never, *never!*" "You mean," drawled Marty, "that little old man leading a donkey and wearing sunglasses and a Pierce Street Annex sweat shirt?"

☆ ☆ ☆

SOCIAL OUTCASTS: For some reason, San Francisco's Paul B. (Red) Fay, Jr., didn't include this anecdote in his best-selling book on John F. Kennedy, *The Pleasure of His Company*, but it should be recorded somewhere, even here.

This happened shortly after Red was named Under Secretary of the Navy and moved to Washington with his wife, Anita. One Friday night, the Fays were invited to a black tie dinner at the home of the then French Ambassador, Herve Alphand—a most coveted invitation. As Anita was struggling into her new gown and Red was working on his tie, the phone rang.

It was the White House, JFK's secretary speaking:

"The President would like you and Mrs. Fay to dine with him tonight."

Frantically, Red and Anita changed to more informal dress, phoned regrets to the Alphands, and rushed to the White House, where they found JFK with a couple of old friends. The dinner was short and even fairly dull.

On two succeeding Friday nights, the same routine took place. Invitations to the Fays for fancy dinners, last-minute calls from the White House, quick changes of clothes, hasty apologies.

As the Fays walked in, breathlessly, on the third such occasion, Jack Kennedy looked at them with a quizzical expression and said, "Y'know, Redhead, you and Anita really aren't making it in this town, are you? How come you're always home on a Friday night with nothing to do?"

☆ ☆ ☆

HARD CURRENCY: If you happen to have a "K" series dollar bill, look at it. It tells, in its own way, the tragic story of John F. Kennedy's death. The series date is 1963, the year of the assassination. The large number 11, for the Federal Reserve District, could also represent November, the month of the shooting. The four 11s, one in each corner, add up to 44, Kennedy's age at the time. The significance of the big black "K" is obvious. And the bills were issued on the Federal Reserve Bank of—Dallas, Texas.

SENTIMENTAL NOTE (or, what were you trying to say, dear Leon?): The library at University of California Medical Center, which welcomes donations of books, received one with the following inscription penned on the flyleaf: "To Emily, dearest mine always, this book by Dr. Parran, Surgeon General of the U. S. Public Health Service, I give you on New Year's Eve 1937, with all my love and kisses. Lovingly, Leon." The book: *Shadow on the Land*. Its subject: syphilis.

☆ ☆ ☆

IT WAS the occasion of the first visit to San Francisco of Professor Marshall McLuhan, director of the Center for Culture and Technology at University of Toronto, author of *The Mechanical Bride, The Gutenberg Galaxy, Understanding Media,* and *The Medium Is the Message,* darling of the critics ("Compared to McLuhan, Spengler is cautious and Toynbee is positively pedantic"—New York *Herald-Tribune*), the man who stands "at the frontier of post-Einsteinian mythologies."

Hot on the trail of this titan, I thought to myself, "Where is the last place in town you'd expect to see Marshall McLuhan?" and that's where I found him—at Off-Broadway in North Beach, lunching amid the topless waitresses with writer Tom Wolfe, adman Howard Gossage, and Dr. Gerald Feigen.

Being President of the Leg Men of America, I never felt a primal urge to lunch among the topless ladies, but in such distinguished company, who could resist? "Strip steak sandwich," I said to waitress Marilyn, who was wearing blue sequin pasties and not much else. As she walked sternly away, I commented, "A good-looking girl."

"Interesting choice of words," mused Dr. McLuhan. "Good-*looking* girl. The remark of a man who is visually oriented, not tactually. And I further noticed that you could not bring yourself to look at her breasts as she took your order. You examined her only after she walked away—another example of the visual: the farther she walked away, the more attractive she became."

"Actually," I apologized, blushing, "I'm rather inhibited." The professor nodded. "Another interesting word. Inhibited is the opposite of exhibited," he pointed out, "and what is exhibited causes you to be inhibited."

A topless fashion show ensued, commentated by a young lady who was fully dressed and in good voice. "Now here, gentlemen," she said, "is the ideal opera gown for your wife." A gorgeously endowed blonde appeared in a full-length gown open to the waist. The audience, composed mainly of Tuesday Downtown Operator-like types, gaped silently. "You're all dead out there," chided the commentator. "Where's the applause?"

"Now the word applause," interjected Dr. McLuhan, "comes of course from the Latin *applaudere,* which means to explode. In early times, audiences applauded to show their disfavor—they clapped their hands literally to explode the performer off the stage. Hence you might say that the silence here is a form of approbation, at least in the classical sense."

The show over, Tom Wolfe asked waitress Marilyn, "Why do you wear pasties?" "Have to," she dimpled. "It's the law, when food is being served. For health reasons, you see?" Nobody saw. We invited Marilyn and Rochelle to join us for a drink. "Before we can sit with customers," said Marilyn, "we have to put brassieres on." She and Rochelle left and reappeared wearing black bras.

"I think brassieres look sexier than pasties, don't you?" Marilyn inquired. Everybody nodded. "Besides, you can walk faster with a brassiere." Everybody looked blank. "What I mean is," she went on, "you don't *jiggle* so." The discussion switched to the recent police raids on Off-Broadway, and Rochelle said, "I guess it was just a test case, we haven't been bothered since." "I see," said Dr. McLuhan. "To mix a metaphor, it was the thin edge of the trial balloon." I'm sorry to report this, but it's fact that he tittered at his own remark.

We walked out into the sunshine, filled with innocence

and good feelings, to find a young man on the sidewalk, handing out blue pamphlets for the "Scandinavian Massage Studio, Miss Ingrid, Director." The copy read, "Six young and trained Scandinavian girls are ready to serve you. For the tired executive we offer private massage rooms, private telephones, stock quotations, the *Wall Street Journal*, music."

It didn't sound relaxing at all. Not half as relaxing as lunch among the nymphs with Dr. Marshall McLuhan and his merry men.

☆ ☆ ☆

HAROLD LIPSET, a well-known San Francisco private investigator, told a *Daily Mail* interviewer during a visit to London, "In fiction, the detective wakes up at 4 P.M., kicks a blonde out of bed, takes a whisky, showers away the previous night's cuts and bruises, straps on his .45 and goes to the office. One of these things happens to me every day—I'm not going to say which one."

Autres Temps, Autres Scènes

THERE I WAS, walking down Market in my new Glenurquhart plaid suit, with hand-picked peaked lapels, hacking pockets, nine-inch side vents and real buttonholes on the sleeves. I was wearing a modified spread collar shirt in the daring shade called Picasso Blue, and a Countess Mara tie in muted stripes of burgundy and navy. My gold-chained patent leather pumps had been made under Italian waters by Signor Gucci himself. My cuff links: solid gold knots from Tiffany. My watch: a wafer-thin Audemars Piguet with Roman numerals. As I strolled along, I extracted a cigarette from my alligator case and set it alight with a casual flick of my Laykin's solid gold Zippo.

Since it was a fine day, I should have been feeling on top of the world, but actually I was on the underside. Here I was, duded up in all this finery (including Tootal linen shorts from Ireland) and nobody looked twice at me except an old-timer who said, "You look like a walking haberdashery." Like the word "haberdashery"—and what kind of a word is that, anyway?—I was a walking anachronism, surrounded by young men who couldn't care less about clothes, mine *or* theirs. They were standing around in their dirty jeans and crummy sweaters, licking Softees and looking happy. When I was their age, I would have given my teeth to be dressed to the teeth, and now I found myself wishing I could be dressed like *them*. A bewilderment, to be sure.

Talk about generation gaps: the reason nobody over thirty (even dirty) can look like the kids of today is that today's kids are built different. You've noticed this, haven't you? They're all as skinny as malnutrition cases, hipless and buttless, and have long, rather horsy faces that go well with those manes they affect. A generation ago, a lot of learned stuff was written about the American Look that had emerged from the melting pot—crew-cut, short-nosed, jut-jawed, a rather thick and boring look—and now that has gone down the tube, along with saddle shoes and white bobby-sox. In my day, kids came in all shapes and sizes: we had a Fatty and a Skinny and a Curly and a Smokey and a Four-Eyes and a Freckles, a real and wonderful hodgepodge of types, all sharing the American Dream of someday walking down Market Street decked out in the finery I was wearing. Where are they (and it) now?

One of the sharpest comments on the generation gap appeared in the *New Yorker*—a William Hamilton cartoon showing a balding father holding two baseball gloves and looking up hopefully at his son, a shaggy-haired, epicene young fellow who is saying: "No, Dad, I *don't* want to go out in the backyard and throw the old pill around." A real heartbreaker. The pleading, doubting expression on the old man's face, the disdain on his son's. Who *is* there to play catch with in these Catch-22 days?

I continued along Market, my gold accouterments clanking and glittering. I stepped into an anonymous bar for a healer. As I sipped the weak highball and stared at myself in the dirty mirror, I recalled John Raymond's remark as we had strolled through the Haight-Ashbury. "If you think these kids are bad now," he observed, "wait until they discover martinis." Maybe they never will. Horrid thought.

I walked over to the jukebox and played the Sinatra record of "I've Got You Under My Skin," just to make myself feel better. I like Lennon and McCartney, too—they broke the old thirty-two-bar mold and that's quite an achievement —but they still aren't in a class with Porter, Gershwin, or Rodgers & Hart. Or even Hart, Shaffner & Marx. Of this I'm positive. I think. I had another drink.

It's a funny thing: you work all your life toward a certain goal and then somebody moves the posts on you. When I was a kid, I dreamed about Stutz Bearcats, Auburns and Duesenbergs, and what do these kids want? A Harley-Davidson, maybe, and they could be right. I stood at the curb and watched this bony guy and this great-looking girl, in a tight sweater, ride past on their hog. What made the scene arresting was that she was driving and he was seated on the postilion, with his arms around her midriff. Now I must admit *that* makes a lot of sense. I walked on into the sunset, surrounded by emaciated young men hawking underground newspapers that print all those four-letter love words in big-type—those wonderful words that used to give us such a thrill of shocked delight. Now they've become common currency, deflated, all passion spent.

I uttered one aloud, causing a Little Old Lady to flutter perceptibly, and headed for home, reflecting that the snake of life was about to shed another skin—and this time I think it's mine.

Crazy Old Town

I WAS STALLED in traffic, as usual, on Glorious Fourth Street. My roof was open to the Juneshine and I was stuck behind a Muni bus, its rotten old engine spewing Carburn

Munoxide. As I paradiddled my fingers on the steering wheel, I reflected disconsolately that I was getting a sunburn and dying of asphyxiation at the same time. Even a hair-raising performance of the Tchaikowsky violin concerto by Henryk Szeryng on KKHI didn't help much. I tried to exhale only, remembering an idle statistic I had read just the other day: "Each New Yorker inhales toxic materials equal to 38 cigarettes a day." Of course, New York is ten times as big as San Francisco, so at that very moment I was probably inhaling only 3.8 cigarettes. And then again, this is the city air-conditioned by Nature, but the old Mother seems to be falling behind Westinghouse. You can be sure.

The traffic light at the far corner went obediently through its phases without a car moving. Its phase might as well stay red, for all the good it did, and was *Forever Amber* the story of a stuck traffic light? When your mind and engine are in neutral, you think of all sorts of things. The PG&E or somebody is digging up Fourth for the four hundredth time within recent memory. We really dig our streets. I looked at the row of pawnshops, windows filled with electric guitars and other implements of torture. The biggest sign said, "GUNS." "Guns spelled backwards is snug." "Bus Stop" spelled backwards is "Pots Sub." Sighted sub, potted same.

After a short spell, during which dynasties fell, redwood trees went through their life span and the UN reached a decision, traffic moved again. It was terribly exciting. Like James Bond, I went up through the gears, achieving a speed of seven miles an hour. At Third and Mission, I joined the line of cars waiting to make a left turn. Many San Franciscans have spent the best years of their life waiting to make a left turn there. Now and then one car gets through, to the gallant cheers of those left behind. The driver in front of me was in a '37 Hupmobile that was new at the time he got in line. The answer of course is obvious—a "No Left Turn" sign. Now we have one but who pays attention?

Thanks to the machine guns in the bumpers of my Half Aston Martin, I was at last able to bull my way through, and headed north. I stopped at Market because of a cop, a red light and pedestrians, and looked around some more. The cop was wearing a seven-pointed star, which reminded me that San Francisco is the only major city left whose police still wear stars; elsewhere they wear shields (I like the star system better). Most of the young passing by were bearded, which reminded me what Doris Day once said about kissing a man with a beard: "It's like falling face down on a broom." I'll take her word for it.

I drove up Kearny and stopped some more (I'd like to have the brake-lining concession in this town). I sat and looked through my sun roof at the new skyscrapers rising all around. To an old San Franciscan, they look temporary—even the Wells Fargo Building, which was formerly the Fly Trap Restaurant. The Russ Building, 111 Sutter, Shell, PG&E, SP, Phone Building—*they* look permanent. The old Crocker Building doesn't look so permanent since they put that ugly new face on it.

Putting on my James Bond glasses—the ones that make everything look green—I sped all the way to Kearny, Columbus and Pacific, the most impossible intersection in this city of intersectional disputes. It is known as the Gorgeous Gore, in honor of the blood spilled there by tourists. Some of them just drive around and around in circles, like hyperthyroid rats in a maze, never realizing that the only right turn is a wrong one. I finally parked by a psychedelic fireplug, made my way over the smoking ruins of station wagons from Iowa and Indiana, and walked the rest of the way to Enrico's Coffee House. And if you think that's a lot to go through just for a cup of coffee, I couldn't agree more.

☆ ☆ ☆

REMARKS often heard shortly before a quick visit to the doctor: "That's not poison oak. You think I don't know poison oak when I see it?" . . . "You don't have to bring the boat any closer to the dock—I can jump it from here" . . . "I'm sorry, partner, I thought your two-bid was an overcall" . . . "I don't care if John Brodie's father is sitting right behind me, I still say he's a bum" . . . "Say, Luigi, have you heard the latest Italian joke?" . . . "I've got a way with cats" . . . "You truck drivers think you own the road.

Why, for two cents I'd—" . . . "Whaddya mean, squirrels bite? I've been coming to Golden Gate Park all my life and I've never been bitten by a squirrel" . . . "Y'know, bartender, I've had Mickey Finns that tasted better than this martini."

Edifice Wrecks

"I CAN'T THINK of a building I've put up that's one tenth as beautiful as the one I had to tear down to make room for it."

Speaking was one of San Francisco's most successful builders, a veritable Maharajah of Eyesore. He spoke mournfully, and you half expected him to add, as in an old movie melodrama, "Stop me before I kill again!" But kill again he will, and so will all his confreres in the "building" business.

I thought about his words as I stood on Nob Hill, gazing at the gaping hole where the old Sproule mansion had stood. It wasn't a particularly old house, and architecturally it was closer to zircon than diamond, but still it had more charm than the ice-trays-in-the-sky that will rise there someday. In denying pleas that the house be saved, a city official said, "What's so special about it? Did Washington or Lincoln ever sleep here?"

Funny in a tough way, but not particularly cogent, since Washington or Lincoln is not known to have slept anywhere in San Francisco, although Lincoln, had he come West, *might* have slept at the Montgomery Block—and now that's long gone. The Monkey Block (that's what everybody called it, Junior) was built in 1853 by Henry Halleck, who went on to become a general in the Union Army.

Every time the Chinese celebrate "Double Ten" Day, to commemorate the revolution against the Manchu Dynasty by Sun Yat-sen on October 10, 1911, I think about the

Monkey Block, for it was there, at one point, that Sun Yat-sen lived while plotting his coup. It used to be enjoyable for a San Franciscan to look at the Monkey Block and think about the venerable Oriental and the other venerables who lived and worked there: Frank Norris, Kathleen and Charles G. Norris, Maynard Dixon, Charles Caldwell Dobie, George Sterling . . .

The Monkey Block was torn down a few years ago for a parking lot, a flat piece of real estate that sings no songs but tells quite eloquently about our scale of values. Now the Transamerica pyramid occupies the site. Words fail.

I thought about the Maharajah of Eyesore's words again as I watched the wreckers go to work on the old Hall of Justice on Kearny. Here again we have a building that was not particularly old—slightly more than fifty years—but even in its death throes, it has a somber Florentine magnificence impossible to duplicate. To San Franciscans of my generation, it is/was a storybook building, alive with tales of violence, echoing with the arguments of lawyers dead and dying, redolent (especially on a wet-foggy night) of sirens and screams. Another sterile stack of ice trays has risen in its place, a Holiday Inn, and someday, perhaps, this building, too, will tell strange and moving stories of life in Baghdad-by-the-Bay. It doesn't seem like an especially good bet.

The most dangerous men in town may well be our Maharajahs of Eyesore, killing The City That Was—and what a city that was, think you not to the contrary. Day by day, the concrete evidence is being ground to rubble, even when the evidence was as undistinguished as the derelicts that disappeared so that Fifth Street could eventually cross Market. But if anybody cares to know where Painless Parker got his start, the address is now gone forever. Don't laugh: Painless Parker was a historic figure too, and his patients slept there, even if Washington or Lincoln didn't.

Soon, as somebody once said, the only thing old in San Francisco will be the young men's faces, and if you prefer Plastic Inevitable to a fluted column of stone, you're well ahead of the game. If you feel otherwise, miss no opportunity to walk through the Flood Building lobby with its massive pillars and great lanters, its marble floors and polished brass mailbox; it was built to last forever, but it won't. When you look at the gilded and crystal magnificence of the Palace's Garden Court, look twice, for you will never see its like again—not in this city, not in this lifetime. You may even start worrying about the Ferry Tower: its days are numbered. Faster and faster the city changes, and the people in it; those who never heard of the Monkey Block or the Slot can't tell you where Goat Island is, either. Soon, all will be new, bright, shiny and soulless—and then the legends will be gone forever, ground to dust by the relentless jackhammers.

Inhale and Exhale

I CALLED a friend one day and asked in the course of idle conversation: "What're you doing?" "Not smoking, that's what I'm doing," he replied, and I knew exactly what he meant. When you try to kick the smoking habit, thinking about not thinking about cigarettes occupies most of your time, and not smoking is a steady job. Maybe even the most important job you'll ever have.

That's right—I've quit again. The ashtrays stand empty and gleaming. The cigarette lighters, some of them golden and inscribed "To a Great Reporter—the Chief," have been stashed in the bottom drawer of the desk, along with the Dunhill filters (damned expensive and bothersome) and the remaining packs of Pall Mall reds, my crutch for so many years.

It finally came to me, as it came to more intelligent creatures years before, that a death wish is not really a way of life. It is not even necessary to wake up each morning with a mouth that tastes like every refugee from Bangladesh had camped there, bangling and deshing. Besides, I was violating the civil rights of nonsmokers, a truly heinous offense.

Under the tender ministrations of the Seventh Day Adventists, I'd quit smoking once before, but the cure didn't take. After a couple of weeks of being frightened to death by the Adventists, I was right back on those old PMs, sucking away like a newborn babe.

The Adventists, in their Anti-Smoking Clinic at the Palace Hotel a few years ago, used the scare technique. Like color movies of lung cancer operations, with sound effects by the Cleveland Wrecking Company, all crunching and grinding. Awful. Ranged around the room were objects that looked like baseball mitts that had been run over by tractors and then dropped into a sewer to marinate for a year.

"What are those?" I asked a doctor. "Lungs," he said. I must have looked incredulous, for then he snapped, "That's right, fella, lungs. The lungs of people who smoked several packs a day and got cancer and were operated on when it was too late and died. Take a good look."

I did, as my trembling fingers fished through my pockets for the cigarette that wasn't there.

So I signed up for the Seventh Day Adventists' cure, which involved lectures, lots of fruit juice, plenty of no coffee or other stimulants, gallons of water, hours of self-criticism and knocking other people, and "Your Secret Pal."

"Your Secret Pal" was someone of the opposite sex whom you never met. However, she was given your phone number and permission to drive you up the wall. She would call at all hours, day or night, and say in an undeniably sexy voice, "This is your secret pal. You are not smoking, are you? If you feel the urge, don't. Stop right there and let's talk about it."

She sounded so sexy and nice that I asked her if I could go over to her place to discuss the gnawing problem in person. It would give me something to do with my hands, one of the reasons people start smoking in the first place. However, she would have none of it. "If we met," she said severely, "I would no longer be your secret pal and I couldn't help you."

After the third time she phoned me at 4 A.M. to make sure I wasn't smoking—"You weren't asleep, were you?" she always asked politely—I changed my number. I also started smoking again, since there's not much else to do when you're awakened at 4 A.M.

Before you come down hard on me for being an oaf and an idiot, remember that my generation was pretty well brainwashed on the subject, even though my father referred to cigarettes as "pimp sticks" and the authentic nuts (or Naders) of the era called them "coffin nails," a description even more accurate than they realized.

Generally, smoking was all tied up with *machismo,* charisma and sophistication, especially in the movies. There was John Gilbert, a cigarette dangling from his lip, bayoneting a Hun in a World War I epic. We squirmed with envious pleasure to watch Edmund Lowe, impeccable in white tie and tails, extract a cigarette from his silver case, light it with a flick of his Dunhill and blow smoke into Lilyan Tashman's adoring face. There's Bogie, "setting fire to a cigarette," in Hammett's phrase, and Paul Henreid starting a fad by lighting his and his girl's at the same time in the same mouth (his).

World War II made smoking patriotic. Lucky Strike Green went to war ("and came back a dirty Red," somebody pointed out, referring to the color of the new filter pack). "Smoke 'em if you've got 'em," barked every top sarge at every rest period. K and C rations came with cigarettes included. In Europe, we found out that people would do anything and I mean anything, for a cigarette. Tobacco power!

Of course, our generation was also the last that believed the people in Washington knew what they were doing, "or they wouldn't be there." It takes a long time for some of us to grow up.

A forty-year habit, over and done with. The main thing is not to think about it—beautiful red pack, white tube between lips, snap of flame, draw of tobacco, puff of smoke exhaled slowly, pleasurably, sensuously . . . I mean, who needs it?

☆ ☆ ☆

FUTURE REFERENCE: I stepped up to the bar in Enrico's, ordered a Campari and looked around the room. It was just an ordinary day. Scott Beach was at the "family table," playing his psaltery (he made it himself) for editor Blair Fuller and architect Sandy Walker. Nearby, Barnaby Conrad was arguing movies with Mel Tormé. A newly

50

bearded Herb Gold, just back from Haiti, toyed with his eggs-in-hell while listening to Enrico practice his violin. Outside, Richard Brautigan was scribbling poetry on an old envelope, two tables away from Silent Evan Connell, staring into space, and Hard Hat McCabe stood at the bar, contemplating The Odd Couple conferring in a booth: William Matson Roth, the shipping scion, with Paul Jacobs, the only radical in the world who runs a cooking school. As I left, it dawned on me that fifty years from now, historians will make as much of this scene as earlier ones made of the Algonquin Round Table. The nice thing about this one is that it's happening right now and everybody takes it for granted.

One of a Kind

"THAT'S FUNNY," mused a young woman of my acquaintance, "I thought he'd died a long time ago." She was looking at page one headline reading, "Walter Winchell Dead," and her remark, while a little cruel, was accurate enough.

Winchell died when his column died in the old *Daily Mirror*, which also died. He died when his little world died—the "Great White Way" that existed only in his (and Damon Runyon's) imagination, The Main Stem, the Big Apple, the whole phony business of Making It in Bigtown USA, or becoming just another broken heart among the Bright Lights of Old Broadway.

One by one, the points of his compass disappeared. Lindy's, where his nightly appearance caused a stir ("There's Walter!" "Hiya, Walter!"), closed forever. The Stork Club ("Walter is ready to receive you at Table One") is now a minipark. The Astor has been torn down and Toots Shor's is padlocked. The Winchell era is over and three-dot journalism is dead. As one of its last practitioners, I should know.

Winchell was part of the Manhattan that appealed to the

51

small boy in all of us—the New York of Jimmy Walker, Yankee Stadium, Babe Ruth, the *World* and the *Trib,* Cole Porter, Gershwin, the best of the best—and yet he, who chronicled it all for so many years, is already forgotten. At his peak, he appeared in more papers and made more money than any other U.S. journalist, before or since, but serious newsmen belittled him, and in journalism schools, he is a comic footnote, a coiner of words and a teller of jokes.

A year or so ago, the *Atlantic* magazine asked me to do an article on Winchell—a "tough" report that would show up the old man for the bad guy he really was, professionally. But even as I wrote the piece, I knew it would be rejected. It's hard to knock a guy you had admired a long time ago, and the words came out soft and gentle. In rejecting the article, the *Atlantic*'s editor, Robert Manning, said, "I will not have my pages used for the glorification of Walter Winchell." By his lights, he was right, and I was relieved that the project had failed.

In the first place, I was the wrong man for the job. Like my confreres in the business of inserting short sentences and half-baked thoughts between three dots, I owed too much to Winchell to be willing or able to kick him. I didn't want to be one of the many he called "Ingrate!" at the top of his very loud voice.

In the late '20s and early '30s, I must have been the only school kid in Sacramento who pedaled his bicycle downtown every weekday—rain or shine—to buy the old San Francisco *Call-Bulletin.* The *Call* carried Winchell, as did some eight hundred other papers, and his frenetic, splenetic flashes and dashes brought a world of unimaginable excitement into that valley town.

He wrote in an original language called "Winchellingo," and the column was a success because he was a showman, not a reporter. It was also a failure for the same reason. His excesses dazzled the peasants like me, but drew sneers from the cognoscenti—something Winchell was sensitive about (he showed it in his admiration for "real" reporters).

With his scatter-gun technique—"People don't get bored if you change the subject often enough"—he scored tremendous scoops and committed incredible boners. The true mark of the man may have been his constant crowing over his exclusives—"As reported in this column three weeks ago!"—and his refusal to acknowledge his errors. His retractions were grudging, graceless and sometimes undecipherable.

What his critics refuse to concede was the cleverness of the Winchell column. At its best, it moved with what seemed like authentic Broadway rhythm—fast, tough, smart-alecky. He had a great ear for dialogue, punch lines and puns (about Mme. Chiang Kai-shek and her many trips to the U.S. to ask for money, he cracked, "She keeps coming back like a Soong"). He could write dialect jokes better than anybody else in the business. His subheads, like "Sallies in My Alley," were fresh and novel. As a journalistic entertainer, he may have been unique, and, like most of my generation of young columnists, I started out by imitating him slavishly.

I met Winchell only a few times, but he was always cordial. The first time was at the Stork Club about thirty years ago, when he put his arm around my shoulder and introduced me to Sherman Billingsley. "This kid," said Winchell, grinning, "imitates me better than any other kid in the business." He meant it as a compliment and I accepted it as one. In our little world, Winchell was king.

It took years for me to outgrow his influence, and maybe I haven't shed it completely. But even a dedicated three-dotter like myself, even an admirer of his techniques, couldn't accept the rantings, ravings and excesses of the Late Period Winchell. As his hatreds and self-pity took over the column, he began to sound demented. The world changed and Broadway disappeared but Winchell stood still until he was swallowed up by the onrushing past.

Winchell: gone, forgotten. Don't think that all of us who once cast ourselves in his mold aren't identifying like mad.

☆ ☆ ☆

MUSIC DEPT.: The Los Angeles City Council, stung by the worldwide success of "I Left My Heart in San Francisco," is looking for an official L.A. song, and in connection with this somebody sends me the yellowing sheet music of a song written long ago by Jack Lipton and Walter Bedbury. The chorus, a rouser, goes like this: "God took the

53

heart from the Garden of Eden and gave it to the grand old Bay; He made a fairyland out of the prairieland, out of a pasture He made Broadway! He made the skyline the mainline to Heaven. Wonderful Wonderland! The West was blessed with riches grand when God gave California— OAKLAND!" That's what is known in the trade as a surprise ending, but with a few changes here and there, I think it might do nicely for Los Angeles. "The West was blessed with a golden dawn when God gave Los Angeles— Forest Lawn!" And so on.

ADDENDUM: "The song made us rich and comparatively well-known, and at first that all seemed wonderful. But now I'm sorry we ever wrote it. Lately, San Francisco seems to be dying by inches, and all the qualities that appealed to us are vanishing. Maybe we were partly responsible—I suppose the song made thousands of people come to the city and, in various ways, contribute to the changes that are destroying it. San Francisco is no longer the city we wrote about." So, sadly, said Douglass Cross of Clear Lake, who, with George Cory, wrote our official song, "I Left My Heart in San Francisco."

GROUCHO OBSERVED: There he was at the Trident in Sausalito, familiar black beret atop his head, eyes still roguish behind thick glasses, expression alternating between sly smile and Dirty Old Man Leer. Groucho Marx, living legend—"not to mention my legendary liver—" When he enters a room, you know he's something special: conversation stops, people stare and in his wake you hear the voices whispering, "Groucho Marx?"

"I gotta go to the men's room," he complained to his attractive auburn-haired aide, Erin Fleming. "Every time I go to the men's room I meet a man from Omaha. I wrote a song about Omaha once. Sold two copies. I forgot my pills that keep me from going to the men's room and meeting that guy from Omaha." "I'll phone Marvin's wife," said Erin, "and she'll send them up."

At that the octogenarian Groucho became the eternal Groucho. Knees bent into the Marx crouch. Eyes rolled. Cigar was gracefully extricated from mouth. "The hell with the pills," he said, "just send up Marvin's wife!"

Why was he doing an exhausting series of one-man shows? "A man has to do something in his old age," he said. "We've been getting all these letters from people wanting me to do a show. When one came in from Carnegie Hall, I couldn't believe it! Groucho in Carnegie Hall? So I said yes."

"Then," cut in Erin, "we had to figure out a place to break in the act. We went through the files and found a letter inviting Groucho to Iowa State, in Ames, Iowa. Perfect! You could bomb in Iowa and who'd hear about it? The invitation was from a Thomas Wilhite at Ames. His letterhead stationery had 'Thomas Wilhite Productions' in the biggest type you ever saw."

"Yeah," nodded Groucho, taking up the thread. "I figured he had to be the biggest producer in the Midwest. So we land in Des Moines and waiting for us is one seventeen-year-old boy with corn coming out of his ears. 'I'm Wilhite,' he says. A child! Then he leads me over to a hearse for the ride to Ames. 'That's appropriate,' I say, and the kid says, 'I'm sorry, Mr. Marx, I borrowed from our undertaker—it's the only limousine we have in Ames'!"

The show in Iowa was a big success. As Groucho was leaving, he said to Wilhite, "And what're you going to do next, young fellow?" "Well," replied Wilhite, "I had such luck with you that I just wrote a letter to Greta Garbo."

Groucho was wearing the rosette of a high French decoration that has been given to only two foreigners: Chaplin and Marx. When Pompidou presented the medal at Cannes, Groucho held it up, turned to the audience and asked, "How much can I get for this in a hock shop?" Pompidou, fortunately, didn't get it.

"The last time I saw Chaplin," mused Groucho, "all he said to me was 'keep warm, keep warm.' I know what he meant. As long as you're warm, you're still alive. Well, good night."

☆ ☆ ☆

MRS. MIKE CARMICHAEL was taken aback down at Pebble Beach when she heard Clint Eastwood say, "Go on, beat it, kid," to a little boy who asked for his autograph. Her faith was restored, however, when the child pouted, "But Daddy, you're giving everybody else one."

☆ ☆ ☆

STEP UP and shake hands with Greg Rogers, a schoolteacher in Missouri. When a youngster from Santa Rosa moved there and into his class, Greg had all his sixth-graders study the Northern California scene and write reports. Herewith some of the more entertaining excerpts:

"Fort Ross is a famous historic monument that few people have ever heard of" . . . "San Francisco was founded in 1776 but I forget whether it was in AC or DC times" . . . "In Northern California are found such things as almonds, manganese, grapes, chickens and plums. Keeping all this stuff separated is one of the main jobs of Califordians."

Some unsung genius on the growth of San Francisco: "Once upon a time it happened that there was this spot on the map that some people came to. Pretty soon more people came and made the spot bigger. Then it grew bigger and bigger. And bigger and bigger and bigger. And that's about the size of it up to this morning."

LOGIC: "Clear Lake has saved many lives by people not trying to swim across it." Future shock: "Santa Rosa is located in California at the present time." Utter frustration: "The Napa Valley is in California. Maybe it is in Northern California. Maybe it is in Southern California. I do not know. It takes all my knowing to know the Napa Valley is in California." Smugness: "Humboldt Bay is on the Pacific Coast in case I ever want to know."

And finally a touch of poetry from a little girl: "From now on I will put gladness and wonder in my same thought about Northern California."

56

☆ ☆ ☆

ATTORNEY GUY KORNBLUM, aware of my unfortunate weakness for unusual names, forwards the letterhead stationery of a law firm on Hendy Avenue in Sunnyvale called Vermilbeck, Brodanpet & Phlegrillzinger—and isn't that a dinger? Well, yes and no. A couple of years ago, three major law firms (Brobeck Phleger & Harrison and Miller Groezinger Pettit & Evers of San Francisco, plus Verrill Dana Philbrick Putnam & Williamson of Portland, Maine) joined forces to pursue a huge case in behalf of Westinghouse, and it was Robert Ivey of the Miller firm who had this wizard idea of combining the names into one technically nonexistent law firm. The suit won, Vermilbeck, Brodanpet & Phlegrillzinger have disbanded.

☆ ☆ ☆

"SOME PEOPLE," cackles Robbie Orben, "are squeamish about raising their own holiday turkeys but not me. Back in January we bought a live turkey named Clarence who became like a member of the family. We kept him in the house, fed him and took him for walks, but when the time came there was no nonsense about it. We had him for Thanksgiving dinner. He sat on my right."

Laugh, I Thought I'd Die

WELL, NOBODY said life would be easy, but for members of my generation, it's becoming ridiculous. One is reminded of the joke about the psychiatrist's secretary who says, "In my office, I can't win. If I come to work early, I'm anxious, if I'm on time, I'm compulsive, and if I'm late, I'm hostile."

Our group, the over fiftys, is in the same boat, and it has

sprung a leak. Most of us were born poor and are in danger of dying affluent, drowning in a sea of plastic nondisposable luxuries none of us really wants or enjoys. Our pockets filled with inflated dollars to spend on junk, we look back on the Depression as a Golden Age: then, a dollar was big, round, shiny and heavy—and there was that vibrant, confident voice in the White House to give us hope.

Our needs were simple, our ambitions even simpler. "Upwardly mobile" long before the term was invented, all we had to do was get to someplace called The Top. There were green meadows at The Top, under clear and sunny skies. In the middle of the meadow stood The House, shining and white, containing The Beautiful Wife and exactly 3.3 children; and there were two cars in the garage, the Cadillac and the station wagon.

That was our dream, and a record number of us Made It —if not to The Top, at least to within shouting distance. Having achieved this eminence, we find the meadow ruined by DDT and cluttered with 48 billion cans and 26 billion nonreturnable bottles. The sun is seen dimly, if at all, through a blanket of smog. Each person in The House will pollute three million gallons of water in his lifetime and consume food at a rate unparalleled in history. The cars—the very symbol of Making It—turn out to be gas-drinking smog-making death-dealing monsters; Henry Ford put us on wheels so we could get to Oblivion faster. As for the 3.3 children, they're too many. Even if we reduce this to 2.5, the U.S. population would be 330 million by the end of the century. The ideal number is 0.0, but even that won't help much for at least thirty years because most of us live too long.

Our generation can't win for winning. If we think the necessary changes can be made by peaceful evolution—well, we don't know what's going on, do we, Mr. Jones?

The lost group: we worked hard for what we got and what did it get us? Obloquy, that's what, and not all of it unjustified. Good intentions are what our road is paved with, and we know where it's taking us, downhill all the way.

And yet we are too old to be revolutionary. Born to the distant clip-clop of horses' hoofs, we have seen rockets rise to the moon and the destruction of our own environment. Every day we contribute to it without knowing how to stop the cycle.

Well, nobody said the United States As We Know It would live forever.

Our well-meaning generation, living and learning the hard way. Even the welfare state is a disaster; when you see the people jammed into busses, being jolted home after a hard day's work, you can understand their unreasonable anger at people on relief. When we see yet another skyscraper rising, we look at it with foreboding; once we were thrilled and delighted with our growing skyline—each new building a cause for celebration and self-congratulation—and now we see it for what it is; a rising menace that almost literally scrapes the sky out of existence. We sympathize, sincerely and generously, with the blacks, the people trapped in ghettoes, the starving and the hopeless, and yet everything we try to do turns out ill-advised, insulting, condescending or so far wide of the mark as to be pointless. There are still those, nevertheless, who wonder why our generation drinks so much.

We achieved our dreams of the penniless thirties and they turn out to be just a little nightmarish. A house, a car and kids bouncing around at our feet in Norman Rockwell profusion—hi-ho and over the hill; every time your kid flushes the toilet something terrible happens to the environment and the Army Corps of Engineers has to build another dam. We're too young for the retirement centers and too old to learn the new tricks that might save us from ourselves. All we have is a hollow feeling in the pit of the stomach and money to burn, thereby adding to the pollution.

Gallant to the end, we join committees, pay our taxes, buy smaller and smaller cars, and vote for the senator who will support the bill that won't provide half enough money to do the job. Cigarettes may be hazardous to your health, pot is hazardous to your freedom, and as for The Pill, that's getting hard to swallow too. Still, there is always love, but make it the way the porcupines do—very, very carefully. By-by, baby, and amen.

MATT KELLY, vacationing in Marrakech, struck up a conversation with a venerable titled Britisher—an earl, no less—who reminisced: "I was in San Francisco only once—years ago, to make a speech—and struck up a friendship with a lovely lady from Burlingame. Her husband was away on a longish trip and, well, one thing led to another. Then it became a bit sticky. She was overdue, her husband was due home any minute, and she went to take a rabbit test. Let me tell you we were both quite worried. The day after the test, I still hadn't heard from her and didn't dare call, what with her husband being home. I dined alone at the Mark Hopkins, very depressed, and as I entered my room, I heard a strange rustling noise from the bed. I turned on the light and there in the middle of the bed sat a big, white, very lively rabbit, with a pink ribbon around its neck and a note saying 'Relax, darling.' I must say, old boy, it was the classiest thing that has ever happened to me."

☆ ☆ ☆

"I'D LIKE to lunch at some place that's typically old San Francisco," said the Baron Philippe de Rothschild to his good friend, art dealer Bill Pearson—so Bill took him to Tadich's, which, being typically old San Francisco, doesn't take reservations. After they'd waited thirty minutes in the crowded little bar area, the baron sighed, "I dislike doing things like this, but perhaps it would help if you told them who I am." "I dislike telling you this," said Bill, grinning, "but I did—fifteen minutes ago!"

☆ ☆ ☆

DICK VOLK, a good friend of Friends of the Earth, said severely to a young lady wearing a kangaroo coat at Monroe's, "Do you know how many kangaroos it took to make that?" "Well," she replied prettily, "two, at least."

60

☆ ☆ ☆

POLES APART: At the Gold Mirror on Taraval, Jerry Johnstone was shocked to see a friend walk in with another man's wife. Calling him aside, Jerry warned, "You know what it says in the Ten Commandments—'Thou shalt not covet thy neighbor's wife.'" "But, Jerry," protested the friend, "I live in the Parkside and she's from the Marina!"

☆ ☆ ☆

LONGSHORE LEADER Harry Bridges was phoned recently by reporter Alden Whitman of the New York *Times,* who said he'd like to fly to San Francisco to talk with him. "I don't give interviews," said Bridges, at which Whitman explained, "Well, it won't be an interview, exactly. I just want to get some—uh—background material for a piece to be printed later." "Why don't you level with me?" gruffed Harry. "You mean you want to write my obituary, right?" When Whitman admitted it, Bridges chuckled, "You're being premature. I may be seventy and I may smoke too much, but I feel fine. Let's forget it." "Look, Harry," pleaded Whitman, "I'm dying for a free trip to San Francisco." "Now you're *really* leveling," said Bridges, grinning. "In that case, come ahead." Whitman spent a week with Bridges, whose obituary is now up to date. It's enough to make a man stop smoking—and it did.

The Hindsyte Saga

HARVEY SULLIVAN, engaged in some research on early San Francisco, stumbled across a veritable gem: a

Government Printing Office report, dated 1906 and titled "Earthquake in California, April 18, 1906—Special Report of Major General Adolphus W. Greely, Commanding Pacific Division." Browsing therein, we find the remarks of Captain Meriwether L. Walker, Corps of Engineers, USA, who testified, "At about 5:15 A.M., April 18, 1906, I was awakened by a terrific shaking of the house and rushed out. Upon inspection, the damage to my house appeared very slight and I concluded that it was not a very severe shock and returned to my bed and fell asleep."

At this late date, decades later, we salute Captain Walker, a hitherto unsung nonhero of what some historians call "the worst disaster ever to befall an American city." What *sang-froid!* While all about him the city rocked and rolled, he was back in bed, sound asleep and demonstrating what would come to be known as the True San Francisco Spirit. To him, an earthquake was no worse than a bad hangover. I would like to think he slept throughout that entire awful day, awakening at last to find the city in flame and ruin. "I wonder what they put in that last Pisco Punch," one can hear him mutter as he pulls down the blind and stumbles back to bed.

The earthquake and fire continue to haunt San Francisco, and while we're not going to get any expert testimony from the supinely prone Captain Walker, there are still a garrulous few around to remind us that something irretrievable was lost on the day the earth shook and the sky burned. What it was, exactly, is hard to define now, for even the sharpest memories are blurring and the tales are all strangely similar—even a bit boring. Dad ran out into the street in his nightshirt. The chimney fell and almost hit Buddy. We thought the world was coming to an end. We went up to Lafayette Park and watched the city burn. Everybody pitched in and helped everybody else—the spirit was fantastic. I saw a looter shot and hung from a lamppost: fable unto myth into legend.

"We thought the world had come to an end"—that is the key sentence, the one that gnaws perpetually at everyone who is fascinated by this city. From reading the record, we know that all San Francisco is divided into two parts: the city that flowered before the earthquake, and the entirely different one that rose from the flames. What is not quite clear, to this day, is what it was that died in those flames, but we suspect it was something special. "The gayest, lightest-hearted and most pleasure-loving city of the Western continent is dead," wrote Will Irwin as the fire marched across the hills. He knew San Francisco would be rebuilt but he sensed even then that the City That Was could never be again. Whatever it was.

At the time of the earthquake, San Francisco as a metropolis was only fifty years old, yet it had already entered the lists of world-renowned (and beloved) cities. Stevenson, Wilde and Kipling held it in high regard. Years later, when asked to name his three favorite cities, H. G. Wells would say without hesitation, "London, Paris and San Francisco before the fire." A Barbary Coast that was compared favorably with Port Said, Caruso singing at the opera house, W. & J. Sloane opening a San Francisco branch simply to furnish the Palace Hotel, gorgeously robed Chinese mandarins strolling Dupont Gai, tong wars amid bursting firecrackers, saloonkeepers into millionaires, building garish mansions on hilltops—a panoply of sudden riches that existed nowhere else and was never to be repeated.

We San Francisco lovers study the old photographs and wonder what it was like, this tiny city with forests of spars along the waterfront and horse-drawn drays clattering across cobbled East Street. We read the old menus, with their treasures of terrapin and venison, and can almost hear the cry of the street-corner vendors selling wild ducks. Lamplighters and horse-drawn streetcars, bicycles and carriages in Golden Gate Park, the laughter of the bohemians long past midnight in the Montgomery Block and Papa Coppa's and the singsong girls calling softly in Chinatown alleys. These are the legends that haunt us, these are the anguished pleasures we missed . . .

It is not enough to say this is selective history, powdered and perfumed, with all the foul smells filtered out by faulty and faltering memories. We know there was another side to the story: the scandalous ill-treatment of the Chinese, the disease and poverty, the low wages dispensed by robber barons who drank champagne by the bucket at the old Poodle Dog. Yet the suspicion persists that the San Francisco that perished on April 18, 1906, was uniquely blessed: you have only to stare at the faces of the survivors, encamped in the park, to see a rare courage and vitality there. They looked strong and unafraid . . . Of course, they didn't know then what we know today: that they were playing the last act of a tragedy. They had outlived their own city.

A Charmed Life

"IF I HAD my life to live over again I'd live over a liquor store"—Joe E. Lewis, circa 1937.

That's all well and good for bibulous Joe E., but if I had my life to live over I'd like to live it as a rich right-wing Republican, hereinafter to be referred to as RWRs, or Rowsers. In these troubled times, only Rowsers have peace of mind, all questions answered, all passion spent. Richard Nixon? "Not my cup of tea, actually—I mean, we wouldn't have him to *dinner*—but what choice was there? A crook, yes, but who could vote for that other fellow?" Reagan? "Can't imagine spending a weekend with him, y'know—actors not my type—but still he might make a decent job of it in the White House. Wasn't a bad governor, after all."

You hardly ever see a Rowser with deep worry lines or even pimples. Rowsers have clear skins and brains as smooth and shiny as a custard. They won't argue with you because (a) they know they're right; (b) raising one's voice, except to return a bottle of sour wine, is bad form; and (c) one never argues with a social inferior anyway. They'll laugh at a dirty joke but never at one's peers. They don't even fret over fashion. Mr. Rowser knows that the suits he bought in London a decade ago will come back into style next year, and Mrs. Rowser's wardrobe, by Worth, will never be out, having never been in. His watch and her jewels are heirlooms, hence beyond discussion.

With Rowsers, it's not a question of "My country, right or wrong." It's *my* country, literally, at a steady seven per cent per annum, compounded. When a fun-loving Rowser boy makes a little joke about "chippies and clippies," he's not talking about the Tenderloin—he means blue chips and coupons. He may also make some knowing references to "kneejerk liberals," but deep down inside, he's all jerk, throbbing reflexively and invisibly to some rhythm in the past, a nice place to live if you can afford it. Granddad saw to it long ago that he could. He's properly grateful to the old boy, in a well-bred way.

The party in the big house on Washington was crowded with Rowsers, making it look like a men's club into which the women had wandered by accident. Rowsers look so much alike they could all be cousins, and many are ("the very rich are different from you and me"; for one thing, they're related). Most of them had at least three names, some with Roman numerals at the end, and many were just short of handsome, speaking in wan elegance around the silver spoons in their mouths. These are not the Beautiful People, those nouveaux invented by publicists. Rowsers are serenely beautiful all their lives, never having had to struggle. Even their wives are handed down to them.

"All this fuss about environment, really. We bundle up our old papers and put the cans and bottles in boxes—I mean, what more can we do?" What if the Scavengers run out of places to dump them? "Well, that's *their* problem, isn't it? That's what they're paid for." Gary Snyder, the poet, says you can't be serious about the environment without being a revolutionary—you have to be willing to restructure society. "Let's by all means restructure it. Who reads the *Social Register* anyway? Come come, that's a joke. By the way, who's this Snyder boy? Seems to me I went to Yale with a Snyder—" The cool, clear logic of untroubled minds, free of rancor or original thought. When a maverick Rowser accused one of his fellows of being "fascist-minded," the laughing response was, "Really, dear boy, can you see me prancing around with an arm band?" From the police ("Those who have trouble with them are looking for it") to the blacks ("No problem, get along with them fine, always have"), the reactions were as bland as the faces. But have you ever *been* to Hunters Point? "Actually, yes. My old carrier came into the shipyard, and I had lunch aboard with the skipper. Say, do you play bridge?"

Bob Dylan was wrong. Mr. Jones, like the rest of the Rowser Boys, knows very well what is going on, and he plans to rise above it till it goes away. A modern-day Madame Defarge may be clicking her needles alongside the guillotine, but with Mr. Jones-Rowser's luck, she's probably knitting him a pair of socks—and Argyles, at that.

☆ ☆ ☆

CASHIER in a downtown cafeteria, explaining to a Little Old Lady pensioner why the prices have increased: "You see, we all got a raise, so we have to pass it along to the customers." LOL, sadly: "But my dear, I didn't get a raise."

☆ ☆ ☆

GEORGE LEMONT phoned his stockbroker to ask, "If I sell everything I have right now, what would I get?" Broker: "About thirty-two minutes on a parking meter."

☆ ☆ ☆

AT A MASS political meeting of University of California students in Hillel House, off campus, somebody interrupted the heavy debate to report a minibus blocking the parking lot. Chairman Conn (Ringo) Hallinan asked that the minibus be moved. Weary voice: "I move the minibus." Second voice: "I second it." Conn: "The minibus has been moved and seconded. Proceed."

OF HUMAN INTEREST: Around the Sir Francis Drake Hotel on Powell, the staff used to chuckle about Kasson Avery. "What a character!" they'd say in the most loving kind of way.

A bachelor, he was one of the Drake's two permanent guests, having checked into Room 803 ($300 a month) shortly after the hotel opened in 1928. There was nothing unusual about his appearance: tall, slender, neatly dressed. And he was exceedingly polite.

What made him a "character" was his excessive thrift. The staff was amused that every night he'd walk up and down the halls with a paper bag, picking up empty bottles that the other guests left outside their doors, and taking them to a nearby grocery store for cash refunds. And he could never pass the phone booths in the lobby without checking the return slots for coins.

Now and then he'd approach David Plant, then the Drake's general manager, and wonder nervously if his rent were about to be raised, "what with inflation and all." "Don't worry about it, Mr. Avery," Plant would reply kindly. "We are pleased to have you as a permanent guest."

Well, the careful Mr. Avery died at the age of eighty-seven —and left a net estate of $1,848,000. Under the terms of his will, the Salvation Army gets $924,000 and the YMCA and YWCA $462,000 apiece—much to the startled delight of the officers of these organizations. They had never heard of Kasson Avery.

FOOTNOTE: After his death, the Drake's housekeeper was cleaning out the drawers in his room and found a little black book in which he had entered his living expenses for the past few years. Never once had he spent more than thirty-five cents for breakfast or two dollars for lunch or dinner.

THIS YOUNGISH COUPLE got into a cab and were busily engaged in passing a marijuana cigarette back and forth when the cabbie asked, "Say, is that grass?" "Yeah," nodded the man. Cabbie, relieved: "Thank god, I thought it was my brakes."

All the Sad Young Faces

ANCIENT HIEROGLYPHIC found on the wall of a long-hidden grotto in Golden Gate Park: "The good old days really were."

Almost every San Franciscan of a certain age subscribes to that sentiment. Even those of uncertain age. I was thinking about that while walking down Powell toward Market on a particularly cold and nasty afternoon. The hippies were strewn everywhere, in various stages of zonked-outness. Of course, it could have been the miserable weather, but all of a sudden they looked forlorn, pale, sick, drawn. And the startling thought suddenly struck: "Are they really having as much fun as we think?"

Item: He was maybe sixteen, with lank blond hair to his shoulders, and shivering in the icy wind. As well he might be: his soiled white shirt had several buttons missing, revealing no undershirt. Thin tattered jacket and old Levis with holes at the knees and seat. "Got any bread, man?" I gave him some. "Thanks, man." He looked strung out on something heavy. "Y'know," I said, "I know a clinic you could go to. The phone number is—" "That's okay. I'm gettin' out of this town as soon as I can, anyway."

It's an article of faith among my peer group that today's young have it Real Good. The legend is of their own making but we tend to accept it with wry smiles and shrugs: all that hanging around doing nothing, all those guitars and bongos, all that easy-to-get sex and drugs. "The hippies have the right idea," thinks the straight, rushing through Union Square after a hasty lunch to get back to his desk before the boss. "Why am I killing myself?" The answer is simple enough: he's killing himself because that's the only way he can live. He probably feels sorry for himself. No need for you to.

Testimony: "All of a sudden it's over," she was saying, this young girl who has already lived a lifetime. JFK, Montgomery and Selma, the Peace Corps, the Haight-Ashbury when it was good. Now suddenly she's thirty and in the middle of her own gap. Too young for us, too old for the oncoming wave that already regards her as an anachronism. "I feel lost in space," said this beautiful girl. "I can't relate to the new kids or to your crowd." Suddenly she looked angry. "You may be old but at least you have a frame of reference."

She stopped there, but I knew what she meant and could even agree. Our prenuclear world was different and our hangups were simpler, as we were. ("Hangups." There's another justifiable complaint among the young. We take over their language while rejecting their principles.) Our generation knew where it had been—through a scarifying Great Depression—and we knew where we were going: straight to a job as soon as we could get one, no questions asked. We had seen fear in our fathers' eyes and it wasn't going to happen to us, no matter what we had to swallow. There isn't a man in our group who doesn't dread the day he gets fired. Security? What security?

Exhibit: The son of a prominent San Franciscan is now twenty-eight and gradually leaving the street scene. He has cut his hair and is dropping his gear, piece by piece, for the inevitable suit and job. "The real hippies are gone," he says. "The scene is full of young phonies who don't know what's going on—except dope, maybe. Well, I'm off the drugs for good. And I'm tired of the phonies thinking I'm in the same bag with them just because I dress the way they do. I don't think the way they do." He paused. "That doesn't mean I've changed my philosophy. I'm not putting you down, man, but I'm not joining you, either."

Few groups in history have been as vilified as ours—we tried so hard, we did so badly—and yet in many ways we had it better than today's young generation. They had a war they hate, with a multiplicity of good reasons. We had a war with a beginning, a middle and an end, a war that enlisted the support of almost everybody. It was no big deal to become a part of it, it took no agonies of conscience. We were never as young—or as beautiful to gaze upon—as the long, lean, leggy youth of today, but on the other hand we were less confused. In the prenuclear age, our role was preordained: the first date-with-corsage, the dancing cheek-to-cheek, among other contact points, the Mickey Mouse bands playing banal songs, the political naïveté: we bought it all, meanwhile hanging onto the job for dear life.

Down near the end of Powell, on this same wintry summer's day, I passed two miserable-looking teen-age girls in tattered gear. "Got a nickel, man?" one said. I stopped. "A nickel won't buy much," I said, handing over a couple of bills. "How old are you?" "Fifteen," said one, the tears starting down her soiled cheeks. "We're hungry. And a long way from home." "And lost," said the other in a faint voice . . . The good old days really were. For today's young, there may never be any.

Paul

THERE WAS A TIME in San Francisco—maybe even a golden time—when everybody knew Paul. You didn't have to add the last name (which happens to be Smith). For almost two decades his first name was being dropped all over town—"That crazy Paul" and "Guess what Paul has done now" and "Seen Paul lately?"—but it's not like that now, and too bad. A new generation has come along that might ask, "Paul who?"—a fair question. Maybe I can help to answer it.

Few people—and fewer San Franciscans—become legends in their own time (that tiresome phrase), but Paul made it, and made it look easy. At twenty-five he became editor of the *Chronicle,* the youngest editor of a metropolitan daily in the country; "boy wonder," he was called, a tag that would forever haunt him. He entered World War II as a Navy lieutenant commander, resigned his commission, enlisted in the Marines as a private, won the Silver Star in Pacific combat, left the *Chronicle* in 1952 to take over *Collier's* when (as he was to learn) it was already fatally ill . . . these are the bare outlines of the legend. The man is something more.

I first met Paul in 1936, when he hired me away from the Sacramento *Union,* not the hardest trick of that or any other year. As I observed earlier, a lot of older and better men were after the job—that of radio editor—"but," he said, smiling, swiveling in his chair, "I'm hiring you because you're the first guy I've met in this business who's younger than I am." (True; some of the copy boys on the paper then were old enough to be his father.) The next time I saw him, a few days later, he almost ran me down at Fifth and Mission in his mile-long, sixteen-cylinder Cadillac convertible, top down. "Watch it, kid," he called out, with a friendly wave of his gloved hand, as he roared past. I had never seen anything quite so glamorous.

The young Paul hired a lot of kids like me in those years. "Smith's whiz kids," we were called derisively by rival newspapermen, and as for Paul, he, according to *Time* magazine, was "brash, cocky." "Dashing, gutsy," would have been a fairer description, for Paul changed the face of San Francisco journalism: under his impact, the writing became sharper, the make-up better, the point of view broader. You can't believe how bad the local papers were when Paul took over unless you go back through the files.

Paul—the onetime lumberjack, banker, roving correspondent—appeared on the local scene at a time when San Francisco was torn as never since. A general strike had divided the city into two camps, both armed. A disastrous Salinas lettuce strike exploded into violence. Paul had the courage (unheard of, in those days) to treat Harry Bridges as if he didn't wear horns, and to write sympathetically of the lettuce strikers. The young editor learned his first lesson: an advertisers' boycott was clamped on the *Chronicle.* Then the advertisers learned theirs: Paul ran that story, under big

71

headlines, on Page One. The readers reacted sympathetically, and the Smith legend grew.

Never let it be said that Paul didn't help feed the legend. He delighted in the offbeat, the flamboyant gesture, especially in his choice of friends. His chief mentors were (on the right) Herbert Hoover and (on the left) muckraker Lincoln Steffens—a combination that would make a schizoid out of a lesser man. At his fabled two-story apartment— above Julius' Castle on Telegraph Hill—you were as likely to meet Dorothy Parker as Clare Boothe Luce, Noël Coward as Harry Bridges. The combination must have worked: Fascists called him a Communist, Communists called him a Fascist. Democrats called him a Black Republican, Republicans called him a "pinko."

After he had mediated and settled a particular nasty warehouse strike, forty thousand San Franciscans signed a petition asking him to run for mayor, but he declined. It was just as well, for the salary wouldn't have been half enough— as no salary had ever been, for Paul lived in the grand manner: driver, houseboy, cook, dinner parties for 150 (and by now the Cadillac had sprouted red lights and a siren). He bought suits a dozen at a time, smoked incessantly, ate too little, slept even less, and was the single best drinker I have ever met—straight scotches, one upon the other, and keeping his head while all about him were falling on theirs, face down.

The last time I saw Paul, we had lunch at the Palace. For miserably long months, he had been in a hospital, after suffering a stroke, and he entered the Garden Court in a wheel chair. Old friends and old waiters crowded around, and the spark returned to his eyes. When he was driven off, in the old convertible he loves so much—almost the last symbol of his golden years—he waved his hand and grinned "So long, kid." At fifty-five he was no longer a boy, but still a wonder.

Now, a decade later, he wastes away, almost forgotten, in a Peninsula convalescent home. After a series of strokes, he lives in a wheel chair and dreams. I cringe to think of the memories that must torture him at three o'clock on a sleepless night. Outside, the convertible is turning to rust.

72

☆ ☆ ☆

WILLIAM BUFFALINO of Boston gives our thieves full marks for excellent taste. He parked his new Eldorado on a downtown street and came back to find all his clothes stolen except for one shirt, one tie, one suit, one set of underwear and one pair of socks, all blending perfectly. A note read, "I hope you approve of my selections. And I locked your doors so they wouldn't be stolen."

☆ ☆ ☆

I ENVISION the day when the announcer at Candlestick Park will say, "And now, folks, here's the lineup. In left field, Joe Orengo. In center, Dave Falk. In right, Stu Adams. At first base, Blair Fuller. At third, Ida Brown, and behind the plate, Nick Geracimos" . . . The team? No, the attendance.

Pillar of Salt

HE IS A good fellow, his ruddy complexion more a tribute to his steady drinking (accompanied by the clatter of dice boxes) than to healthy exercise; he'll run for a cable car or a pair of pretty legs, but not much else. He feels more comfortable on Post Street than on Market because he feels there is something vaguely wrong about really scruffy people, and he still looks twice at women who smoke on the street. On Straw Hat Day, he buys a new straw hat, although he's beginning to notice that fewer and fewer men are following suit. He is touchingly square.

He is aware, in an indeterminate way, that something has gone wrong with morals, as he knew them, but he takes what he calls "visiting firemen" to the topless joints. He cheats as much as he dares on his income tax and overtips cocktail waitresses, especially those who allow him a friendly pat. He

73

is shocked that his children talk openly about things he only thought about darkly when he was an adolescent, and he wonders where they got all their highly accurate information from in the first place. Certainly not from him.

He knows a few blacks and feels that because he addresses them by their first names he is making a meaningful contact ("I get along with them just fine—I don't know what the problem is"). He still regards the Fillmore District as "sort of colorful"; Hunters Point, to him, is something temporary that will go away if ignored long enough. He eats in Chinatown once in a while, calls the waiter "Charlie," and asks for the "beetle juice"; patient Charlie knows he means the soy sauce, and is so far beyond caring, one way or another, that he can even grin.

The old-time San Franciscan, salt of the earth, pillar of the community. He votes conservative, for the people who represent The Real America ("but that was a real shock about Dick Nixon, I still can't believe it"). He feels at ease only with those he went to school with, and believes his generation was the last that had its feet on the ground ("I mean wasn't the town better when it was open? Kids should learn about sex from old pros, like Sally"). He likes Dixieland music, especially "When the Saints Go Marchin' In," and has gone through several sets of his early Sinatra albums. Even though he's an old Cal man, he never could figure out what those kids were up to over in Berkeley, but he was against it. Mainly because their actions struck him as rude, and he's polite; that's why he has held the same job for thirty years.

He has a sense of values and he knows what's important. The proper address, for one thing (Cow Hollow is about right; not too flashy, not too snobbish, damn decent neighbors). A good martini at 5:30 P.M. in a good bar (meaning all the men wear neckties and the girls will flirt with you, but not enough to make it uncomfortable). Being addressed by name by the headwaiters, the mailman, the cop on the beat. Belonging to one club that isn't overpoweringly elegant— perhaps the University. Having one friend with a house at Tahoe, another with a pool down the Peninsula, a third with a sailboat. Being able to say about Joe DiMaggio that "I've known him for*ever*." And, in his own salutary phrase, keeping his nose clean. Which means not rocking the boat that may be sinking, whether he knows it or not.

Like all old-time San Franciscans, he is sentimental. About Lowell High and Old Rec. About the tennis courts in Golden Gate Park. About Dancin' with Anson and the Ferry Building clock. About the Russ Building (to him, it's still the pride of the financial district—all the newer, taller buildings are strictly jerry-built-come-latelies). His favorite mayor was Roger Lapham, because Lapham represented everything he believed in. His favorite restaurant is any one that once was a speakeasy. His favorite dish is no longer available: crisp corned beef hash on an SP ferry bound for Oakland to hear a traveling Big Band (Goodman, Dorsey, Miller) at Sweet's Ballroom.

All in all, a decent, God-fearing family man who somehow has avoided cirrhosis, the more serious neuroses, and even more serious thoughts about problems that didn't exist when he was a kid so what can he do about them now? Culture is the Opera House and the museums and what more do they want? Anybody can get a job if he wants to, unquote. And hey, Joe, one more time on that Beefeater martini, hey?

Root-root-root for the home team, things will work out because they always have, and let's drink a toast to San Francisco, the greatest li'l town in the world . . . and so it is. In spite of or because of him?

Wasps' Nest

EMMETT WATSON, a man who worries a lot, wonders why there isn't any WASP cooking. "There's Chinese, Japanese, Jewish, black, Italian, all kinds of ethnic dishes," he muses, "but no White Anglo-Saxon Protestant specialties." The only one he could think of, offhand, was mayonnaise on white bread, and that started a lively discussion.

Polly Pitkin Ryan, a self-styled "card-carrying WASP," described the situation in her home state of Vermont: "I knew a family of farm kids there who relished sandwiches made of white bread and butter with white Saltines as filler! This same family ate lettuce sprinkled with sugar. Of course, the most usual rural dish was fried salt pork with cream gravy, a triumph of the genre."

Catherine Sang offered, "The unique WASP contribution to world cuisine is that thing that looks like a staphylococcus culture but actually is gelatinized carrot shreds." As for mayonnaise on white bread, which Watson suggested as the epitome, Marguerite Pendergast dissents. "That may seem WASPish," she observed, "but mayonnaise is definitely French, first whipped up by the Duc de Richelieu's chef in 1756 during the siege of Mahon, when no cream or butter was available for sauces." So mayonnaise was originally Mahonnaise. That's instructive.

Reported Sara (Mrs. Stuart) MacRobbie of Berkeley: "I, a nice Jewish girl, married a WASP and for thirteen years I've been picking peanut butter and wads of Langendorf white out of my teeth. Every now and then in sheer desperation I spread one slice of the soft white with a little chicken schmaltz and what do I get for my troubles? A roar from the other room, like 'What the hell is wrong with this peanut butter???'"

Priscilla Wegars nominated tuna-noodle casserole, macaroni and cheese, and Jell-O and peanut butter-and-jelly sandwiches. Jim Lyle suggested "the infamous" chicken-fried steak and iceberg lettuce in chunks, covered with bottled so-called "French" dressing; Jean Miller's list included all franchised foods, fried chicken to go, any sandwich with limp lettuce on white, and anything fried beyond recognition and drenched with catsup.

Of course, let us not overlook the good WASP inventions —hamburgers on a bun, hot dogs, corn on the cob, ice cream and milk shakes, although this last art form had its golden age long years ago. Anyway, considering their diet, it's amazing how well the WASPs have done in this country. And their dentists.

FOOTNOTE: For me, the pinnacle of WASP cuisine is and shall always be creamed chicken and green peas in a patty shell. The stomach churns.

☆ ☆ ☆

MARION CONRAD paused at the No Name Bar in Sausalito long enough to hear one girl say to another: "I don't care if he *is* married, that doesn't prove he's a fairy."

☆ ☆ ☆

HISTORY CLASS is now in session: In 1890, San Francisco had 3,117 saloons, one for every ninety-six residents, which made it the true golden age; it has been downhill ever since to the present one for six hundred. Cocaine and morphine were easily available for a dime to fifteen cents a fix, and opium was a drug on the market. Same year, there was a bar with topless waitresses at Kearny and California; the police eventually made the Glamazons put on blouses, but didn't specify that they had to be buttoned so they weren't. On June 14, 1876, a local ordinance was passed that "the hair of every male imprisoned in County Jail be cut or clipped to a uniform length of one inch from the scalp." Shortly thereafter, the U. S. Circuit Court declared that unconstitutional, especially after finding out that the ordinance was aimed at and enforced only against the Chinese and their pigtails. It was quite a town, quite a time.

☆ ☆ ☆

THE ENCYCLOPEDIA AMERICANA contains the histories of the twelve largest U.S. cities—and ever since 1950, historian Oscar Lewis has been writing the San Francisco section. But then came this sad note from S. J. Foderaro, the encyclopedia's executive editor, reading in part:

"We are dismayed by the new Federal census figures—San Francisco has been superseded by Indianapolis among the

77

12 largest cities in the country. So, we must substitute Indianapolis for San Francisco and cancel our request for your article. Somehow, the substitution seems unsatisfactory—we wish we could enlarge our space to include the 13 largest cities, but unfortunately we cannot."

Wrote back Lewis: "While I understand space limitations, I find it harder to comprehend why the decision must be based on population figures alone. Surely there are other factors worth considering. To take one rather far-fetched comparison, if the rule of 12 were applied to Italian cities, Milan and Turin would have to be included with Florence and Venice left out, a manifest absurdity."

Replied Foderaro posthaste: "Your letter has convinced us. Indianapolis will have to go and San Francisco stays, even if its population goes down to 10!"

☆ ☆ ☆

POOR PITIFUL PEARL: "The drinks are on Pearl!" read the invitations to her friends—and they all turned out for the big party one night at Mike Considine's Lion's Share in San Anselmo. It began at 8:30 P.M. and it went rollicking on till 6:30 A.M. . . . the music was sensational: Big Brother and the Holding Company, with members of the Airplane, Dead and Quicksilver joining in. The tab for food and drinks added up to about $1,600 but there was no sweat. Pearl's budget for the party was $2,500 . . . The only sad note was that the hostess wasn't there. A couple of weeks earlier she had been found dead in a Hollywood motel room—but in her will she had left $2,500 "so my friends can have a ball after I'm gone." . . . Pearl? Well, only her closest friends called Janis Joplin by that nickname.

☆ ☆ ☆

STATEMENTS I don't quite believe: "So what if it blocks the view—it'll broaden the tax base" . . . "By the time they're thirty-five they'll be just like the rest of us" . . . "I

78

went to school with that Meter Maid—she'd never tag me"
. . . "I found a little California wine, made up at Crepesole
Vineyards, that makes Chateau Lafite look sick" . . . "It's
too cold to rain" . . . "I don't think the color of a person's
skin has anything to do with how bad they are" . . . "It'll be
the funsiest party of the year" . . . "It doesn't look like much
from the outside but the food is better than anything you'll
find in Paris" . . . "If you can't find a parking space, use the
neighbors' driveway—they won't mind" . . . "Don't let his
lack of small talk fool you, he has a beautiful mind" . . .
"She may be loud and flashy but she's all heart" . . . "Commuting is fun" . . . "A man who likes good music can't be
all bad."

☆　☆　☆

EDUCATOR Clark Kerr's finest line: "The circumstances
under which I assumed the Presidency of the University of
California and those under which I left were identical. In
both cases I was fired with enthusiasm!"

Lost in a Fog

IT WAS ONE of those good San Francisco days—gray
and misty. If you could keep from looking at the Bank of
America Building, it could have been a day in the 1930s, the
city's last golden age. Drench coat weather. Dashiell Hammett might have been puttering around at Bush and Stockton, setting the scene for Miles Archer's murder in *The Mal-
tese Falcon.* Jake Ehrlich and his latest girl, a blonde nine
feet tall, should have been drinking Cutty in the far corner
of Fred Solari's bar. Bill Saroyan, in sneakers, sneaking up
to Anita Zabala Howard's penthouse at 1001 Californi

John's Grill in the Tenderloin, the bookies are gathering for a 2 P.M. breakfast, dividing the spoils over steak and eggs (hi Marty, hello Benny).

A day to churn memories and stomachs. At Fifth and Mission—Filth and Mish' to the regulars—Mel Ravella, the good traffic cop, was dodging signal jumpers and muttering, "They're crazy, they're all crazy." A Volkswagen jumped the light and swerved left, narrowly missing two pedestrians, Mel whistling at the driver in vain. What makes it funny is that the driver was wearing a safety harness. And he had a Flag decal on the back window to show he's a good American light jumper.

Like a homely pigeon, I headed northward, toward all that is left of the old town, if you don't count the back yards of the Deep Mission and the Victorians of the Western Addition. I walked along Grant Avenue, past the ornate lampposts with their dragons entwined around tourists. Grant *Avenue,* young-timer. Just because City Hall is so chintzy these days that the street signs don't tell you whether you're on a street, avenue, boulevard or what is no excuse for not remembering it's Grant *Avenue.* Still sniffling 1930, I kept trying to avert my eyes from B of A, Crocker, Alcoa and all those other dark buildings thrown up by newcomers with cold New York hearts who think this town is Chicago. It's hard to measure how much damage they've done to San Francisco, but it's considerable. The old-timers, who knew what San Francisco was all about, built their buildings to scale and made the city grow beautiful. The giants have passed on and now we have rich pygmies with ego problems.

I slid down the Chinatown hill toward Kearny, past crated ducks and winter melons, staring at a freighter moving slowly across the leaden Bay. It's not a sight you'll be able to see much longer; once Mr. Rockefeller, his blessings to bestow, gets up his sixty-story tower and the adjoining blockhouse, you'll have to use your imagination. I passed the irascible Cookie Picetti's Star Bar, where the prosecutors, the defense lawyers and the cops used to gather when the Hall of Justice was next door. Now the Hall lives only in *Ironside* and memory. In its place rises the strangely designed Holiday Inn, which, in the words of Jimmy Price, "looks like a Trojan horse somebody wheeled over from Alameda."

Lost in a foggy memory, I wandered around North Beach, reliving the vanished summertimes. Past La Tosca (uptight Italian, where Allen Ginsberg was once thrown out), past Vesuvio (where Ginsberg licked his wounds), past the cellar where Mona Sargent once reigned over the jam-packed dykes, past Finocchio's, where Joe grew rich on the labor of his fruits. On Columbus, Carol Doda came swinging past, jaunty in brown tam, jacket and bell-bottoms; with her clothes on, she's one pretty girl. Across from the Gold Spike, the tiny shoeshine stand run by a sad-looking woman and today she looked even sadder—who gets a shine on a drizmal day? I stepped into the little Italian newsstand nearby and bought an *Oggi* and a *Domenica del Corriere*. I don't read Italian but it seemed the thing to do and besides somebody has to keep these little places alive.

Back on Broadway, I felt a pang that could have been nostalgia or hunger. Deciding it must be the latter, I fell into Yank Sing, which the most knowledgeable Chinese favor for dim sum (teahouse-style food). The place was crowded with knowing-look Chinese, chattering at round tables. And prebeatnik bohemians who know where to shop for a buck. Also some straight Montgomery Streeters with their secretaries, smugly sure they wouldn't bump into anybody who knew them. You can imagine how delighted they were to see me. Yank Sing. It sounds like the title of a World War II movie about a GI stool pigeon caught by the Japanese. In my phony phonetic Chinese, I ordered Poy Nay tea, steamed pork buns (it's the same in English), Hai Gow, Sei Chai, Sei, Sei Mai and Chai Sei Bow. French touch in this very Oriental place: at the end of the meal, the waiter counts the plates—just as a waiter does in a Parisian sidewalk cafe— and figures out your check.

It was less than an hour later that I felt hungry again, so I stopped at an Italian bakery and bought a cream puff. There is only one way to eat a walking-around cream puff without getting goo all over yourself: you take off the top and use it as a spoon to scoop up the cream. That's the way we did it

81

in the thirties, when spring came every day to San Francisco, and it still works here in the winter of the malcontents.

EVERY MORNING for eleven years, Dick Wagner awakened at 6 A.M. to take his dog, Blitz, for a walk along the streets of Millbrae. Then, one Thursday, Blitz died. Next morning at six, Dick woke up, stared at the ceiling for a few moments, and then nudged his wife Jan. "Hey," he said. "Wanna take a walk?"

"TO A TENNIS player, love means nothing," disc jockey Carter Smith said on Station KNBR, to which Joel Pimsleur instantly retorted, "To a lover, tennis means nothing."

IN CASE you're tired of eating sole and sand dabs day after day, try these: sarcastic fringehead, hornyhead turbot, bonehead sculpin, Southern spearnose poacher, shovelnose guitarfish, smooth stargazer, bearded ellpout, swell shark, grey smoothhound. These, according to the State Fish & Game Report, are just a few of the fish trawled regularly in Santa Monica Bay, and it all sounds like more fun than bird-watching, even.

AT THE OPERA HOUSE Artur Rubinstein had standees, a full house and three rows of people seated onstage behind his Steinway. As the house lights darkened, a late-arriving lady emerged from the wings and walked across the length of the stage to find a seat, whereupon the audience burst into ritual applause. "Wouldn't it have been a groove," said the man next to me, "if she'd played 'Chopsticks'?" Another golden opportunity blown.

It's hard not to cry a little when Rubinstein plays. It must be his great age plus his irrepressible gaiety. His face radiates humor; you wouldn't be surprised if he stopped in the middle of Chopin to tell a joke. His publicity says he's eighty, he says he's eighty-two, his intimates say he's eighty-five but it doesn't matter. He's always the youngest member of the group.

Later, at the St. Francis, he nodded at a compliment. "Yes, I played well today. It's because I have this terrible cold. Like Maestro Avis, I tried a little harder." He had once explained in a classic phrase why he didn't play Mozart —"It's too simple for children and too difficult for artists"— but he is now playing Mozart again. "I stopped," he said, "because I had lost my innocence. But now I am so old I have regained my purity—call it retroactive virginity."

Bundled up in a greatcoat, with a thick scarf around his neck, he strode through the St. Francis lobby, spry as a teen-ager. I remembered the time he was riding in a cab to Fisherman's Wharf, and the cabbie had said: "You look familiar, what's your name?" When he replied: "Artur Rubinstein," I said, "Why didn't you let him guess?" "Because," smiled Rubinstein, "when I let people guess they always say I'm Leopold Stokowski."

☆ ☆ ☆

UNCLASSIFIED CABLE, spotted by one of my spies, from Navy medics at the Third Field Army Hospital, Saigon, to superior officers at Pearl Harbor, 6 Mar 69: "Psittacosis, suspected. Patient (Carlos H. Spain) bitten by parrot four days prior to admission. Temperature ranges from 100.9 to 104.8. Patient has been given initial 2 million units procaine penicillin, then 500 milligrams tetracycline every six hours. Request instructions for disposition of parrot."

BuMed Pearl Harbor's reply 10 Mar 69: "1. Parrot should be thoroughly plucked, cleaned and washed well. 2. Julia Child recommends plain bread crumb and herb stuffing. 3. Roast in 350 degree oven approximately 30 minutes per pound, baste occasionally. 4. Side dishes should include crisp watercress salad, wild rice, asparagus tips. 5. Highly recommend properly chilled Schloss Johannesberg vintage 1966. 6. Bon appetit."

You can count on the Navy.

Meanderings of a Monkey Mind

YOU CAN FEEL reasonably secure as a San Franciscan when a tourist stops you on Powell to ask directions, you know that it's 4:30 P.M. when the Ferry siren blows, and 5 P.M. when the Presidio cannon barks, you don't even know what the "other" room at Trader Vic's looks like, you have never sat inside on a Powell cable, you walk up to your favorite bar and your favorite drink is already waiting for you, and the sidewalk photographer no longer bothers to take your picture . . . On the other hand, suggests Dean Webber, you're in trouble when you go into a strange restaurant and order ham and eggs and the waitress sets a bottle of catsup in front of you. While you're talking, the guy you're talking to wanders away and turns on the TV. The phone wakes you up and it's your wife. After studying the wine list for some time, you make your choice and the waiter captain winces. At a party, you wink at a sweet young thing and your eye stays shut. Your wife comes home drunk with one of *her* old Army buddies. The day after you've told your best friend what a jerk you think his estranged wife is, you find out they've reconciled. Ah well. The only way to face life is as Mark Twain recommended: "With the serene confidence that a Christian feels in four aces and the composure of the man who said to his wife, 'If one of us dies I shall move to Paris.'"

THAT FELLOW sitting there with the bemused look— that's John Herrell of Burlingame. He ordered two motorcy-

cle crash helmets from Montgomery Ward in Oakland. And
they arrived in a big box marked "Fragile."

A Singular Man

HOWARD GOSSAGE'S middle name was Luck, and he
needed all of it he could get, but it ran out for him at 4:30
A.M., July 10, 1969, in Presbyterian Hospital. He died of
leukemia, a kidney infection and other complications, but
mainly, I think, he died because he didn't want to live as a
vegetable, never having had any experience at it.

If there were any justice, the flags would have been at half
staff all over town, for he was one of the most valuable of
San Franciscans. He would have understood why they
weren't, though. As he once said in that wild Irish way of
his: "Of course there isn't any justice, buddy, and isn't that
wonderful? We'll never run out of things to be angry about."

Only, the buddy would have come out "b-b-buddy." He
had an ingratiating stammer, along with a dramatic appearance that made him an unforgettable figure around town:
flowing white hair, a perpetually gaunt, drawn and handsome face, the sad-sweet smile that seems to be the signature
of so many Irish philosophers.

Nominally he was in advertising—he hated the business—
but realistically, he was the archetypical San Francisco Renaissance man. Like most of the best men I've ever met, he
never haggled over a bill and he overtipped recklessly.
Money meant nothing to him and he probably died broke.
But he knew more about classical music than most musicians, he was better read than most critics and he composed
more graceful prose than most writers. I never met a more
unbigoted man, even about bigots; the worst he would say
about anybody was, "Well, I can t-take him or l-leave him—
not n-necessarily in that order."

What was important about Howard Gossage? It's a matter

of style. There was nothing cheap or shoddy there, and his everyday presence made you feel that just being a San Franciscan was important. If a guy like Gossage picked this place over all others—in the face of constant offers from New York and Europe—then San Francisco had to be okay. Editors, authors, tycoons and advertising men were forever seeking his advice, and he'd say, "If they want to see me all that much, they'll just have to come *here*."

And come here they did, to his firehouse on Pacific. Talk about style: he was the first to buy an abandoned old firehouse and convert it into offices that were the last word in cool modern elegance. His lunches there were legendary. He'd call up David's Deli, order a ton of everything, ask you to drop in at the last minute, and you'd drop everything to be there.

You'd find yourself building a pastrami sandwich next to Dr. Benjamin Spock. Or pouring a beer for John Steinbeck. Or listening to Buckminster Fuller. Or laughing at the bad jokes of Marshall McLuhan. (Gossage, more than any other person, was responsible for the launching of McLuhan as a household name—a job he took on, like so many others, just for the hell of it, "let's see if it works.") Robert Manning, editor of the *Atlantic Monthly,* was a Gossage luncheon regular. And writer Tom Wolfe.

Along with Ogilvy and Doyle Dane Bernbach, Gossage was responsible for changing the whole concept of American advertising. Before they came along in the '50s, the approach was serious, heavy, bombastic. Gossage was the first to inject sophisticated humor and even—amid cries of "Sacrilege!"—the poking of fun at one's own product. His first ads for Qantas, long ago, are still classics. For the then unknown airline, he devised a contest he headed: "Be the First Kid on Your Block to Own a Kangaroo!" And when a winner was finally selected, his headline read, "Bronx Girl Wins Her First Kangaroo." The style won the accolade of instant imitation.

Did I say he had no interest in money? In '53, Volkswagen was ready to begin advertising heavily in the U.S., and narrowed the competition to Gossage and Doyle Dane.

Howard's final presentation to VW's directors lost him the million-dollar job: "I've been driving your car for years, and it's a great little product. I don't think you *need* any advertising." Later he confided wryly, "I've always hated automobile accounts—but wow, I had no idea they were going to advertise *that* much!"

The last time I saw Howard, he looked worn and dazed, but he was trying bravely to keep up the old style. Marshall McLuhan had phoned him long distance to say, "I can't send you flowers, you've read all the books, so I'll give you a joke." Then followed a typical McLuhan pun that made no sense. "For a genius, he sure tells lousy jokes," Howard mumbled. A couple of hospital technicians wheeled in a complicated kidney gadget. "That's okay, boys, you can have the machine tonight," he grinned weakly. As I started to leave, I said, "I'll be back to see you tomorrow," and he sighed, "W-why would you w-want to do that?" And when I reached the door he called out, "Hey, b-buddy, you're not going to be m-mad at me, are you?"

It just dawned on me that I don't even know Howard's age. I guess he was fifty-something, but he never talked about it, as he never talked about his years as a Navy combat pilot in the South Pacific and a lot of other matters he considered trifling. But to answer his last question, yes, I'm mad that he died. Damn mad.

☆　☆　☆

DONG KINGMAN, the most celebrated artist ever to rise out of Chinatown, stood at the corner of Grant and Bush the other noon and shook his head. "It's terrible," he said. "Proportions all wrong. It doesn't even look Chinese. Instead of adding to the scene, it detracts." Object of his scorn: The tile-and-concrete "gateway" to Chinatown, which cost $70,000—a sum that could have been spent to better purpose in the Silken Ghetto. Besides, the two institutions flourishing at Bush and Grant tell the story of New Chinatown much more eloquently than the $70,000 arch they flank. On one side, Burger Town. Opposite: the Hot Hoagy

Sandwich Shop. Both, according to their signs, serve "Breakfast 24 Hours a Day." The twain has met over an order of ham and eggs.

ZOUNDS: Jim Butler overheard this in the lobby of an Oakland hotel, guest to the desk clerk: "This is my first visit here—I'd like a map of the city, please." Obtaining same, the tourist walked away, stopped, turned around and said, "Hey, you gave me a map of San Francisco." Clerk, a bit huffily: "You said you wanted a map of the City, didn't you?"

OUR NATIVE WITS at work and play . . . Dean Webber: "You know it's going to be a long day when the alarm goes off and you get up and shower and shave and start to get dressed and your shoes are still warm" . . . Bob Orben to Lawrence Welk: "What do you think about violence?" Welk: "I like dem. Alzo I like pianos und drumz" . . . Paul "Red" Fay, Jr., gazing at Telegraph Hill across his tortellini at Julius' Castle: "What a fantastic view. It chokes me up. Do you realize my father's construction firm installed all the sewer pipes on this hill?" . . . Jay Gordon, postcarding from Lahaina, Hawaii: "When Captain Cook named these the Sandwich Islands, he must have anticipated that someday that would be the only meal ordinary people could afford here" . . . Writer Collie Small in the Beverly-Plaza bar, brushing off an amorous lady with an unfortunate snout-like nose: "Why don't you go to France and root for truffles?" Lady: "What's truffles?" Collie: "A French soccer team and good night" . . . George Lemont, preparing for Thanksgiving: "I crossed a turkey with an ostrich, figuring I'd get something with monstrous drumsticks. Instead I wound up with a queer bird that runs over and sticks its head into the mashed potatoes."

NORMAN LIVERMORE, chief of the State Resources

Agency under Ronald Reagan, coined the word "proserva-
tion" to replace "conservation"—because, he explained to
Congressman Don Clausen, "I'd rather be pro than con."
Don: "Perfectly brilliant. Now what do you propose to do
about 'Constitution'?"

Baghdad-by-the-Bay

SOMETIMES, in the cold wintry dusk, the city looks positively Florentine. You drive West on Geary Parkway toward
a sky all Dante-dramatic, and a false antiquity gilds the twin
spires of St. Ignatius; they seem as real and as far away as
the Renaissance. Dark mystery on Lone Mountain: the
school and its innocent tower become a castle on a hill. A
thousand lights flicker against the black mass of Mount
Parnassus, beacons glow on and off in a nervous pattern,
and the far-off rumble of a ship's horn makes you realize the
sea is ceaselessly near, surf pounding in rhythm to the beat
of the old but not-so-old city . . .

No, not so old. Nothing is allowed to grow old except people—the city is still too young to have a decent respect for
age. Once in a while, in the half light of a dusk-thou-are-to-
dusk-returneth, you can play optical tricks on yourself: put
on the sentimental blinders and see only what you want to
see—familiar faces in familiar places, the hills full of yester-
days, dear old waiters in dear old restaurants, the spotless
Victorian mansion on California with its windows always
shining clean, lawns cricket-cropped. Downtown, the beloved old buildings (St. Francis, Shell, Russ, Standard,
PG&E and a precious few others) begin to look as majestic
and impressive as cathedrals. Perhaps they are.

But it's only a trick, an innocent exercise in self-delusion.
On Geary Parkway, even as you are hypnotizing yourself
with that baroque sky, the pattern of the future is much
more discernible than the shades of the past, and it would

appear that tomorrow will be colder than the wind after sundown. Concrete blockhouses rising out of the warm ashes where hundreds of families once lived, procreated, ate, slept, fought and died—each with a backyard where the wash flapped on the line and dogs yapped, stoops where old people rocked and children shouted and there were games to be played. But they were poor (even though they had a fern in the front window) and so they had to go. Poverty must be paved over, and out of the real mud grows the real dross.

Geary Parkway, a race track across a stone desert, but let us not be bitter when the plumbing promises to be better. East of Van Ness, the old city struggles to stay alive, the old bones getting thinner but still showing through the new layers of drab. (Drab: a good name for a detergent guaranteed to make your clothes grayer.) There's architect Bernard Maybeck's Corinthian-columned showroom for a car no longer made, the marble temple that outlived the Packard. At Powell and O'Farrell, the steel bones of a dead cable car line—one chorus, please, of "O'Farrell, Jones and Hyde, it's the world's most famous ride"—and here and there the old cobblestones jutting out of the pavement. On Mission near Third, the sign that marks Opera Alley (I put that sign up myself) which once led to the stage door of a Grand Opera House, and later to a bookie joint well patronized by the young Saroyan. Gone and forgotten now, sign and all, but not quite; the city buried within the city is never dead as long as somebody is still alive who remembers.

Well, who really gets to know a city—even his own, the one he loves best? You think you've mapped the trails and the landmarks, and you wake up one morning to find the signposts have been changed, and all the streets are one way going the other way; everything familiar has been towed away to a garage you can't find. Even the old downtown apartment houses, with the ancient cooking smells and the distant sound of a toilet flushing—even these become nostalgic objects, for you know they are doomed, dead as the life that once flourished behind the ugly doors (speakeasies, call girls, kept ladies). In North Beach, a topless joint where the man in the fedora used to sell Marca Petri cigars, stronger than the garlic on his breath. At Grant and Green, you stand on the corner and remember the Co-Existence Bagel Shop and Kerouac and Corso and our own lost degeneration; only one shred of evidence remains—the legend, "A Square Is a Square Is a Square," etched in the cement below the fire alarm box. A beatnik—how old-fashioned the word sounds —had made his neverlasting mark; Kerouac died respectable.

Baghdad-By-The-Bay: Young/old city of the young and old. The young gather in Winterland and listen gravely to Bill Graham's latest discoveries; how appalled they would be by the jitterbugs we knew. Ken Kesey's psychedelic bus grazes Lotta Crabtree's fountain on Market Street, and there very definitely are cracks in the walls of the Opera House.

☆ ☆ ☆

ONE OF PROFESSOR C. Northcote Parkinson's latest laws, suitable for framing or needle point, is "Delay Is the Deadliest Form of Denial." At an Esperanto Society tea, advertising man Dennis Altman ran into C. Northcote, and asked him to explain it. "I will," replied Parkinson, "in a few minutes."

The Splendid Anachronism

"IF YOU DON'T like opera, why do you go?" people have been asking me over the years because of this tendency I have to make fun of it. It so happens that I like opera and I like to make fun of it. That's one of the things I like about it.

Unless you're sobersided beyond belief, you have to admit there's something inescapably comic, even ludicrous, about this particular art form. All those fat sopranos falling into the arms of skinny tenors who try not to stagger under the load. And fail. Conversely, all those fat-bellied tenors trying to get close enough to a skinny soprano, if any, to embrace her. Heroes and heroines stretched out on the stage, fatally wounded, singing at the top of their lungs for twenty minutes as they die.

Contradictions by the score: opera houses jammed to the rafters and still losing money. In a recession, people lining up to buy high-priced tickets for a show presented in a language they can't understand, and, if it's in English, it's worse. Standees stacked three deep, half a block from the stage, straining eyes and ears—and feet. In an age of supersonic speeds, an entertainment as slow and cumbersome as a dinosaur, which it sometimes resembles in everything but longevity.

Grand opera has been pronounced dead more often than the dodo, but it not only survives, it flourishes. Why? Because in an age of schlock, it's the real thing. In a "cool" world growing cold, it is blood-hot. Compared to the tawdriness of TV and the plastic corridors of high-rises, it is still grand and romantic. And finally, there is the genius of the music and the integrity that goes into its presentation.

Even when they are bored by it—and much of opera is boring—the maligned "people," whose brains and judgment supposedly have been beaten to a pulp by Modern Life, respond in growing numbers because they know they are being treated to something rare, special, unusual, even bizarre. As W. C. Fields said about sex, "I don't know whether it's good and I don't know whether it's bad, but I do know there isn't anything quite like it."

As I started to say at the beginning of whatever I'm trying to say here, the funny thing about opera is that you can make fun of it while still respecting (and even enjoying) it.

If there's a six-foot woman in the audience, she'll be wearing her hair piled another twelve inches on top of her head —and you'll be seated behind her. If you don't get her, you'll get the frizzy guy whose hair runs north and south, three inches on each side. A woman you've never seen before will fall asleep on your shoulder and here you have to go to the bathroom even though your favorite aria is coming up and if you leave you can't get back in till intermission anyway.

People snore, stomachs rumble, the barking coughs sound like mating season at Seal Rocks. The opera drones on through a dry spell. You stare at the ceiling to stay awake, thinking about the chandelier hurtling down, as it did in *The Phantom of the Opera*. You are directly beneath it. You straighten up: the music grows glorious again, the singing brilliant, the harmonies rich enough to make you cry, even though the libretto at this point reads, "Here King Fluoristan orders the death of Prince Dristan, unaware that he is actually his own wife, Queen Bufferin, in disguise, who as she dies, sings the unforgettable aria, *'Où est la route à Brisbane?'* "

We sat through five hours of *Parsifal*. "What's it about?" someone asked Robert Cromey beforehand, and he replied, "About two hours too long"; but he is wrong. It's not too long at all and besides it's another example of how to have fun while being deeply moved.

Parsifal is Wagner at his Druidical-mystical best or worst, so there is this opening scene in the forest. The longer you look, the more the scene begins to resemble the Bohemian Grove. There ensues a lot of mumbo-jumbo in guttural German, a long ritual involving what purports to be the Holy Grail. Okay, so it's initiation night at the Grove, except that everybody seems reasonably sober.

The acolytes open the mysterious receptacle to reveal the Grail itself. All your life you've wondered what the Holy Grail looks like, and there it is. It looks like the sign on a Tenderloin "cocktail lounge"—an oversized Manhattan glass glowing with a huge cherry. You can see the electrical cord running across the stage. Our hero raises the glass with a visible effort and cries his heart out because he was expecting a martini (it sounds better in German).

But five hours! A tremendous achievement. Five hours in which to make mistakes, like dropping the Grail or dumping the wounded knight out of the stretcher, or falling off the tilted stage, and yet there were no mistakes and the music was unfailingly sublime. Thank you, Richard Wagner, singers, musicians, listeners, guarantors, ushers, impresario Kurt Herbert Adler, thank you all for these riches. And for the laughs, too.

Through a Glass Lightly

I WAS SITTING at Enrico's Coffee House with a twenty-one-year-old hippie girl from Berkeley who had an annoying and flat opinion on everything (i.e.: "Classical music is a drag—who needs it?"). Actually, I would have invited her to get lost early in the game, except that she had fantastic legs of unbelievable length and symmetry; Dirty Old Mannism uber alles. She left of her own accord when, after one of her didactic didoes ("Nobody listens to opera any more"), I snapped, "Do you plan to remain callow all your life?" At this she retorted, "You're just jealous because I'm young and beautiful. I'll bet *you'd* like to be twenty-one again." "Sweetheart," I said in my best Humphrey Bogart imitation, "I wouldn't even like to be fifty again."

As she swept off, her stern riding high and proud, I reflected on what I had just said. Drat that hippie girl, who, by the way, was hipless, as they all are. Of course I wouldn't want to be twenty-one—a rotten age to be in the Nuclear Age. I'm delighted to be exactly where I am, neither here nor there; well, maybe a bit more there than here, but still here for all that.

Breathes there a generation still alive whose members have had to adjust and readjust so many times? Certainly not. When I was a child, horses were delivering the ice, the milk and the coal, and here we are on the moon. Today, satellites bring us TV programs from all over the world; my first radio, which I remember vividly, was a crystal set with a cat's whisker that, after much fiddling, delivered the first music I ever heard through the airwaves—a record on KFBK, Sacramento, of "Bye-Bye Blackbird." Infinitely more exciting than a live telecast of a prize fight in Germany transmitted by Early Bird. Pathé News showed us ex-Kaiser Wilhelm chopping wood in Doorn, Gertrude Ederle swimming the Channel and Babe Ruth hitting home runs, a bare two weeks after the occurrence; the anticipation made it all the sweeter.

My generation has seen it all, from the machine gun ("So horrible it will make war impossible") to nuclear bombs (ditto, and don't you believe it). They talk about electric cars today as though they were a big deal—but we had them in all their glory: marvelously romantic broughams driven by fierce old ladies wearing huge hats. Autos lost their running boards, their silk shades and their flowers in cut-glass vases, and does this put us ahead? A skyscraper was something ten stories tall and that still seems high enough, or haven't you waited for an elevator on the twenty-ninth floor lately? Butchers gave you bologna and threw in a piece of liver free ("for the cat"), barbers gave you all-day suckers, and "mother" was still an acceptable word. God was alive but not in the White House.

How tell the kids of today about the glories of the bridgeless Bay and the curving beauty of the ferryboats? The steam train that curlicued its way to the top of Tamalpais? The pasta at Papa Coppa's? They were part of a generation's innocence: we thought homosexuals were simply "sissified," that all the dikes were in Holland, and that girls were divided into two groups—those who Did and those who Didn't; anybody who went to a psychiatrist should have his head examined, as Sam said. As for not trusting anybody over thirty—ridiculous; in our lexicon, age and wisdom went hand in hand, and a successful man was simply anybody who made $10,000 a year or over; that he might also have been an exploiting, thieving summbitch was unthinkable.

The hippies and other youngies are getting their own kicks in their own way, and good luck to them. At sixteen, I had my first shot of bootleg booze in an upstairs speakeasy in Sacramento and at eighteen I was turned on to my first marijuana cigarette by a Sacramento police sergeant who smoked one too. Benny Goodman came to McFadden's Ballroom in Oakland and I haven't heard a more exhilarating sound before or since, and that goes for the Rolling Stones. We drove Model T Fords that would run over you while you were cranking them, but they were worth the trouble: they had front seats you could remove to neck on in

William Land Park. We were probably all neurotic as hell but we didn't know it because there was nobody around to tell us.

Memories that bless and burn and to hell with that hippie girl. If I were twenty-one again I'd probably ask her for a date and have a lousy time. But she did have great legs, no getting around *those*.

ADD LEGENDARY characters I have often heard about but doubt actually exist: Former All-American football stars dying out their tragic lives as winos on Skid Road. Young women working as cocktail waitresses while getting their Ph. D.s. Hookers with hearts of gold. Old waiters who own "a dozen apartment houses" and are "richer than the bankers they wait on." A cabdriver who is not only writing the Great American Novel but gets it published. An old-time native San Franciscan "who can tell you enough about this town to fill a dozen columns." A topless dancer who took the job only to put her husband through law school. A politician with a heart of gold.

But what the heck, I've never seen a deer at a "Deer Crossing" sign, either.

WALDO HUNTER of Eureka is a man with a long memory. He had never forgotten or forgiven that I once chided the natives up there for pouring catsup over their fried eggs, and has been plotting revenge ever since. Here it is in his own undeniable words:

"On our most recent trip to San Francisco, my wife and I had breakfast at one of those famous restaurants of yours down near Fisherman's Wharf. Upon entering the place, my wife tripped over a plastic tube that pipes in brown gravy from the oil-reclaiming plant in Richmond. The scrambled eggs tasted like they had been hauled across the country from Ashtabula, Ohio, in the trunk of a '41 Studebaker. The toast seemed to have popped right out of the refrigerator freshly glazed with fireproofing compound for shake shingles, while the chef du jour, in an inspired flash, added a fillip of Dr. Snoramorfles' Iron Mountain Spavin Liniment to the coffee.

"Moral: Never go anyplace without a bottle of catsup."

☆ ☆ ☆

I SUGGEST Honorary Sanfrancitizenship for Dr. Story Musgrave. He's the space scientist (and U.C.L.A. grad) who was running the console at Mission Control in Houston when Major Jack Lousma of the Skylab crew did his space walk, remarking, "It's just an all-round beautiful sight—I can see from Baja California to Los Angeles and almost to Frisco," at which point Dr. Musgrave interrupted with a tart *"San Francisco!"* Major Lousma sheepishly, "Yeah, San Francisco." Don't call it Frisco, even 270 miles above it, a new record.

☆ ☆ ☆

FELINE FREAKOUT: It was a few years ago, in the Good Old Summertime, that June and Fred Dutton, then living in Sausalito, asked Dick Tuck to house-sit while they took a vacation. Everything went smoothly for the first few days and then Tuck, backing out of the driveway, ran over and killed the Duttons' beloved cat. Racing to San Francisco, Tuck double-parked outside Ansel Robison's pet shop, in Maiden Lane, rushed in with the dead cat, showed it to Ansel and gasped, "Quick, can you match this?"

☆ ☆ ☆

BALLAD OF WATERGATE: Hanley Norins, the legendary advertising figure (Young & Rubicam), dashed off this doggerel on his magic typewriter up at Little River, and it swings right along . . . "Ehrlichman did it to Ziegler, Haldeman did it to Dean. Dean, then, what did he? He did it to Liddy, who'd done it to Hunt in between. Magruder he did it to Mitchell, and Mitchell got Martha aboard, who did it to

97

Gray, who had to repay by doing it twice to McCord. Kissinger did it to Agnew, and Spiro, his back to the wall, said, 'Frank, put the fix on, let's do it to Nixon, the one who's been screwing us all!' "

Color Lines

THERE IS a certain kind of San Franciscan—not a bad fellow, really—who is forever sighing helplessly, "Why can't the blacks be more like our Chinese?" I think he is the sort of person who says during opera season, "If they just did *La Boheme* and *Butterfly,* I'd go every night," and who thinks the '29 Seals could have licked the present-day Giants, and who says, "I don't know what the younger generation is coming to" and "Some of my best friends are—

"I respect the Chinese, I really do," this nice fellow continues, "and I think they respect me. They have dignity and a strong family sense and they mind their own business." He always stops short of saying, "They know their place," but he doesn't have to verbalize it. "What I mean is," he finishes, "why can't the Negroes learn something from them?"

The most obvious answer is that the black is not Chinese, and please observe the "No Smirking" sign. I quote a Chinatown scholar: "In the first place, the Negro was brought to this country as a slave. Even those Chinese who were imported a hundred years ago to work on the railroads were free men who were paid wages. The Chinese have thousands of years of culture behind them, and a homeland of great history. The Negro—degraded by the white man, torn from his native land, denied a family role for generations—is just beginning to find an identity, something the Chinese has always had."

But getting back to my friend, the earnest San Franciscan,

with his illusions and delusions, I wonder if he knows how an earlier breed of San Franciscan acted toward the Chinese he professes to respect so much. (I assume he knows that even today certain residential areas are off-limits to all Orientals, not to mention blacks, and that the so-called "Chinaman's Room"—for the servant—still exists in the nether regions of some of our finest houses, and that the good American who orders "flied lice" in a Chinese restaurant still considers himself a wit.)

The other night, I was browsing through historian Oscar Lewis' book, *San Francisco: Mission to Metropolis,* and he supplies some salty and painful reminders. In the High Sierra, during Gold Rush days, mobs of whites attacked Chinese settlements and burned their cabins. Lynchings and shootings were common and went unpunished.

In enlightened San Francisco, a few years later, things weren't much better. Because the Chinese constituted "cheap" labor, workingmen raised the infamous cry of "The Chinese Must Go!" The State Legislature passed an Exclusion Act—literally to exclude them—that was later declared unconstitutional, but that didn't change anything. As the Chinese grew more prosperous, especially in the garment and cigar-making industries, white businessmen got nervous too.

In 1873, the Workingman's Party, founded on a straight anti-Chinese platform, won the city elections, and installed a mayor, Andrew Bryant, who decreed all manner of restriction on the Chinese: higher taxes, stiffer jail sentences, and even a curfew (they had to be off the streets at 2 A.M.). Thus encouraged, a firebrand orator named James D'Arcy organized a mob of five thousand on Market Street that set out, howling, for Chinatown. All night, they raided, looted, set fires, and severed the firemen's hoses with axes.

Even Mayor Bryant was taken aback. He called for federal aid, and two warships, the *Pensacola* and *Lancaster,* tied up at the waterfront, with marines and sailors armed and ready to land. The mob dispersed—for a time—but this was a violent city. In comparison, the riots of late September 1966 at Hunters Point were a tea party.

Soon, another "Chinese Must Go!" orator, Dennis Kearney, was working up the mobs on the issue of "coolie labor." No punch-puller he: "The monopolists who make their money by employing cheap labor have built themselves fine mansions on Nob Hill and erected flagpoles on their roofs. Let them take care they have not erected their own gallows!" At one point, he led a mob of three thousand to the steps of Charles Crocker's mansion on California Street, which must have frightened the old gentleman out of his wits. "If I give an order to hang Crocker," he bellowed at the front doors, "it will be done!" Fortunately, he didn't give the order.

One of the ugliest scenes took place along the Bay, when white workmen, hired to fill in the tidelands at $1.25 a day, were replaced by Chinese (then known as "Crocker's pets") who'd work for half that. A mob of whites attacked them as they worked, killed one, injured fifteen, and burned their shacks to the ground. This scene of violence was—Hunters Point, to this day the most racially troubled area in the city.

A Bus Named "Further"

I WAS lounging at the corner of Fifth and Mish', minding anybody's business, when along came Ken Kesey, the successful author (*One Flew over the Cuckoo's Nest, Sometimes a Great Notion*), who has opted out of The Big Money Machine and is trying to fly free. He rolled up in his famous bus, the one painted all those psychedelic colors ("The Rolling Rorschach," he calls it) and he reached out his hand to this square and said, "Climb aboard!" His friend, Babbs, was behind the wheel wearing captain's bars on his jacket and marksmanship medals on his chest. There was a blond young man called Ramrod and another named John and a bright-looking kid wearing thick glasses. Mrs. Kesey and her three small children. And a pretty, thin girl named Susie.

They had driven over from Fairfax, where they live aboard the bus (officially named "Further"), to show me San Francisco. As we drove down Mission toward the Ferry Building, Babbs and Ramrod spoke to the people on the streets via amplifier. "It's a beautiful day!" Babbs called out in a voice that carried for a block. The people looked startled. "The sun is out, let's all enjoy ourselves!" Pedestrians looked at the bus with hostility.

We rolled back up Market, Babbs keeping up a constant stream of good-natured chatter, Kesey playing reflectively on a harmonica. From my vantage point inside the crazy-wonderful bus, the square world never looked squarer or more ridiculous. Men in hats and little dark suits, striding along. "On your way to the topless and bottomless?" heckled Babbs. They scowled. Women shoppers in drab clothes stared deadpan, compressing their lips. Only the young people were able to summon a grin in return for a smile.

As we headed for Golden Gate Park, Kesey perched on a box in the middle of the aisle. He was wearing a red, white and blue striped shirt tucked into tight gold striped pants stuffed into scuffed cowboy boots. As has been remarked before, he looks like Marlon Brando, despite his tonsure of curly blond hair, and he has the same sad, sweet smile. His capped right front tooth looks red from a distance, but actually is a tiny American Flag. He is a man of charm, sympathy and, obviously, talent.

"I've got to get away from the Bay Area," he said. "There's too much going on here, it reaches out and encircles you. I've got to get back to the high country." He glanced around the bus. "I'm sorry it's such a mess today. We're going to fix this old bus up and travel. This is our home. Wonderful things have happened here—two babies born on it in Mexico. We're going to install a navigator's bubble in the roof, revolving, so we can really observe." The famous bus inched through the crowded Haight-Ashbury. Now we were surrounded by beaming, bearded faces: everybody knew it was Ken Kesey. He lit a stick of pungent incense—"to cover up the other smells around here," he said, grinning. At a street corner, he impulsively jumped out and handed the incense to an old man waiting for a bus. The oldster refused it, growling, "I don't use dope." "A real clean old man," sighed Babbs.

We went through the park toward the ocean. "Some professors at University of Texas want to put me in for a Rockefeller grant, hoping to get me to write again," he said, shaking his head slowly. "But I don't think I could ever write another big chunk of a book, like a telephone directory. Still, it's fourteen thousand dollars, and I could go to Europe. *Cuckoo's Nest* still sells—it's in its fourth or fifth printing. A royalty check always seems to arrive just in time to keep me going."

A motorcycle officer pulled alongside the bus, eyed it curiously, and roared away. Kesey followed him with his eyes. "San Francisco cops are okay—they leave us alone," he said. "Soon as we get outside the city, some cop has to stop us and come aboard and look around." He was arrested once on a marijuana charge, and the jury hung 8–4 for conviction. "I know the jury liked me," he said. "But then the prosecutor told them, 'Don't let emotions sway you,' like if they didn't convict me they wouldn't be doing their duty."

"My parents made a break-through the other day," he said. "They live in Oregon, very proper people, and they hate this bus—they think it's responsible for my decline and fall. But they finally came aboard, which was a very hard thing for them to do. I think they feel better about it now." At Pacific and Fillmore, the bus stopped to let me off, back in Squaresville. We waved good-by and I watched it roll away, riding high above the Cadillacs and Lincolns, looking brave and defiant. And quite a bit poignant.

☆ ☆ ☆

THINGS I hate to see: A funeral cortege on a bright, sunny day—moving past a park where children are playing; an empty Victorian house, its dusty windows shattered; a row of empty seats, fourth row center, at a theater opening; an old man, still wearing his hat, eating dinner alone off a tray in a cafeteria; a hate message scrawled inside a Muni bus whose seats have been slashed by the hateful; a storekeeper standing in a forlorn slouch at the front door of his empty shop; a Silver Star medal in a pawnshop window; an elderly widow in a downtown grocery store, shopping for the lonely dinner she is about to have in her tiny room (one lamb chop, one potato, one roll, one tomato).

☆ ☆ ☆

I'M NOT ONE of those who are forever saying: "The old days were better," because maybe they weren't. But Neil Davis, when owner of the No Name Bar in Sausalito, made me start wondering all over again by sending over a piece of doggerel titled, "The Ballad of Steam Beer," the first stanza of which goes like this:

> You may talk of Moet and Chandon, and all the cuvees of Champagne,
> Of Burgundy ruby and royal from Romance's storied demesne,
> Of Lafite and Lacrimae Christi, or the warm blushing vintage that grows
> Where Yquem and the Premier Grand Vins gush forth from the hills of Bordeaux;
> Of crusty old ports and Madeira and all of the sherries of Spain,
> All the liqueurs of castle and convent that ever came over the main;
> But I chant out a hymn to Gambrinus, the god of small change and good cheer,
> For I sing you a song of the nickel that buys the big glass of steam beer.

That rollicking, rolling bit of verse was written at the Press Club in 1902 by Billy Barnes—who, at the time, was district attorney of San Francisco, and obviously a man of parts. The old days might not have been better, but they were certainly different in the nicest possible way.

A Crock of Chrysanthemums

IN THE WORDS of Shakespeare, we "shall not look upon his like again." John Steinbeck, who could only have died too young, was uniquely American and peculiarly Californian—a strong, shaggy wolf of a man who came ranging out of the Salinas hills to make an indelible mark on his time and place.

Along with his honesty, which spilled over so often into memorable outrage, he had a strong sense of privacy. I met him first in 1939 at the old Bal Tabarin night club here, and he was not particularly pleased to see me. "All I ask," he said gruffly, "is that you don't turn me in" (translation: "Don't mention that you saw me"). Some writers court publicity, but Steinbeck was not among them, and so I was doubly pleased that we became friends, and that he would write, on the twenty-fifth anniversary of my column:

"He has made a many-faceted character of the city of San Francisco. It is very probable that Herb's city is the one that will be remembered. It is interesting to me that he has been able to do this without anger and without venom and without being soft. Then suddenly I see the anniversary—25 years!! Now where in hell did those years go? Well—they went into his column, for one thing."

Where did those years go? I remember John Steinbeck in 1961, lying ill in a suite at the Clift Hotel after returning from a trip to the Orient. He was propped up in bed, a pad of yellow foolscap on his knees, pencil in hand. "I'm so sore at myself for being sick," he growled, "that I'm making myself write epigrams. Confucianisms. Or maybe confusionisms."

He had already scribbled sixty-four of them, in his laborious longhand, and I take the liberty of reproducing a few of them here. So far as I know, they have never been published before—these feverish (102) thoughts of an angrily ailing John Steinbeck:

"I didn't know I had political ambition, but I must have—I am ill.

"For cultural interchange, the first book translated should be the Sears Roebuck catalogue—as Marco Polo demonstrated.

"Courtesy thrives on a potential kick in the pants. H-bombs may well be jet-propelled doves of peace.

"Hospitality is the most charming torture we have devised.

"I wonder who appointed the Americans to world leadership. Could it have been the Americans?

"Some men so love the world that they wish to own it.

"Since Thoreau's time, desperation has grown noisier.

"The final test of gentility is solvency.

"There are two roads to privacy—smallpox and poverty.

"Confusion is the child of speech. Silence gives no misinformation.

"Dignity is elusive. If a man wants it, he can't have it. If he has it, he has never heard of it.

"An author is an entertainer with tail feathers.

"Honor is the hell of the unhonored and the hell of the dishonored.

"Sympathy is what you feel for a man you wish were somewhere else.

"Love of women keeps pool rooms open.

"To be loved, get rich and hide your will.

"All people have this in common. They are good and those others are bad.

"Ambition is the lust for something to avoid when you have it.

"Hell must be a pleasant place. Nobody wants to steal it.

"A bird can fly but can't thread a needle.

"Government is the evidence that as individuals, we have failed.

"A man who loves cops is studying to be one.

"Swans are free-swimming public buildings.

"Without the devil and the weather we would lack work and conversation.

"A gift is a bribe with bells.

"A good woman is the best of women. A good man wants watching.

"Mankind has at least reached the eminence of a child with a stolen dynamite cap.

"Loyalty is conditioned friendship.

"Ignorance is the solidified wisdom of the ages.

"Thought is for Monday after the game.

"An evil man is never evil to himself nor a good man good.

"Time is the only critic without ambition.

"Force is the reasoning of failure.

"A man too well insured may find it economically unsound to be alive.

"A man will break his ass to avoid trouble, forgetting that a broken ass is troublesome.

"Art is a scream of loneliness.

"We can have peace if we can make it dangerous and expensive."

Four sheets of yellow foolscap, covered with these, and other, thoughts of John Steinbeck. "I would love to have those," I said, and, although he carefully guarded everything he wrote, he said, shrugging, "They're yours, on the altar of friendship." Then he scrawled across the top, "For Herb Caen—'A Crock of Chrysanthemums,' by John Steinbeck." I reproduce them also on the altar of friendship, and in sorrow at his passing.

CANINE FOOTNOTE: While he was gathering material for his book *Travels with Charlie,* Steinbeck arrived in San Francisco to relate a tale of one shining moment in the life of his beloved Airedale. "When Charlie and I were driving through the redwood country," he told a group of us at Enrico's Coffee House, "I looked around till I found the largest redwood in the area—an absolute beauty, probably 2,000 years old, a considerable tree before Christ was born. And then I let Charlie out of the camper so he could go and pee on that tree. Now I ask you, what is left in life for that dog?" The silence which followed the question was broken at last by Howard Gossage. "Well," he ventured, "he could always teach."

☆ ☆ ☆

EASY ANSWERS to hard questions dept.: "Why is it that the Cleveland Wrecking Company, which has torn down so much of San Francisco, has offices in almost every principal city except Cleveland?" Answer: because Cleveland has already been torn down.

☆ ☆ ☆

GOOD BETS: If the stranger you're chatting with at a cocktail party graduated from Yale or Harvard, you'll find out about it within five minutes, sometimes less. If the male hairdresser you meet isn't homosexual, he'll drop the fact within ninety seconds. A woman who feels she looks too young to be a grandmother will produce photos of her grandchildren within fifty-five seconds, not a record. A wife who says: "I don't want anything for Christmas and I mean it" doesn't mean it, as the husband will find out twenty-one seconds into Christmas Eve.

☆ ☆ ☆

THE AMA POLLED 628 doctors on the best hospital in the country, but I won't keep you in suspense, local hospital fans. We didn't make it. Closest is in Los Angeles, but I'll be danged if I'll print its name. Fine reply, though, from a doctor at Yale Medical School to the question "Which would you choose if suddenly taken ill?" "The nearest Holiday Inn," he stated . . . I want to leave my body to medical science, since it's such a marvel, but it seems I can't get into the school of my choice, Stanford, dead or alive. First it was my grades and now it's my address—I live too far away, even if I deliver myself personally. Your suggestion that I drop dead on the premises is a good one, but not guaranteed to be effective, either. U.C. Medical has a long waiting list, and one hates to stand in line. Of course, you can always wait at the bar, I guess . . . Bloody Mary, please.

107

Distant Heroes

I REMEMBER when the spitball was legal, and when Three-Finger Mordecai Brown had five fingers, and when the '29 Seals had a club that could have beaten most of the majors, and when the White Sox wore socks that were really white, except when they turned black in 1919 and the little urchin looked up at Shoeless Joe Jackson, accused of taking a bribe, and allegedly whinnied, "Say it ain't so, Joe," and . . .

Well, never mind. I'm not parading my age and devotion, I'm simply establishing my bona fides as a longtime follower and admirer of the great old game of inches, baseball.

This requires a certain nuttiness. And to be a nut about baseball, you have to be an old nut, for baseball is an old man's game, even when the old man is young. Put a kid in a monkey suit, and he immediately becomes an ancient, adopting a grave and sober mien, chewing reflectively on his tobacco cud and occasionally spitting with tremendous dignity. There is no room for youthful hijinks in baseball, and a "showboat" is regarded with suspicion (hence the coolness toward the Charlie Finleys and other stunt men).

I remember when I got my first uniform, as a member of the Sacramento American Legion club. As soon as I put it on, my manner changed. When I played in sweat shirt and jeans, I was just another sandlot joker, a true busher. But once in uniform, I became a man, gazing out over the field with steely eyes. Undue laughter was out. Life, which was baseball, became a serious matter, and we all aged overnight. Cops and ball players are very much alike: out of uniform, they look ten years younger, a discovery that always comes as a surprise.

There are two major reasons why I believe today's youngsters cannot truly appreciate baseball. The first is the Westward move of major league teams, and the second is television.

When I was a kid, big league ball was played exclusively in the far-off, mysterious East. We read about it, dreaming impossible dreams, but we never saw it, except maybe at World Series time in the Pathé Newsreels, which showed the players performing with incredible speed and agility. We didn't learn till much later that this was because those primitive cameras tended to speed up the action. Big leaguers were all supergods in a distant Olympus, possessed of a genius beyond mortal capabilities.

My first trauma came when Stanley Hack, a kid I had occasionally played sandlot ball with in Sacramento, was purchased by the Chicago Cubs. I knew he was good, but no superman, and I figured privately that he'd last maybe a week in that rarefied company. Well, he not only lasted for years, he became one of the great Cubs, to be ranked alongside Kiki Cuyler, Hack Wilson and Gabby Hartnett. That was a shock.

Then—oh, the awful propinquity of it all!—everything began to cave in. Television, the great leveler, began showing us weekly that major leaguers—at least, those of today—were all too mortal, and that a big league game can be every bit as tedious as the kind we had grown up with. And when the major leagues came to town, in person, the reality became stark. These are good ball players, to be sure, but were they fit to shine the shoes of George Sisler and Eddie Collins and the Big Six and the Big Train and all the other heroes who had strode through our childhood imaginations? Growing up is always painful, and never more painful than this.

That's why I say you have to be an old man of whatever age to enjoy baseball—and how are the kids of today to get the message when it no longer exists? To them, Candlestick Park is just Windlestick Park and those guys out there are just guys out there. To us who refuse to let the dream die, we are sitting in the Polo Grounds and we're watching Davey Bancroft and Freddie Lindstrom and Fat Fred Fitzsimmons and Mel Ott with his foot in the air as he swings and Heinie Groh advancing to the plate with that crazy bottle bat of his.

We have to squint a little to get away with it, but squint we do, to bring a little of the glory back into focus. I can well understand why most of the shaggy-haired beautiful kids of today couldn't care less about baseball. It comes as a pleasant surprise that so many of them do, when they can't see the ghosts in the infield and the angels in the outfield, playing the dream game that we old-timers are forever watching from out of the past.

The Moving Finger

AS YOU GET older in this racket, you find yourself spending more and more time writing of the deaths of those who made the city an exciting place to be alive in—among them Beniamino Bufano and Lefty O'Doul, Jake and Louis, the Great Gossage, Gaetano Merola and Pierre Monteux, Amelio, Joe Vanessi and now—Johnny.

I first met Johnny Kan in '38 or '39 when he was working as "host" in a long-gone and quite beautiful tearoom called the Blue Willow. A handsome young man, he cut a striking figure in long silken robes topped by a ceremonial headdress. In educated and urbane English, he would welcome Caucasians with a deep bow, pouring out Confucianisms. And as they passed, starry-eyed, into the pretty tearoom, he would chuckle to a friend, "White devils velly surplised hear young Chinee boy speak so good English, eh what?"

Chinatown at that time was still a mysterious world to most Caucasians. The restaurants were small, generally, with bare marble-topped tables and waiters who looked more hostile than they really were. The whites ordered chop suey and, if they were daring, chow mein. The wondrous subtleties and intricacies of true Oriental cuisine were beyond them, and there was no one in Chinatown prepared to offer an education. Except Johnny Kan.

Around 1940, he founded the Cathay House, a good-looking restaurant with a splendid location at the corner of Grant and California, and began wooing the tourists—not by "selling out" but by going to the trouble to introduce them to great Cantonese dishes. Chinatown elders muttered about Johnny Kan "catering to the white man, forgetting the traditions," but he and Cathay House were an instant success. A generation learned from him about Peking duck, winter melon soup, fried squid, sea bass, gold coin chicken—and the proper use of chopsticks.

And to tourists (and natives) who would innocently order chop suey, Johnny would purr, "I'm sorry, we serve only Chinese food here."

After the war, he opened the restaurant at Grant and Sacramento that was to become, quite literally, world famous (a lot of San Francisco eating places advertise themselves as "world famous" but few are). With the help of his master chef, Ming, he created dishes that captured the essence of the Cantonese art and yet appealed to wide audiences. Politicians and princes, Cary Grant and Danny Kaye and Benny Goodman, Gianni Agnelli, Merle Oberon, Joe Doakes from Topeka and Whitney Warren from Telegraph Hill—these were part of the legions that trooped through Kan's.

After Johnny, Chinatown cooking was never the same. Chop suey has all but disappeared and you seldom hear anyone calling for beetle juice. In his wake came restaurateurs who tried to emulate him, and patrons who know the infinite variety that stretches beyond chow mein. Not long ago, at sixty-six, he died, a man who worked too long and too hard for the perfection he often achieved. In Canton and Peking, they should be aware that there lived in San Francisco a man who raised their cuisine to the highest level.

Winning and Losing

IN MANY WAYS, this is a city of losers. Maybe that's why we have so many more saloons than churches; we figure our prayers may never be answered, but a couple of stiff shots will get us through the day. The natives have always been kind to panhandling bums; they know if they hadn't got a lucky break somewhere along the line, they'd be standing there with their hand out, too. They are perversely aware of the cirrhosis and bridge-jumping rate—and of the thin line that constantly separates them from contracting the former and performing the latter. The city's favorite shade is gray (even the sightseeing busses carry the name). If it's clear and sunny for two days running, they say: "It can't last." It's one of the few bets they win.

The old San Franciscans always blow their money on slow horses, fast women and sick stocks. But they're never too broke for a shoeshine and a manicure plus a fat tip; they still send corsages and open taxi doors for ladies, being gents. They're suspicious of newcomers to the town who make it too fast, too big and too loud—like, what are they trying to prove? That's why characters have always been more popular in San Francisco than winners. Anybody can win. A character is a loser with color and a little class. It's more important to live rich and die poor than the other way around. The San Franciscan wants only one epitaph: "When He Had It, He Spent It." And when he lost it, faded away without regret or whimper.

It's always the end of an era in San Francisco. Barbary Coast, bonanza kings, champagne nights, ferry boats— something or somebody nice is always dying. The cable cars will probably go next. And the views, sacrificed to those new money guys who like to build big mothers in the sky. The San Franciscan will raise a little hell about it because he knows he's supposed to, but if he wins he'll be surprised. He's used to living with defeat. When he dials a number in a phone booth and the line is busy, he doesn't even get annoyed when the dime doesn't come back. He expected it.

Take Joe Alioto. He doesn't know it yet, or maybe it's slowly dawning on him, but he's a loser, too. He was a rich, happy, respected millionaire lawyer and then he ran for mayor. And won. Another famous Italian, Enrico Banducci, is more in the San Francisco tradition. When he was riding high and making a ton of money with his Hungry I, nobody resented it. They knew he was a loser at heart. They knew he'd blow it one day in great style and sure enough he did. So everybody respects him.

The Giants were the perfect baseball team for San

Francisco. They couldn't win for losing in New York, and were going broke. Now they are going broke here. It figures. A lot of old-timers got nervous when they won a pennant in 1962, but they managed to lose the Series and everybody relaxed again. Who could live with a winner? Still, the Giants were coining money at Seals Stadium till Charlie Harney went and built Christopher's Crock, otherwise known as Candlestick, and that did it. "S.F. in Big Leagues!" read the headlines when the Giants arrived, but the old-timers just yawned. Cincinnati has had a major league baseball team longer than any other city in the land, and what is there to say about Cincinnati?

Please Don't Eat the Frisco

IT SADDENS ME to report that column readers in Minneapolis are sharper than our own. At least, readers of Will Jones's column in the Minneapolis *Tribune* are, judging from the evidence as it pertains to games. While we have been playing around with childish punmanship, like Tom Swifties ("I'm crestfallen," ejaculated Tom prematurely) and the Animal Farm (the people who named their aardvark A Million Miles for One of Your Smiles), Sweet Will's readers have been going at a really grown-up pastime called Eclectic Sequels. This is a game for movie buffs invented by Attorney Bruce W. Burton, the idea being to combine two hits into a sequel that could conceivably save the entire film industry from going down, drainward . . . Herewith some of Burton & Friends' better combinations, complete with plot summaries:

Garden of the Finzi-Kontiki. Anti-Semitism flares aboard a raft in the South Pacific when the Jewish captain tries to keep a kosher kitchen but the crew is hungry for pork.

I Am Curious (Yellow Submarine) Four singers from

Liverpool meet a liberated Swedish girl who tackles them in all sorts of unnatural positions on the ocean floor.

Moby, the Bank Dick. Gregory Peck suspects that W. C. Fields is an escaped whale and pursues him into the bank vault.

Snow White and the Magnificent Seven Year Itch. A tuneful, animated Disney training film for service personnel of the Mexican Army.

What's Up Doc's Rear Window. Hitchcock, Stewart and Streisand in a madcap chase across, over and through Grace Kelly's San Francisco vestibule.

Auntie Maims the Godfather. Watch the sparks fly as zany Roz Russell finds Brando hiding in the main kitchen of Puzo's retirement home.

The Sound of Music Man. Sentimental musical caper in which Julie Andrews and Robert Preston smuggle a seventy-six-nun marching band out of occupied Poland.

NOTE: the game isn't as easy as it first appears. For instance, verbs like "meets" are out, so discard *Ryan's Daughter Meets the Last of the Red Hot Lovers.* Also, no credit is given for ad-nauseam titles: *Gidget Goes Bananas with the Wild Bunch on the Waterfront Under the Planet of the Apes.* Moreover, warns Burton, international mixtures such as *Seven Brides for Seven Samurai* are discouraged on the grounds of cultural shock.

Cabaret on the Waterfront. Neo-Nazis infiltrate the Longshoremen's Union dance hall, with Liza Minnelli starring as the unforgettable Harriet Bridges, hostess.

The Legend of Nigger Charley's Aunt. Invited to chaperone a square dance at a frontier university, a black drag queen becomes the scourge of the Old West.

Fanny Patton. A musical masterpiece about a crusty American general who finds love while taking a few days off for R & R in the waterfront cafes of Marseilles.

A Star Is Born Free. The tragic show-biz biography of Leo the Lion, his rise to fame and his fall from Tinseltown grace after eating the emcee at an Oscar ceremony.

Bob & Carol & Ted & Alice's Restaurant. A social document about a hippie hangout where they swap organic recipes almost as casually as they swap wives.

Rachel Rachel Tora Tora Tora Curtain. A spinster speech correctionist from New England (Joanne Woodward), working in Tokyo just prior to Pearl Harbor, becomes romantically involved with a double agent (Paul Newman) who is the identical lookalike of stammering Admiral Yoshomato.

The Wrong Man for All Seasons. Hitchcock's semidocumentary tells the true story of a struggling trombonist who is mistakenly arrested and tried for heresy when the king's sterile wife identifies him in the lineup. Parental guidance suggested.

Nanook of the North by Northwest. If an Eclectic Film Festival is ever held, honoring the all-time great directors, this is a must. A primitive ice fisherman and his naked wife (Eva Marie Saint) desperately flee from a gang of neo-Nazis led by James Mason, across Hitchcock's lower lip.

2001 Paths of Glory, or, How I Learned to Stop Worrying and Love the Clockwork Orange. Kubrick's savage antipeace satire brilliantly exposes the double standards inherent in the Xerox 3400 photo-copying process; with Peter Sellers as Everyman.

Now that you have the idea, forget it. We are not starting a new contest or inviting entries. Besides, there is no way to top "A Night to Remember the Ten Commandments": a mammoth luxury liner, while crossing the Red Sea . . .

CASTING ABOUT for a "noncontroversial" Charter Day speaker, U.C.-Berkeley decided on Jacques Cousteau—but there is no way to win these things. When the chancellor, Albert Bowker, announced Cousteau's selection, he was immediately attacked by a young radical woman who exploded about the famous deep-sea diver: "But he's so—so—shallow!"

ADD REMARKS you wouldn't hear ten years ago: "You going to the big football game in Oakland Sunday?" . . .

"It's such a nice day I think I'll wear my boots downtown" . . . "The one with the short hair is the girl" . . . "Look, there goes Grandma in her new red Porsche!" . . . "Gee, my watch stopped—the battery must be dead" . . . "Isn't he awfully old to be wearing a beard?" . . . "Leave my hair long, barber, I want to look younger" . . . "It was a good party, by Pacific Heights standards, but they ran out of pot by midnight" . . . "Do you think this dinner jacket is dressy enough to wear with my turtle-neck sweater?" . . . "He's six feet tall—in his high heels, I mean" . . . "Oh-oh, I think I just got a run in the seat of my stockings!"

☆ ☆ ☆

ORIN CASSMORE, after suffering through yet another 49er defeat on Sunday: "Slowly but surely those guys are driving me back into the arms of the church!"

Small Thoughts at Large

A DISTINGUISHED national magazine asked me to write a few thousand words about San Francisco's irresistible attraction for hippies and beatniks (if not vice versa), and while I was, of course, flattered at being taken for an expert in this arcane field, I declined the offer for two middling good reasons. First, in the manner of most distinguished magazines, the fee offered would not exactly put me on the sunny side of Easy Street, and second, I'm damned if I know why San Francisco has been Mecca, through several generations, for so many round pegs in a largely square world. It's a puzzlement, as I believe Square Old Alice said in her Wonderland daze, little wotting that the Mary Janes she wore would someday become a euphemism for pot. Or, indeed,

116

that Brillig and the Slithy Toves would be memorialized as the name of a rock 'n' roll group.

However, in the interest of basic research, I put on my eight-button double-breasted Brioni jacket, a pair of bell bottoms and my boots and went out to the Drogstore on Haight Street, looking more odd than Mod. The pants were so tight I could inhale only, a situation not devoutly to be desired in the Drogstore. To the sound of splitting seams, I settled down next to an adenoidal young man.

"You new on the scene?" I asked. Examining my attire, he inquired, "You from the fuzz?" "No, man," I replied. "I am a journalist from the overground press, seeking truth." He grunted. "I want to know," I continued, "why you happened to come to San Francisco." "Because this is where it's all happening." "What is?" I asked. "Everything," he said, shrugging. "You know, the whole scene."

"Well," I ventured, "would you say you came to San Francisco as a gesture of protest against the sterility of middle-class morality and the puritan ethic that has been so inimical to the mental well-being of America? And if so, do you feel that total alienation is a viable stance vis-à-vis the military-industrial continuum? To put it another way—"

He looked at me for the first time. "You crazy?" he said. "I came out here like everybody else—to get laid and get high." I threw down a few coins and left, feeling that perhaps there was less to this story than we had been led to believe.

However, still searching, I consented to participate in a panel discussion at a school of higher learning. The subject was, naturally, the hippies (has any group been discussed with greater earnestness and less enlightenment?), and I threw in a question, "But why San Francisco?" The answers from the erudite panelists were murkily articulate. "Because this is where the winds of freedom blow." And "Because there has been an atmosphere of abandon here since the Gold Rush days." And because "This city has always taken the oddball and the alienated to its heart—the care and feeding of characters is part of the San Francisco tradition."

And so on, round and round, and where it ended was nowhere, as usual. Several obvious untruths were spoken, such

117

as "The hippies are antiestablishment, and so is San Francisco." Actually, San Francisco is very much an establishment city; it makes just as much sense to say that *that's* why the hippies are flocking here—the "enemy" is so visible. I also think it's a mistake to look upon the hippies as characters in the sense that Emperor Norton, Oofty-Goofty and even the beatniks were characters. Norton and his ilk were establishment characters, more than willing to play the role of court jester to the condescending lords (this goes for the Barney Fergusons and Tiny Armstrongs of a latter age, as well). Even the beatniks, especially the talented writers and artists among them, were not averse to the rewards that only the establishment can bestow. The hippies are an entirely different pot of tea. Except in their music, and closely allied activities, they couldn't care less about the approval and acceptance of the straight world. And as for the fond, self-gratifying notion that there is something especially alluring about the San Francisco tradition, forget it. Take it from me, these kids never heard of Lotta Crabtree or Belle Cora's parlour house. Our police are more sensitive and understanding? "Fuzz is fuzz," said one of the more talkative hippies.

The hostess at a polite dinner party the other night wailed, "How did this hippie thing ever happen to our lovely city?" All I could think of was the reply of the Vassar girl (Smith? Bryn Mawr?) found working in a house of prostitution. "Just lucky, I guess."

☆ ☆ ☆

JACK CARNEY, updating Voltaire: "I may not agree with your bumper sticker but I will defend to the death your right to stick it."

☆ ☆ ☆

ADD PLASTIC CITIES: Insurance executive John Schwobada is back from six months in San Diego, and quite pleased to be home. "It's nice to eat in some real restaurants again," he told Ed Stackhouse. "San Diego is pretty enough, but I didn't have one unfranchised meal the whole time I was there!"

☆ ☆ ☆

NOW THEN: Why do the Salvation Army belles ring their bells over black kettles during the Christmas season? The reason that's a good question is that I just discovered the answer. Back in 1894, there was a shipwreck off the Golden Gate, and the survivors were sheltered and fed by the Salvation Army. When the food supply was exhausted, an Army lass grabbed the empty kettle and walked through the Barbary Coast, calling out, "Keep the kettle boiling— help the shipwreck survivors!" That's such a nice story I hope nobody tells me it's untrue.

☆ ☆ ☆

WHY IS the new Hilton Hotel tower here exactly 509 feet tall? Because Conrad Hilton is one tycoon who never forgets, and he well remembers that the owners of the Fairmont, the Mark Hopkins and other major hotels once strove mightily to keep him out of town. So when the tower was planned, he told architect John Carl Warnecke that it had to rise higher than the Top o' the Mark and the Fairmont's tower—"and not one story higher, *two* stories, so there will be no room for doubt." That added up to 509 feet.

☆ ☆ ☆

FOOTNOTE: In his *Pleasures of Archaeology,* Karl E. Meyers recalls philosopher Morris Raphael Cohen asking his class to imagine that a superhuman being appeared on earth and offered to teach mankind a trick that would make life incomparably more pleasant. "In return," Cohen went on, "the god demanded only the blood sacrifice of 50,000 lives a year. With what indignation would this proposal be rejected! Then came the automobile."

A Day in the Life

THE WEATHERMAN had predicted gales, but by 9 A.M., the clouds parted and the sun came out, followed by children, dogs and people on the way to church, their prayers already having been answered. I whistled a merry tune, feeling the day was already a great success: nothing makes a columnist feel better than to find somebody else's prediction turning sour in cold print.

I leaned across the breakfast table and patted young Christopher on top of his young and pointy dome. "A beautiful morning, my boy," I said paternally. "Why?" he asked. "Because the sun came out for a change." "Why the sun came out for a change?" "Look, Christopher," I said, "don't ask 'Why' all the time." "Why?"

Our conversation having come to its usual dead end, I stared out the window at the neighborhood cats chasing the robins, which were disgustingly drunk on pyracantha berries. "Take me out to the music-go-round," commanded Christopher. "Why?" I said childishly. "And anyway, it's a merry-go-round." "Why?" he asked. Not a bad question. Music-go-round is quite descriptive, and don't ask me why.

We got in the car and drove in the general direction of the park and the beach. Sun glinting off the neo-onion domes of the neo-Byzantine Orthodox church on outer Geary (so what else is neo?). We rolled along the empty streets, every inch of curb space—legal or otherwise—crammed with cars. San Francisco has one car for every two residents and only one garage for every two cars. This is a real mink-lined poverty pocket, filled with two-car families.

We walked across dewy morning lawns to the Children's Playground in the park, past fine old neo-Gothic buildings of sandstone. They built things to last in the old days, not having figured out that there's money in obsolescence; it'll cost a fortune to tear down those buildings but they won't fall over by themselves. Sooner or later we have to pay for quality.

The merry-go-round was dark, cold and gloomy, haunted by the laughter of children grown old. I strapped Christopher onto a big rooster and climbed aboard a green frog that had seen better days. A bored young man reading a comic book punched a button without even looking up, and we were off to the strains of "La Ronde." Such sophisticated neo-Viennese music in this drafty temple of innocence. An old man wearing a beret and raincoat stood just outside the door, beaming at Christopher and dreaming dreams of sunnier days. At least I hoped that was what he was dreaming.

"Let's go again, Daddy," said Christopher at the end of the interminable ride. I was tempted to ask "Why?" but we went again. I never liked "La Ronde" in the first place and now I hated it.

We bought some peanuts and went over to the Arboretum, its majestic fountain splashing silvery in the thin sun, a giant Chinese magnolia supplying a distant early warning of spring. I guess it was a Chinese magnolia; I'm a little weak on flowers but there were some nice red, pink, and—oh, maybe lavender ones. Elderly ladies wearing coats down to their sensible shoes, and fedora hats redolent of Berlin in the thirties, strolled about, chatting in German. A group speaking French stood on the tiny wooden bridge, feeding the ducks. Golden Gate Park early on a Sunday morning is European, alive with brisk walkers, deep breathers and memories of Potsdam.

The squirrels, so aloof during the tourist season, came running for peanuts. Winter is the thin time of year for them, and they put on a great show of friendliness and spurious charm, standing on their hind legs and cocking their heads in a manner they know to be irresistible. Christopher was enchanted. To one squirrel that grabbed his hand while reaching for a peanut, he said huskily, "I love you." The squirrel cocked his head at him uncertainly before scampering away.

We walked across the road to the Japanese Tea Garden, looking for goldfish in the murky ponds. The pretty, run-down place—it could use a refurbishing—was crowded with out-of-season tourists, potting at each other with their In-stamatics and spilling Cracker Jack along the pathways. The people looked like members of that mysterious group called the Silent Majority; that is, the men wore their hair short, their ties thin and their pants wide, while the ladies were gorgeous beyond description with their bouffant hair, flowered dresses and little mink stoles. On the curved bridge, I stood next to one of these paragons as he threw his empty Cracker Jack box into the pond and hated myself for remaining as silent as the majority.

We drove out of the park, now filling rapidly with all those cars we have too many of, over back roads cracking and pitting under the strain. Back home, I said to Chris-topher, "Now, you have to take a nap." "Why?" he wailed. "Because I'm tired," I said sternly, secretly pleased that I'd found an irrefutable answer.

You Should Live So Long

PEOPLE, places and things we can do without:

Bars that don't have a back mirror. When you're having a drink alone (hi there) it's nice to have a familiar face to stare at, even your own.

Most movies and books advertised as "The heartwarming story of—"

Politicians who think they know what the Silent Majority is thinking.

Silent majorities.

Married couples who call each other "Mama" and "Daddy" (greetings, Dr. Freud).

"Personalized" letters written by a machine, especially when your name is misspelled and fits badly into the space provided.

Merry morticians who sign off *their* "personalized" letter with "Eventually yours."

Merry morticians.

The host who greets you with "Nice to have you aboard," walks you to the bar saying, "Name your poison, podna," and beams as you're leaving, "Here's your coat, what's your hurry?"

Hosts who call champagne "shampoo."

Perhaps the most distasteful of all TV commercials: the chewing gum plug that featured the girl who has "the cleanest mouth in town." I can understand why her boy friend might know, but why those gossipy old biddies? Erggg.

Interviews with Elizabeth Taylor in which she tries to fob herself off as the most courageous woman in the world ("That's me, Mother Courage in a sable").

Guys who wear those deep-sea diver watches with their dinner clothes.

Any recorded announcement by the phone company except the time and the weather. Especially nominated for oblivion: "The number you have rea-uched is not in servuss at thee-us time. Plee-us—"

People who say, "May I ask you a question?" when they already have.

Or, "I like oysters but oysters don't like me."

Executives who end an argument with "What do you know about it, mister, have you ever met a payroll?" (I never met a payroll I didn't like, especially if I happened to be on it.)

Readers who seem terribly put out because I don't write the way I did twenty years ago. I don't do anything else the way I did twenty years ago, either. And I'm terribly put out about it.

Being taken to look at a dam while on a vacation.

Ladies who can't resist giggling, every time they decline a cigarette or a drink: "none of the minor vices, hahahaha."

Wives who call their husbands by their last name.

Statements in newspapers attributed to an unidentified "official spokesman."

"Official spokesmen."

Automobile ads that read exultantly, "Over 30 standard features at no extra cost!" That's what "standard" means, isn't it?

Creamed spinach with too much nutmeg.

TV station managers who, in their on-the-air editorials, pronounce nuclear "nucular."

TV station managers' on-the-air editorials.

People who hang up after letting your phone ring only three times.

Politicians who complain they were quoted "out of context" when the gist of their statement is unchanged. Scares hell out of them to be edited down to the point where somebody might understand what they're struggling to avoid saying.

Deejays who forget that their primary function is to identify the tune and the group performing it; after that simple chore, they may be as witty and windy as they please.

Executives who practice their golf swing, their eyes far away on the imaginary flight of the ball, as you're trying to talk to them.

That frog-voiced guy who croaks "Braaaaavo!" from his grand tier seat at the symphony, even when the performance is good.

Critics who write, "I find all this emphasis on sex very boring." Okay, so that's *their* hangup.

"Speed Checked by Radar" signs a mile before you come to a sign that tells what the speed limit is.

Envelopes bearing the stirring printed announcement: "Place Stamp Here." Where else?

Lists of pet hates.

DO YOU remember the Seattle earthquake of April 1965? It scored a rather exciting 6.5 on the Richter scale, and George Lemont recalls it vividly because he was in a crowded restaurant there at the time. As plaster fell from the ceiling and plates crashed to the floor, our hero arose and shouted coolly, "I'm from San Francisco—we always stand in doorways!" Loud male voice from across the room: "I'm from Chicago—where the hell do *we* stand?"

The Season of the Witch

NO, I DON'T KNOW what it means. "The Season of the Witch"—neatly printed in white chalk on a wall opposite Fifth Street on Market. This is the wall of graffiti that first gave us "Ecology—The Last Fad," a chilling piece of writing. And "Support the Blind—They're out of Sight." Not an obscenity to be seen. Just gentle nastiness, such as "Happiness Is a New Governor."

Religion is very much with us, here on the scorched and seamy side of Everybody's Favorite City. "Praise Jesus, praise Jesus," chants the old black man in his sackcloth robes. He is wearing a wooden sandwich board on which is written, "America, Come Back to God." On sidewalk newsstands, wooden plaques implore, "Don't Go to Hell's Fire, Jesus Loves You." "You Are Entering Wino Country," reads a chalked inscription on the sidewalk. The old black lady with the Aunt Jemima kerchief is huddled on the stone steps, covering herself with newspapers. Shivering in the heat. There is enough irony there to make you shiver with her, for she is on the steps of the United States Mint, sick and penniless.

The wailing wall. You stand there in the smoggy air and go on reading it, dizzy in a miasma of patchouli oil, sweat and poverty. "You think police are bad—try calling a hippie," somebody has chalked. The meaning has been changed: somebody else has inserted the word "one" after "calling." Okay, try calling one a hippie. "Rock's Grass Is Beat Grass," reads another inscription. I don't dig it. Is beat grass good or bad? A few yards down the line, the police lover is back again. In black letters, he has written, "For a

125

cop not to be aggressive is fatal to you and others. Think a minute."

Out there in the middle of the street, the new folk heroes, the hard hats, are lounging on their equipment. They look relaxed and should. Their jobs will go on forever. They demonstrate their virility by making loud cracks at passing girls in tight pants. The Silent Majority has found its voice, but the girls look straight ahead, pretending not to hear. Back at the wall, I read the white chalked words: "Herb Cain"—sic-sic-sick—"is still over there and I know that the paranoia exists between him and that funny paper." Yeah. "It's all part of the total experience."

Oh, there are stirring sights to see if you don't get mugged, slugged, bugged or jugged. At Fifth and Mission, the cap is off the fire hydrant and water gushes into the gutter, alongside the Pickwick Hotel's trees that are dying for lack of it. The newsboy with the ratchet voice crouches in his wooden stand, listening to blaring rock music as his headlines go unsung—headlines that tell of the death of kings and the triumphs of Herr Kissinger.

You sidle along the wall, past the pale young girls carrying pale babies that look older than their mothers. Two young beards fall into a conversation. "Hey, how you fixed for grass?" "Depends. You buyin' or sellin'?" "I'm sellin', man." "Well, so am I." They split. Around the corner, the flower stand with its corsages wrapped in foil, looking as dated as the gambler who stops to buy one for his henna-headed girl. A better-looking girl whispers hoarsely: "How about a little fun, baby?" But the Adam's apple gives him away. In front of Bank of America at No. 1 Powell, the sweet-faced lady, so proper in her neat gray coat and hat, is selling *Awake* and the *Watchtower*. I've seen her for years. I have never seen her sell one. But she goes on smiling blankly at a world she can't possibly understand.

"The Season of the Witch," it says there on the wall. I don't understand it but it makes sense.

I ONCE REMARKED that "All the guests at the Clift

126

Hotel look like they come from Santa Barbara." This observation returned to mind one noon while I was lunching in the Clift's Redwood Room and examining the crowd from behind a Campari. Good Santa Barbara bones, clear and slightly tanned skin, but faces a little on the dull side. They matched the hotel perfectly: the Clift is safe, clean, well run, expensive and conservative. Very Santa Barbara.

As I was thus ruminating, probably unfairly, an elderly gentleman walked over slowly, with the aid of a cane, to say hello. I jumped to my feet to greet a great newspaperman and a man of irresistible charm: then ninety-three-year-old Tom Storke, publisher emeritus of the Santa Barbara *News-Press,* Pulitzer prize winner, undisputed leader of the Santa Barbara Establishment.

And yet he had won his Pulitzer not with a series of articles exposing the lurking Reds that proper Santa Barbara dowagers look for nightly under their king-sized beds. He won it because, down there in the heart of ultraconservatism, he was the first to take on and expose the un-American aspects of the John Birch Society. Further, when Ronald Reagan began criticizing the State university system, it was Tom Storke who was the first to say: "In these attacks by Reagan I see the slippery hands of Robert Welch and his Birch Society."

I watched him slowly thread his way through the dining room, nodding and waving to all the Establishment people who greeted him warmly. Truly, here was one of those "contradictions of capitalism" that the Marxist tacticians used to talk about—one of the precious contradictions that may yet save the system from being smashed by its noisiest so-called friends.

"Love It or Leave It"

IT STILL SEEMS to be a popular bumper strip— "America: Love It or Leave It!"—and it sticks in the craw as well as to the chromium. Along with its gag writer's glibness, it has an oddly non-American ring, stern and dictatorial, the words of a zealot. Actually, it *was* originated by a gag writer, Walter Winchell, who used it first in his column circa 1940 when he was campaigning against the German-American Bund. "Love it or leave it"—patriotism reduced to a Tin Pan Alley rhythm. A far cry from the warm words of welcome inscribed on the Statue of Liberty: "Give me your tired, your poor, your huddled masses yearning to breathe free . . ." Along with the bumper strip goes the inevitable tiny American Flag affixed to windshield or window—decalcomania as a way of life. "It's like hiring Madison Square Garden to announce that you love your wife," said the *New Yorker* about this form of patriotism. The Melting Pot has grown cold.

"Patriotism is dead in America," publisher William Randolph Hearst, Jr., lamented one recent night to a group of us. "They think it's corny or something." He's an American and the rest of us are "they," and anyway, it turned out he was talking about nationalism, not patriotism—the kind of nationalism that has wracked Europe twice in half a century: "These little countries still have their pride, their people will stand up and fight." Another World War II veteran nodded vigorously. "He's right," he growled. "I really worry about our country. It's the kids, damn 'em. You think they'd stand up and fight the way we did?" For a draftee, he was talking pretty big.

The message of the bumper strips, the Hearst message, is clear enough beneath its simple-mindedness: "My country, right or wrong." An American even more celebrated than William Randolph Hearst, Jr., had this to say about that and about a war:

"An empty phrase, a silly phrase . . . Each must, for himself alone, decide what is right and what is wrong, and which course is patriotic and which isn't. You cannot shirk this and be a man. To decide it against your convictions is to be an unqualified and inexcusable traitor, both to yourself and to your country, let men label you as they may . . . Only when a Republic's *life* is in danger should a man uphold his government when it is in the wrong. There is no other time.

"This Republic's life is not in peril. This nation has sold its honor for a phrase . . . The stupid phrase needed help and it got another one: 'Even if the war be wrong, we are in it and must fight it out; *we cannot retire from it without dishonor.*' Why, not even a burglar could have said it better." So wrote Mark Twain in 1901. He was discussing the U.S. occupation of the Philippines, while anticipating a Vietnam. His closing quotation is remarkably apt: "An inglorious peace is better than a dishonorable war."

Fred Dutton, one of a tiny band of courageous people still remaining on the U.C. Board of Regents, said something that should be graven in stone: "A society that hates its young has no future." This is not to say that the young are not difficult and demanding. "What do they really *want?*" an anguished parent said one night, wringing his hands, as though the problem could be quantified. What they want is what they're not getting: honesty, straight answers, an end to the war psychology, a feeling that something real is being done about the real problems inside this country. Sometimes the generation gap seems as impossible to bridge as the credibility gap that caused such erosion in American life. As Lyman Bryson put it: "The younger generation thinks intelligence is a substitute for experience, the older generation thinks experience is a substitute for intelligence." In the long run, if there is one, intelligence should carry the day.

DID YOU KNOW that Senator Stuart Symington has a sense of humor? I didn't either till Congressman Pete McCloskey sent me the following excerpt from the *Congressional Record*—Symington's advice to future Democrat batsmen after they lost the annual congressional baseball game to the Republicans: "First, on the fast ball, I suggest that if you hear the ball hit the glove, it is probably fruitless to swing. Second, in handling the curve, do not be alarmed by the noise. It is the normal sound of the landing gear falling into place. Finally, if you have been standing there for 60 seconds and have not noticed anything, perhaps you should walk with dignity back to the dugout. You are out."

QUOTESVILLE: "The weather is unpredictable, of course, but that keeps it from being monotonous. A bit more windy than San Francisco, and more fog. But it's really a lovely place. At night, my wife and I can take a stroll and know we're not going to be hit over the head. And when we go to bed, nobody is going to come through our window and attack us. I guess you could say it's the safest place around." So says John Hart, the caretaker of Alcatraz, who lived on The Rock for twenty-one years.

WELL, IT WAS a lovely warm evening in Washington Square, and here was this naked guy prancing around, doing calisthenics and generally enjoying himself. Passers-by either laughed at or ignored him—you know how it is in San Francisco—while Frank Marianetti, owner of Fior d'Italia, watched from across the street. After about thirty minutes, Frank reluctantly called Central Station, where an officer asked, "Is he bothering anybody?" "No," said Frank, "but the fog is starting to come in and I wouldn't want him to catch cold."

A KID carrying a balloon wandered into the Hansen-Fuller Galleries on Grant Avenue and accidentally exploded it against the sharp corner of a Bruce Beasley metal sculpture. As he burst into tears, co-owner Wanda Hansen observed: "Well, I must say it's the first time I ever *heard* pop art!"

☆ ☆ ☆

HELLO: When James Brown was director of the Oakland Museum, he attended a party in a Hillsborough mansion, and was introduced around by the host with "This is Jim Brown of Oakland." Immediate reaction from a Peninsula dowager: "How anonymous can you *get?*"

☆ ☆ ☆

IN HIS WINE journal, Fred Cherry tells the delightful story of the English wine expert who visits the Napa and Sonoma vineyards, and, in the course of an interview, is asked by a brash newsman: "Which do you think is more important, sex or wine?" to which the Britisher replies: "Claret or Burgundy?"

☆ ☆ ☆

DR. DON ROSSMAN and his wife Claire, driving to San Francisco from Chicago, stopped in Nevada for gas, and Claire, who had never played a slot machine before, happily ran inside to try her luck. "Nothing," she said as she returned to the car. When they checked into their Reno hotel later in the day, Don played a machine in the lobby as Claire watched with considerable interest. "Oh," she said at last, "I didn't know you were supposed to pull the handle."

☆ ☆ ☆

"A YEAR AGO, when I was only 82, I wrote somebody that 'I don't feel like an old man, I feel like a young man who has something the matter with him.' I have now found out what it is: it is the approach of middle age and I don't care for it."

Thus begins a note of Christmas greetings from Bruce Bliven, who was editor of *New Republic* magazine for thirty remarkable years and now lives in retirement in Kingscote Gardens at Stanford. He goes on cherrily:

"I walk with a slight stagger, thus acquiring a lot of new friends; everybody welcomes the approach of what they feel is an amiable, elderly drunk. I forget a lot of words, thus reducing the size of my whaddayoucallit. The floor is covered with memos to myself, which I hope I'll be able to reach down and pick up . . .

"What have I learned in 83 years? I have learned that if you are mugged on the street, don't yell 'Help!' Yell 'Fire!' Nobody wants to come to a mugging but everybody is interested in a fire."

Season's greetings, dear Mr. B. And many more.

☆ ☆ ☆

SWORDS INTO plowshares or something: Do you remember the XB-70 bomber program? You should, since it cost you close to $2 billion, although only three prototypes were built (for *you*) at North American Aviation in L.A. The first was destroyed in a mid-air collision in 1966 and the second now reposes among the other dinosaurs at the Air Force Museum in Dayton, Ohio. And the third? Well, it wound up in crates scattered here and there. Sculptor Tom Van Zant bought a lot of the stainless steel and titanium, and fashioned the metal into huge abstract birds that now adorn the walls of the Crocker Bank branch in the Transamerica pyramid. I guess that closes the books on the XB-70.

☆ ☆ ☆

WILLIAM RANDOLPH HEARST, JR., dropped into the Post-Powell branch of Roos-Atkins one day and bought a suit from Dave Falk, who said, "Y'know, I sold your father an Inverness cape for the opera opening in 1939, down at the old Roos store on Market." At this, Hearst, Jr., turned to his son, William Randolph Hearst III, and said, grinning, "Billy, buy yourself a suit so Mr. Falk can go down in history as the only salesman who sold clothes to three William Randolph Hearsts." Done and done.

☆ ☆ ☆

SMALL OBSERVATIONS guaranteed to shake you up a little:

Your psychiatrist's hands tremble every time he opens a fortune cookie.

The man in charge of the hair-restoring salon is bald.

Your banker opens his attaché case and a copy of the *Daily Racing Form* falls out.

Just after you've congratulated the owner of the French restaurant on his authentic Provençal cuisine, the kitchen door swings open and you see that the chef is Filipino.

You finally meet the noted symphony conductor, and he has to cup his ear to hear you.

Your barber goes elsewhere to have his hair trimmed.

The renowned surgeon, who comes to your cocktail party for "just one drink" because he has an operation in the morning, is the last to leave, nine drinks later.

The guy who used to date your wife drops around to pick up your daughter.

Changes

"WHERE DO YOU RUN?" The question was propounded by the editor of one of San Francisco's most distinguished underground newspapers, and as I struggled to sort out the language, he amplified: "I mean, where is your turf, man, your terrain?"

The editor was a presumably clean-minded young man, about twenty-four, who happened to be wearing a very dirty shirt. Not revolting, more a symbol of revolt, I should think. His hair and manner bristled, and he couched his question in the faintly hostile tone characteristic of what may or may not be the New Left. The manner has been explained to me by a Berkeley psychiatrist: "The reason the New Left shouts down a Ted Kennedy, say, is really quite simple. They drown him out for fear he might say something with which they could agree. That they could never bear."

"Where do you run?" Well, it was a good question. The reply I tried to put together sounded vapid: "Oh, you know, the north side of town, I guess." I'd never been asked the question before. "Uh—North Beach, Telegraph Hill, Russian, Pacific Heights, downtown." Pause. Then, too brightly: "I get out to the park once in a while. The zoo. The beach."

There was a silence, and we regarded each other across a chasm. Not a communications gap, exactly. It's just that we lived in two different worlds in the one world of San Francisco, and the realization grew on me that I was running in a pretty constricted circle.

We were on his "turf," a hamburger and coffee house near

133

Fourteenth and Valencia in the Mission. The Mission. What did I even know about that? To me it was a vast and even mysterious section of old Irish and Spanish families with an uncommon number of churches. Tree-shaded streets, some of them quite pretty. Desolate alleys and old frame houses and a large black population.

"Rather a conservative part of town," I ventured, remembering the sturdy God-fearing native San Franciscans I'd encountered in the Mission over the years. "Not any more, man," said the young editor with finality. "All sorts of wild and beautiful things are happening in the Mission. Lots of Hashbury people make it here now. Communes all over the place. Whole new scene."

It was only twenty years ago that one of my mentors, the late Joseph Henry Jackson, talked daily about "the singular homogeneity of San Francisco" (he lived in Berkeley, which might have had something to do with it). He had me convinced that the people of the Marina cared desperately what happened in the Mission, and vice versa. "San Franciscans are one people, bound together by their devotion to the city and each other," he would say with pride. As he headed for the East Bay hills.

Forgive me, Joe Jackson, but San Franciscans no longer know their city. Put it down to fear or apathy. They go to Hunters Point about as often as they go to Cypress Point at Pebble Beach, which is never. Car doors locked, they circle around the Fillmore; in the past, they at least used to go "slumming" to the jazz joints there. In Pacific Heights, rent-a-guards patrol apartment house entrances. On the mansions, iron gates, barred windows . . .

"It's a sick scene, your part of town," said the young editor equably, "but we'll change all that after the revolution." The words "What have you been smoking, buddy?" crossed my mind, but then I remembered Susan Sontag's conclusion that America (read San Francisco) "is in its pre-revolutionary stage." It's young vs. old, tradition against outright rejection of same. The editor's dirty shirt is a symbol, as are bare feet and costumes (castoffs) instead of straight clothes ("Cheap Is In!" and the merchants are nervous). Pot? It outsells Pall Mall.

134

"A revolution is unthinkable," I said, picking up my hamburger. "The Establishment won't give up without a fight. The streets will run with blood." I bit fiercely into the burger to underline my conviction, but the young editor was unruffled. "It will be peaceful," he said. "We're winning already. Our people are moving in everywhere. We will take over by sheer force of numbers. We will just *be* there. Money will be out of the window. One big commune. Right now we're handing out free pictures in your part of town. Beautiful. Don't buy pictures, get them free. We're turning on the world." He displayed a photo of a little girl smoking pot. "How old is she, maybe eight? They're starting at six now. Your values are dead. What do you think of ours?"

I finished my hamburger and arose. "Not bad at all," I said. "Really an excellent hamburger." He gave a tiny smile as I left, and that was something of a victory. I forgot to tell you—the New Left is humorless, maybe because they think the joke is on the rest of us. But who gets the last laugh?

Our Finest Hour

Here today, here tomorra,
We ain't Sodom or Gomorrah . . .

EPIC TIMES call for epic poems and I'm sorry that's the best I could do on the latest anniversary of the roaring climax to San Francisco's Belle Époque, the great earthquake and fire. But the truth is that the authentic poets of the time didn't do much better, bogged down as they were in heavy Victoriana. The revered Ina Coolbrith, whose salon rang with the hearty jibes of Jack London, Ambrose Bierce, Bret Harte and Joaquin Miller, was so undone by the events of April 18, 1906, that her anguished heart turned to treacle: "In olden days, a child, I trod thy sands, Thy sands unbuilded, rank with brush and briar And blossom—chased the sea foam on the strands, Young city of my love and my desire" and so on to "But I see thee ever as of old! Thy wraith of pearl, wall, minaret and spire, Framed in the mists that veil thy Gate of Gold—Lost City of my love and my desire!" Later, for reasons that are perfectly obvious, she became poet laureate of California.

Jennie Crocker Henderson of Hillsborough, a member of the pioneer Crocker family, was in New York in April 1906, and attended a lecture by Mark Twain a few days after the earthquake. The ordinarily wry author, moved to tears by the fate of "one of my favorite cities," read a poem hastily written for the occasion, and Mrs. Henderson, then a teenager, wrote it down as he spoke.

"The Stricken City" was the title. "I am swept across the desert by the sorrow of my soul," began Mark Twain, "To the glowing golden city where the waves of anguish roll/I can see the sheen and shimmer that enveloped sky and street/I can see the smiling faces of the friends I used to meet." I won't detain you further except to mention such memorable images as "Supreme Pacific wonder, fair Goddess of the Gate!" and "Behind the smoke and horror let your prophetic eyes/Perceive God's chosen city from your own ashes rise!"

The Mark Twain scholars at the University of California concede that Mark Twain did recite that poem in New York at the time, but they have "serious doubts" that he was the author. This defensive attitude is understandable.

Not all the contemporary poetry was so overblown, of course. Charlie Field's memorable quatrain still has the rollicking irreverence we like to think was the style of those times: "If, as they say, God spanked the town for being over-frisky; Why did He burn the churches down And spare Hotaling's whisky?" And Larry Harris's "Damndest Finest Ruins," written while the city was still smoking, remains the best of the "epics," with its Kiplingesque, Robert W. Serviceable lilt: "Put me somewhere west of East Street where there's nothin' left but dust./Where the lads are all abustlin' and where everything's gone bust/Where the buildings that are standin' sort of blink and blindly stare/At the damndest finest ruins ever gazed on anywhere." Harris managed to sustain the cocky mood for four stanzas, and he deserves to be remembered lovingly. Shortly before he died in 1966, he murmured: "It was a great show but it wasn't worth the price." If it happens again, I like to think that our present-day bards (Ferlinghetti, Snyder, McClure, Duncan, Ginsberg) will do as well as Harris—and infinitely better than the others.

It was a time for extravagant rhetoric, of course, and understandably so: a great and well-loved city lay stricken (the style is contagious). Will Irwin wrote a moving newspaper eulogy entitled "The City That Was," sensing wisely that while the city would be rebuilt it would never be the same. Major General A. W. Greely, the martial law administrator, wrote: "It is safe to say that 200,000 people were brought to a state of complete destitution. Yet I never saw a woman in tears nor heard a man whine over his losses." (Maybe he didn't get around very much?)

Act of God? Yes. Even an atheist would have to describe another disastrous earthquake as just that, and hence San Franciscans, for the most part, seem unconcerned about the possibility. "Uh—I'd run and stand in the doorway. What else?" Today it's the man-made problems that concern us all, and they are of such a magnitude—so far beyond any Richter scale—that any act of God must rank far down on the list. Nuclear weapons, warfare, pollution of earth and sky, Pentagonism, the youthquake, the decaying cities and so on. No act of God will solve those, although it could only improve the crumbling ghettoes. There are greater faults around us than those that produce earthquakes.

From Here to Eternity

(On the 30th anniversary of my column in the San Francisco *Chronicle*)

HORACE MANN, father of public education in the U.S., said this in 1858 when asked to write a magazine article: "I have not the time to prepare it for the press. Besides, this printing exhausts a man too rapidly. If one could, like a domestic fowl, lay new eggs just like the old ones, then production would be easy. But when each new one much be more tasteful in shape and larger in size and richer in quality, who can lay one every day?"

As one who has been laying an egg in public daily for years, I can attest that Horace is correct. Born July 5, 1938, died somewhere along the line, but limping along like a dog in a Soviet experiment. If this thirty-year stretch demonstrates anything, and I doubt it, it simply implies a fairly strong constitution, a thick skin to go along with a hard head, and a decided lack of imagination. A rut is not a groove, and all that. I live in dread of the day my young son finds out what his old man does for a living. I suppose I had better tell him myself. I'd hate to have him pick it up in the streets.

As long as this mood is upon me—confession is good for the heel as well as soul—I might as well tell you that this is my last anniversary column. If memory serves, I wrote epitaphs on the tenth, twentieth and twenty-fifth, and no use overdoing a bad thing. As has been noted by sharper minds than mine, it's okay to be bored but not to be a bore.

I don't know how you feel about it, dear friend and/or enemy, but it doesn't seem that long to me—these thirty years of six columns a week adding up to about eight million words, including time out for my generation's edition of war. The hard evidence is there, though, in a wooden case against the office wall, facing me every day: the bound volumes, year by year, of all the columns, for bitter or better. (The wooden case is now filled, and Volume 30 will have to go elsewhere—on the floor, out the window.) I seldom look back over them, and when I do, it is usually with embarrassment—they were written by a stranger about dead people and places, and it is hardly credible that the jokes were even funny then. However, *autres temps, autres scènes,* and maybe someday I'll write that One Perfect Column.

To look on the brighter side, perhaps those thirty volumes will prove helpful a hundred years hence to some historian digging for the essence of a San Francisco long gone—but I don't envy him his job of trying to distill some meaning out of those yellowed pages filled with fact, fancy and trivia ("Is Three-Dot Journalism Dead?"—and herewith the evidence, gentlemen.). I used to be inordinately fond of trivia, and even wrote pompously of its Significance, along the lines of "When the story of our time is written," blah-blah-blah, "the truth will be found as surely in these tiny kernels"—of corn—"as in the headlines of presumably more major events," drip-drip-drip. A crock, old friend. Trivia is trivia is trivia and forever will be, but the important is never trivial, nor is the trivial ever important.

Change is always painful, even for those who chase ephemera with a butterfly net, and when I occasionally run into a contemporary who complains, "Why don't you write the way you used to?" I know exactly what he means; and I sometimes wish I could. But unless we (you and I) are certified cases of arrested development, we aren't the same people we were twenty years ago, as this is not the same San Francisco. I hate to shake up the nostalgics, but it could just be that this is a better city in some important ways than it was twenty years ago. Certainly there is a greater awareness of the complexities around us, and a firmer resolve to confront them. We know now, because we wouldn't face it then, that there is more to San Francisco than the naïve, nonironic, fog-through-the-harp-strings-of-the-bridge approach that is reflected in some of the early columns in those bound volumes. Not innocence—a failure of perception.

A true story comes to mind, passed along by a friend who happened to ride in from the airport on a bus crowded with tourists and natives. A tourist reading a guidebook leaned across the aisle and asked a man, "You live in San Francisco?" The San Franciscan nodded. "Well," went on the tourist, "do you still have that great sour-dough French bread?" "Sure," said the San Franciscan. "Reason I ask," said the tourist, "is that Herb Caen says it isn't as sour as it used to be." "I'll tell you why," said the San Franciscan. "Herbie-boy has gotten so sour that even the sour-dough bread tastes sweet to him." So be it, and I salute the San Franciscan, whoever he is, for a funny crack. (Actually, I don't feel sour at all, but my taste buds might be wilting.)

In closing, may I say thanks to all you people who have

been reading me, and writing to me, for so many years: I have long felt that the readers write better than the writers, and your wise letters keep me humble. May I thank my many enemies; I'm proud to have them, subscribing as I do to the gospel according to St. Luke: "Woe unto you, when all men shall speak well of you." No chance, amen, and never trust a column under thirty.

Your Humble Servant

WHAT I CONSIDER the most cynical utterance in the entire literature of Americana—H. L. Mencken's "No one ever went broke underestimating the taste of the American public"—presents a point of view I eschew enthusiastically. In fact, I not only eschew it, I spit it out.

Unlike some of my colleagues in this children's art form, I have a possibly sick respect for the public, and I genuflect before the readers. Mine—or at least those who bother to write—are possessed of such a knife-edged intelligence I can only marvel that they bother with my poor tripes à la mode. They seem overbred to the point of extinction, better read than Gore Vidal, trilingual at the very least, and so civilized that they offer their criticisms with an air of genteel embarrassment.

To come to the point, I love them, especially those who have stuck patiently with me through thin and thinner, forgiving my foibles and my feeble French, putting up with my crotchets and carelessness, even swallowing the dumb jokes without once saying: "Get thee to a punnery." As I reflect upon this excellent body of Americans, I can only think that history has long overestimated H. L. Mencken. For all I know he died broke. (A dozen letter writers will assure me tomorrow that he didn't, citing his net worth at death.)

What started all this, somewhat to my surprise, was a letter to the editor from the aptly named Fred Anger of San

140

Francisco, criticizing the entire ineptly named stable of *Chronicle* columnists. I will not repeat the contumely he directed at Charles McCabe, since the contumacious Mr. McCabe is well able to fend for himself. Mr. Anger's displeasure with Stanton Delaplane will likewise be ignored; I know Mr. Delaplane as a saintly man beyond reproach and a writer of infinite style. His opinion of me, however, engages my ego-ridden attention. "Herb Caen," he said, "has been writing the same column for 30 years."

A couple of years off, on the kind side, but pithy and possibly true. Since Mr. Anger is a literate member of the reading public—my favorite people—I do not take his charge lightly. Have I been in a groove or a rut, is a rut much different from a grave and whatever happened to Walter Winchell? He sank out of sight in a sea of three little dots . . . and here I am still using them. He said-she said jokes, punchless punch lines, Names that no longer make News, all the dreck that's unfit to print and all the trivia that's dead by noon—those perishable items that die in the dark of the ink.

Well, *mea culpa* and all that, Mr. Anger, but every bone in my aching head assures me this is not circa 1940, and a glance in the mirror convinces me it's later than I ever thought it would get. But if the column doesn't reflect this, at least once in a while, then I've been wasting everybody's time and a lot of type, garbled and otherwise.

In 1940, I didn't know anything and was sure of everything. Today I'm not even sure about columns (value thereof in relation to reality, unperceived). Thirty years ago, I thought there was nobody in journalism to compare with Winchell and his three little dots. Thirty years later, the statement is still true but for a much different reason; I have reversed my opinion but the schoolboy addiction caused permanent damage. I'm punchy from those short, punchy items.

I began as a sentimentalist and a callow nostalgic. In the manner of a schoolboy in love, I thought San Francisco was the greatest city in the world—there were no warts on my lady. I still think San Francisco is the greatest city in the world, but now I can see the warts and they bother me, perhaps too much.

Thirty years ago, I could sit for hours at the knee of

graybeards as they spun their tales of an older and better San Francisco, being put down as a Johnny-come-lately and accepting it—"Kid, this was some town in the old days, too bad you missed it." But, as writer Nick Browne has put it, "Nostalgia is a wretched witness who cannot describe the accident, gets the details all wrong and is very likely in the pay of an interested party."

Nostalgia also gets the names and dates wrong and has a fatal sense of direction. Old San Francisco was wonderful, as youth is wonderful, but I'll take San Francisco now and onward, with all its faults and problems. At least we've been shaken out of our self-satisfaction, and that clears one big boulder out of the way.

As for Mr. Anger, who started all this, give me thirty more years of writing the same column. Maybe by that time I'll have got the hang of it.

The Moving Finger

HE HAD beaten the odds so many times that I thought he might even win The Big One, but nobody does, even multimillionaires, and so Louis Lurie died at eighty-four. His sycophantic acquaintances, and he had many, called him "Uncle Louie." The late A. P. Giannini, who patronized him while supplying easy loans, called him "Luigi." He would announce himself on the phone as "Dr. Lurie," for reasons never explained. In many ways, he was a baffling man, this epitome of the Horatio Alger legend, an easy laugher whose eyes suddenly could turn to ice, a man who enjoyed seeing his name and picture in the newspaper and yet was essentially private and lonely. He knew who his real friends were, and they were few. There were many after his money and he knew who they were, too.

A rich man has died, and what is the significance? The cliché about an era ending is true, as always, and not all that interesting. The San Francisco that Louis Lurie helped to build as a real estate tycoon has changed almost beyond recognition and, not surprisingly, he resented the change. He was conservative to the core—the stubborn conservatism of the poor boy who struck it rich. His interests, aside from money, were few. In unguarded moments, the eyes that usually twinkled would look back for a moment at his impoverished past. The fear of being broke again never leaves those who experienced it at a time when to be poor was a disgrace. It explains a lot about the very rich of a certain age.

Hollywood's central casting, in its palmiest days, could not have created a millionaire who looked more like one. The façade was perfect: the pince-nez perched on his nose with those Foxy Grandpa eyes behind them. The homburg was worn at a rakish angle, the shirts were tailored of Sulka's finest silk, and the suits never varied: black or dark gray with silk piping on the vests, lapels and cuffs—his only sartorial foible. The suits were made, year after year for half a century, by the firm of Edlin & Regolo in the Russ Building, which, ironically, went out of business only two months before its best customer's death. The Lurie limousine was a nine-passenger leather-topped 1960 Cadillac driven by chauffeur Herman Cameron. The Lurie hobby was backing Broadway shows that smelled like hits. He had little interest, financial or otherwise, in opera, the symphony or museums. "Too high-tone," he'd say. "Not my people."

Louis Lurie, creature of habit and habitat, a colorful figure, humorous in manner. In his day, getting up in the world was to be taken literally. When I first met him, he was living in mirrored and gilded splendor in the penthouse of the Sir Francis Drake (in fact, his luncheon guest that day was his old friend, Herbert Hoover). Still moving up, he selected 2100 Pacific, an elegant apartment building, as his next abode. The fact that 2100 Pacific was filled didn't stop him: he simply bought the building and kicked out the people occupying the floor he desired.

The Lurie legend, the legendary Lurie who lunched at Jack's restaurant almost daily since 1916, presiding like a proud papa over his table under the stairs, ordering for everyone. Whenever you walked into Jack's, you peeked to the right to see who Lurie had as guests that day—Gertrude Lawrence or Noël Coward, Somerset Maugham or Arthur Godfrey, Maurice Chevalier or Sammy Davis. Sometimes it was only politicians or newspaper bums, as he called us. He was unabashed about his love for publicity—getting your name and picture in the paper was a sign of success. When he was angry with me, which was quite often, he would call me "Herbert." We had a bad falling-out over a proposed cultural center, and he barked on the phone one morning: "Herbert, I never want to see my name in your goddam column again"—pause—"for the next few days."

Louis Lurie, a man to be missed. He had this thing about riding alone in the elevator of 333 Montgomery, the building he built. "Get out," he'd snap at people trying to enter with him. The building itself, torn down for the new Bank of America, was a replica of 333 North Michigan in Chicago, in front of which, according to Lurie legend, he sold Chicago's first Hearst newspaper as a crippled newsboy. In some versions, the Imperial Hearst himself came by and bought the first copy with a twenty-dollar gold piece. When his son, Bobby, was ten, Father Lurie gave him a ten-dollar check for being a good boy; Bobby went from store to store in the neighborhood, but nobody would cash a check for such a small boy. "Dad," said Bobby, handing it back, "your credit is no good."

And so it ends. The story of his death and his picture were on the front page—he would have liked that. And when we go into Jack's for lunch, we will still instinctively glance over toward that table under the stairs. But from now on, it will be occupied by mere mortals.

Something to Live For

MORE PEOPLE, places and things we can live without:
Manicurists who put polish on your nails when you didn't ask for it and wouldn't be caught dead with it.

Such unresolved advertising comparatives as "The *Daily Blatt* is more interesting and you'll be more interesting, too." More interesting than what—a wombat or a wallaby?

Plastic chopsticks.

Sixty-mile-an-hour motorcycle escorts for visiting dignitaries who couldn't possibly be in that much of a hurry.

"Personal" jet aircraft, the one luxury status symbol that literally reeks to high heaven of tax-dodgerism.

"Food at It's Best."

The incredible police toleration of signal-jumping motorists, bus drivers and pedestrians. What kind of accident will it take?

People who can't hold a tennis ball for more than thirty seconds without bouncing it.

Double-parking delivery truck drivers who don't even *try* to stop as close to the curb as possible (they're getting away with traffic murder).

Newscasters who pronounce "negotiation" as though it has a "c" in the middle.

Greeting cards that contain confetti.

Dog owners who allow their pets to turn sidewalks into obstacle courses, thereby providing an answer to the question, "What's dumber than a dumb animal?"

Garages that don't tell you they're "Full" until you're halfway into the entrance.

"Whatever's right."

People who tear pages out of directories in phone booths. People who tear out the entire directory. People who use phone booths as convenience stations. People who say "convenience stations" when they mean lavatories. Public lavatories that require keys.

Fat-haunched women in pedal pushers and wedgies who sneer at the way hippies dress. Barefoot hippies downtown, pausing to peel gum off their arches.

The same old tired people, growing more tired by the year, holding a drink in one hand and a cigarette in the other in society page photos.

Any more postage stamps like the one "honoring" FDR, which, for color, workmanship and imagination, wouldn't do justice to an underdeveloped country.

Inserts in magazines and advertising stuffers in store envelopes that contain your bill, if you'll just look hard enough for it.

Bills arriving in envelopes that can be used for your check if (1) you opened it carefully enough, (2) tore along the proper dotted line, (3) refolded it correctly, following the simple directions, (4) found where the gummed edge is hidden and (5) found enough mucilage thereon to make it stick.

TV newscasters who self-consciously shuffle their papers while the program is being introduced, a gimmick that looked phony and corny the first time it was tried.

Architects who describe their new buildings as "lithe, clean-limbed and relevant" when what they mean is "We cut every corner we could to stay within the budget."

Memos headed "From the desk of—" Business stationery so elegant that such trivia as the address and phone number is not included. People who surreptitiously run a finger over your business card to see if it's engraved.

Cocktail bar pianists who solicit your request and then say, "Sorry, I don't know that one—how does it go?"

Two hour two-dollar movies padded out to three-hour five-dollar movies by the inclusion of an unnecessary intermission and a long overture cribbed from the works of great composers.

Financial ads that tell me I'd have been a millionaire today if I'd invested eleven dollars in JQR Pfd. nine years ago.

Waiters and waitresses who fill your coffee cup to the brim. What if you have the shakes so badly you can't pick it up without spilling? What if I have? If you haven't, I salute you. Shakily.

☆ ☆ ☆

A NATIONAL magazine reports that "the best-dressed women in the world walk the streets of San Francisco," and several industrious readers have troubled to clip and mail in that doubtful observation. I don't know what intrigues them exactly—the implication that our best-dressed women are prostitutes, or the wild extravagance of the statement?—but if it's the former, the remark is not too wide of the mark. Historically, anyway.

In the Gold Rush era—twenty men to one woman—the prostitutes were quick to appear on the scene from New Orleans, Chile and Nukahiva, and an elegant lot they were, by all accounts. Mme. Belle Cora arrived in 1849, mothering a herd of talented demoiselles from her parlor house on the corner of Dauphine and Burgundy in New Orleans' Vieux Carré. By 1851, Frenchwomen dominated Commercial, Dupont and Pike Streets, and their clothes were the *dernier cri,* copied not only by second-class courtesans but eventually by actresses like Lola Montez and Lotta Crabtree, and then "respectable" matrons.

They wore dainty British boots, crinoline petticoats, Paisley shawls, coat scuttle bonnets, Russian gloves and Chinese fans, and parted their hair in the middle. As de Russailh wrote at the time: *"Il y a aussi des honnêtes femmes dans San Francisco mais pas de trop"*—and the only way to distinguish "honest" women from the others was by the absence of paint on the faces of the former.

The myth of San Francisco fashion—or shall we be kind and say legend?—began with Mme. Cora's soirées and the Sunday promenade of her girls down Kearny Street. Whether our women are particularly well dressed today is a matter of opinion, although some pretty Tenderloin tarts and cocktail-hour secretaries on Montgomery Street exert themselves to uphold Mme. Belle's tradition. A pity they never make the published lists of best-dressed women.

☆ ☆ ☆

IN THE COURSE of one Sunday's idling chatter, I wondered how you get chewing gum off your shoe, and the readers were quick to respond, in their usual generous manner. "Place shoe in freezer for a short while; gum becomes brittle and is easily removed" (Jannette Spitzer, Los Altos Hills). "As most Brownies know, the time-honored infallible way is to apply gasoline or lighter fluid" (Priscilla Joffe). "I thought everybody knew the way to remove gum is to get it cold and brittle with an ice cube, then it just snaps off" (Joyce McBeth, Books Cooperative, Berkeley). I can hardly wait to get some more gum on my shoes so I can test these methods—especially the shoe-in-the-freezer gambit.

AND THE SKY was filled with chuckles: Captain Bud McGauhey of Air West was flying into S. F. International one 8 A.M. when he heard the woman control tower operator saying to an American Airlines pilot: "Is my transmission fuzzy?" American pilot: "I don't know, dear—how old are you?"

JUST FOOLIN' AROUND: After you've been told "You look just great!" a certain number of times, you begin wondering how sick you really look . . . Nobody in San Francisco can jaywalk with the celestial dignity of an aged Chinese woman, looking neither to the right nor the left but straight ahead—fiercely. As traffic stops—respectfully . . . Along with getting tired of protesters, I'm getting tired of their critics who protest, "But what are they *for?*" For the opposite of what they're against, I guess, if it matters. As one student rebel puts it: "We didn't create the problems, we're only pointing out their existence. We don't have to worry about solutions until we have power to put them into effect." . . . I never read the ads for the new automobiles— "72 improvements! . . . New Safety Devices!"—without wondering what kind of a dog they were trying to palm off last year . . . You know you're getting old when it comes up rain on the morning you were supposed to play tennis and you're glad . . . *Modern times:* I pointed to the sky the other night and said to my young son Christopher, "Look, there's the Big Dipper." Christopher: "What's a big dipper?" Good question. Anybody seen one the last twenty-five years or so? . . . Add things that make me nervous: Manicurists who gaze at TV while cutting your cuticles.

☆ ☆ ☆

HELPFUL HERBERT: Since the S. F. Landmarks Board is in danger of running out of landmarks—they are torn down faster than they can be designated—I would like to suggest historical markers on the following addresses: 610 Leavenworth, 1526 Franklin, 929 Bush, 1224 Stockton, 1001 Vallejo, 1144 Bush and 676 Geary. Each of these was, at one time or another, the bedquarters of Sally Stanford, our greatest living ex-madam—and it's sad to relate that her most famous bed-a-wee, 1144 Pine, has already been flattened. It was there in 1945 that the United Nations Charter came to full flower: "Every night" (as Sally recalls it) "the place was jammed with UN delegates, tackling the subject with great vigor and getting down to the business at hand. You know, details. I would have to say that 1144 Pine was the true seat of the United Nations— all those rich Arabs, all that French champagne—I could cry when I think about it." And sure enough a tear trickled down her cheek and into her cleavage, another noble landmark.

Please Have Exact Change

A LOT OF people like to think I roll around town in a chauffeured limousine, or a Ferrari Berlinetta, at the very least. I'd like to think so, too, but such splendid equipage accrues only to columnists in comic strips, TV series and movies; the late Lucius Beebe covered his beat in a Rolls-Royce, but he was born with a silver spoon in his mouth and died untarnished.

No, the sordid truth is that I generally travel to the posh luncheon spots by Muniserable bus, since waiting for cabs in this town can cause ulcers (in the case of Yellow, jaundice). Not that I'm complaining. Our busses may be dirty, hot and vandalized, but they're filled with people and getting close to the minds, hearts and armpits of the people is an experience well worth missing.

Don't believe those subversive foreign accusations that Americans are so hung up on cleanliness and deodorants that they have no smell at all. We smell as rich and ripe as any old Camembert that ever came out of northwestern France. Who's hiding the Right Guard?

Nevertheless, riding the Munis is instructive. After you get tired of trying to open a window you can read "The Traveller's Times," those white cards on the overhead racks that print bright sayings by Ralph Waldo Greenleaf, or whoever, and occasional conundrums.

One of the latter has been fascinating me for miles. It's about Jack and Doris, as follows: "Jack and Doris are engaged but—sigh—they live 400 miles apart, Jack in San Francisco, Doris in Los Angeles. Jack wants to plan a weekend somewhere between the two cities. He can leave at 9 A.M. and drive an average 50 miles an hour. Doris can't leave until noon, and, since her mama is coming along as chaperone, Jack knows she will be lucky to average 25. When Jack telephones to reserve rooms in a resort motel at the exact point where they will meet, what arrival time shall he advise the manager?"

My advice to Jack is to forget the whole thing. Who needs a girl who brings Mama along, especially since Mama is obviously a nagger. Doris can only average twenty-five because Mama is always saying, "Frevvinsakes, Doris, not so *fast,*" right? She's also suspicious of Jack and will want her own room between his and Doris's. Three rooms in a motel is ridiculous. Jack should advise the manager that he broke down in King City and to give Doris and her mama one room.

Another great thing in Muni busses is all that badly lettered gobbledy-gook over the rear exit. It's bureaucratese gone berserk. I've been marveling at it for so many years I can recite it from memory:

"At passenger stops YOU operate rear safety door BY YOUR WEIGHT ON TREADLE STEP—Doors Close After Releasing Weight—THEREFORE keep your foot on bottom treadle step until children with you have alighted and are CLEAR OF DOORS," and so on.

What they mean is "Step Down to Open."

After you get tired of contemplating that and the girls'

legs, you can make lists. I recently rode all the way to the end of the No. 30 line, making two lists, one headed "People I've Never Met but Think I'd Like" and "People I've Never Met but Don't Think I'd Like."

On the former list I put Pierre Elliott Trudeau, Wally Schirra, Valery Giscard d'Estaing, Shirley MacLaine, Andrew Wyeth, Patrick McGoohan, Gunther Sachs, John Lennon, Gary Player, Zubin Mehta, Diana Rigg, Satchel Paige.

On the "Don't Think I'd Like" list I placed James Gould Cozzens, Joe Namath, Al Capp, Howard Hughes, Roman Hruska, George C. Scott, Herbert Von Karajan, and Brigitte Bardot. I would have included Curtis LeMay but I met him once during World War II, and I think he put me on *his* list.

Whenever I ride the No. 15, one of my favorite noisome busses, I pass the new Bank of America World Headquarters, and I would like to make one minor suggestion: tear it down and start over. Not that the building isn't imposing, it's just that it's so *dark;* with those sunspec windows, it looks like it's filled with oil. This must be a trend. The Alcoa Building looks like an oil sump, too. San Francisco has always been a "white" city—or at least Mediterranean-pastel—and—and . . . Say, Doc, can a person go nuts from riding Muni busses?

☆ ☆ ☆

"POOR BENNY" (Born—?, Died—August 18, 1970): So many of the people who knew him were forever saying that, with a sad shake of the head, and they were saying it again as the news flashed across the city that sculptor Beniamino Bufano was dead. "Poor Benny"—meaning he was always broke, always involved in bizarre episodes, always cast by his inferiors in the role of eccentric, or "Bufoono." It was said condescendingly—"Poor Benny"— and we of the press were as guilty as anyone else.

Too many times we made him out to be the clown, too many times he went along with the gag—because he was genuinely sweet and wanted to be liked. We wrote about the odd clothes he used to weave for himself and the way he'd try to make himself look younger by applying shoe polish to

151

his hair. We'd indulge his fantasies: that he had chopped off an index finger and mailed it to Woodrow Wilson to protest U.S. involvement in World War I, that he had posed for the profile on the old Indian head five-cent piece. None of his stories checked out and eventually it seemed insulting to him even to try.

"Poor Benny," and yet there was no reason to call him that, since worldly goods didn't interest him anyway. He was truly bohemian, a beatnik before the word was coined, an ancient hippie; like Saroyan, Bridges, O'Doul and Izzy Gomez, he lived in a vanishing world of San Francisco—and like them was a legendary figure before his death.

All he cared about was his art, and there we all let him down. Critics elsewhere applauded his work, but here, typically, he was more an object of fun than reverence. He had no doubts about posterity—"A hundred years from now they'll know I was a genius," he often said—and posterity may well judge him so. "Who cares, I belong to the ages," he would say when reporters tried to pin him down on his exact age. An old passport of his said he was born in 1889, but when he went to Russia recently, he recorded his birth year as 1913, even though he often boasted of working on the 1915 exposition here.

Only yesterday, before I knew he had died I walked past Moars Cafeteria on Powell, where he executed some spectacular mosaics in return for a gold pass good for a lifetime of free meals. "Home of the Famous Buffano Murals," reads the sign in the window, and I said to myself, "They can't even spell his name right. Poor Benny."

Thousands of words have been written about Bufano, but his own are best at defining his lovely, poetic spirit. He wrote me this letter in 1955, about his first celebrated statue.

"Well, here I am in Paris working like a beaver on my statue of Saint Francis that I made here in 1928, '29 and '30, and as you know, gave to San Francisco. They financed my trip here so I could get it ready for shipment. But the money they allowed me is so small that I have been living for the past two months on black bread, figs and milk while working in this damp and cold warehouse where Saint Francis has been in prison so long.

"But the Saint is still smiling. So I keep on polishing, rub-bing and warming his face and find myself singing a half-sad and half-joyful song, 'Brother Francis, we will be out of here, we will be out of here in a week or so, and then out in the sun the sun, the sun of California, California, California . . . There we will dry our tears and share our song with the people, all the people, peace and good will!'

"In a little while his years of imprisonment will be ended and he will have a beautiful place on the steps of The Church of Saint Francis of Assisi. There in all his humility and grandness Saint Francis will call upon the people of all nations to live in peace with one another. Now I pray this time his message will be heard.

"Herb, our greeting comes to you from 6,000 miles away and God Bless you and all our friends, including our enemies. Beniamino."

The great statue that Bufano labored so long over didn't last long on the steps of the Church of St. Francis of Assisi here. People complained, "It gets in our way," and it was moved, first to Oakland, then to Longshoremen's Hall—as restless and sad-eyed as the man who created it.

☆ ☆ ☆

C. B. DeMILLE'S *Greatest Show on Earth,* an Oscar winner in '52, was on the telly one recent night, and Jack Abad faithfully recorded some of the dialogue (Betty Hutton to Charlton Heston): "You don't need me, Brad. You've got all you need—the circus" . . . "I crippled The Great Sebastian, Brad, just as surely as though I threw him off that trapeze myself" . . . "You crazy wonderful fool! Brad, you're—you're—CIRCUS!" . . . "Take it easy, Brad, or you'll finish this performance under that big top in the sky" . . . "Round up every animal that can walk or crawl! You heard, Brad—we're going to give a show!" . . . They don't make 'em like that anymore and now you know why.

☆ ☆ ☆

ONE DAY I printed what I thought was a fascinating array of occupations listed by the U. S. Department of Labor—crotch piece boaster, bung dropper, bladder blower,

153

clinker cooler and so on, to which Charles Roumasset, a Department of Labor official here, adds a sidelight. From the Dictionary of Occupational Titles, the following jobs have now been dropped: beachcomber, button marker (boot and shoe), circus detective, coconut shaver, flat-fifties checker (tobacco) and rumble-seat assembler. I must say the Department doesn't rush into things . . . Newly added to the list are these: assembler (rocket engines), audiovisual specialists, flight information expediter, baker (pizza) and artificial inseminator. I don't think that last one is as exciting as it sounds, and how come it took Labor so long to discover pizza?

☆ ☆ ☆

ONE ZOO TO ANOTHER: Barnaby Conrad gave four beautiful, full-grown macaws to the Santa Barbara Children's Zoo, whose delighted director, Arthur Locker, wrote him: "We await the delivery of the birds and meanwhile would like some information about their present habitat. Sudden changes in atmosphere can be harmful and we want to simulate the conditions they have been accustomed to."

Replied Barnaby: "They should be placed in a dark, smoky room filled with noisy drunks. A recording of bongo drums would also be helpful. And since they don't go to sleep until about 3 A.M., it is recommended that a 'Do Not Disturb' sign be placed on their quarters during daylight hours."

For the past fourteen years, these macaws occupied a glass cage in the Matador night club on Broadway, then owned by Barnaby.

☆ ☆ ☆

INSIDE: At S. F. Airport, Dick Rafferty of Fresno, Hawaii-bound, gave his hand luggage to a security guard who, while rummaging through it, accidentally set off the flash attachment on Dick's camera. "Wow," said the guard, jumping back in alarm, "that scared hell out of me!" "Well, Charlie," said another security guard, "it's better than a wet diaper."

The Big Martini Mystery

ITEM: Among my most prized possessions is an original blue glass pitcher from the days when Shirley Temple was the most famous little girl in the world. Her smiling, dimpled face is embossed in white on the side of the glass pitcher; this renders the vessel ideal for the mixing of a perfect martini, the formula being: "Gin to the chin, vermouth to the tooth" . . . Item: When elegant ladies like Mrs. Suzy Strauss go to bars like Breen's or Hanno's, they order a "Geranium." That's bartenders' code for "a gin martini onna rocks wit' a twist steada an olive," which, ladies like Mrs. Strauss insist, doesn't sound ladylike . . . Customer to bartender at Joe's in Hillsdale: "Gimme a mental martini." Bartender: "Whazzat?" Customer: "You pour the gin, I'll think vermouth," which, as martini jokes go, is fairly dry.

The foregoing is merely by way of illustrating that the martini, the straight world's hallucinogenic, is still very much with us. It also leads us to a pair of provocative martini-angled ads running in the national magazines. The first, devised by the S. F. Convention & Visitors Bureau, begins: "When you come to San Francisco, why drink the water?" and goes on to state that "This is the birthplace of the martini and the Mai Tai." The second, on behalf of Lejon Vermouth, shows in ravishing color a perfect martini with bleeding olive, resting on the bar of the Vesuvio. "It's hard to get a bad martini in San Francisco," reads the copy, because "The martini was invented there." Meaning here.

Maybe I should mention *en passant* that I'm all *for* the idea of the martini having been invented here; it's just that in thirty years of desultory research, I've uncovered no hard evidence. Even Charles Clegg, who, as the late Lucius Beebe's drinking and business partner, has access to all known writings on the subject, admits he draws a blank on the martini's origin. "I do know, though," he adds, "that the Gibson was invented in San Francisco." Oh? "Certainly," he goes on with brash confidence. "By the stockbrokers on

Montgomery." Oh? "They like to drink martinis in the morning, you know, and they switched the olive to an onion because the onion kills the smell of the gin, which was offensive to old ladies." Oh.

The other folklore is equally fanciful. Even so steady a researcher into Californiana as Peter Tamony buys the unwieldy tale that the martini was invented about 1860 by the noted bartender, Jerry Thomas, at the Occidental Hotel here. I won't bore you with the details, but a customer asked for "a special drink for my hangover" one foggy morning, and Jerry came up with something he then named "The Martinez" because that's where the customer was bound for. Ridiculous. Even more ridiculous are the ingredients, which Professor Thomas listed in his *Bon Vivant's Companion,* published in 1862: "1 dash bitters, 2 dashes maraschino, 1 pony Old Tom Gin, 1 wineglass vermouth (!), 2 small lumps ice." A long way indeed from the 16–1 martini, and anyway, if the drink *were* named in honor of Martinez, wouldn't that town have a statue of Jerry Thomas in the main square? (If it has any other claim to fame, forgive me.)

My own research at one time led me to the Public Library, whose redoubtable reference department unearthed the information—equally ludicrous—that the martini was invented in Germany in the late eighteenth century by one J. P. Schwarzendorf, whose nickname for unexplained reasons was "Martini." (All fables contain at least one afterthought like that.) Old J.P., reports one musty volume, put together Belgian *ginevra* (from the juniper berry, and later shortened to gin), with a touch of dry white wine, "probably Chablis," and one-sixteenth teaspoon of cinnamon to produce "the first recorded martini." Schwarzendorf died in 1816, probably because he got sick of hearing his friends complain: "Too much Chablis, J.P.!"

Well, no need to stagger on. Maybe "martini" simply came from Martini & Rossi vermouth, since the early cocktail was made with Italian, rather than French, vermouth. (Even the origins of "cocktail" are cloudy, although it is known that the word *coquetel* for a mixed drink was current in Bordeaux in the eighteenth century.) The point, if any, is that these latter-day attempts to establish San Francisco as the martini's birthplace go along with our general reputation for constant inebriation. As Jim Murray, the Los Angeles wit, once observed, "San Francisco has the only bay in the world with an olive in it," and the average San Franciscan is thought of as the reincarnation of W. C. Fields, who said, "I always keep a supply of stimulants on hand in case I see a snake, which I also keep on hand." The rumors that Mr. Fields is alive and drunk in Oakland may now be laid to rest.

☆ ☆ ☆

SARTORIAL NOTE: You have to be properly dressed to arrest an improperly undressed lady in San Francisco, and if you don't believe it, ask Police Captain Charlie Barca. On second thought, don't ask him. All you'll get is a sputter.

One night, Good Charlie figured he'd had enough of the nudity in North Beach. Topless, okay. But—BEAVERS??? Not by a damn sight. So he strode to the bar in the Roaring 20s and waited impatiently for two plainclothesmen and a photographer with an infrared camera. He would do it right: photos, witnesses, signed complaints from eager antibeaverites. The Beaver Must Go!

As Charlie was waiting fretfully at the bar, the photographer rushed up with bad news about the two plainclothesmen. "They can't get in!" said the photographer. "The doormen won't let 'em in because they aren't wearing *ties!"* "What?" yelled Charlie. "You gotta wear a tie to see a beaver?" Sure enough. "You win this time," snapped Charlie to the owner, "but we'll be back, we'll be back."

The following night, Captain Barca trapped the beaver in its lair, and it appears that patches are back in season. Maestro, one chorus of Air for the G-String.

☆ ☆ ☆

FRIEND OF MINE wandered into an after-hours joint in the Tenderloin at 3 A.M., ordered coffee and was asked by the waitress for his ID. "For coffee?" he complained.

157

"Well," she said, "you could be a cop, after all." After displaying his various identifications to her satisfaction, she said briskly: "Okay, now what kinda coffee do you want—scotch or bourbon?"

Tale of Two Cities

NEW YORK: The constant need for reassurance—nowhere is it more apparent than here in this dying metropolis where the American dream began and is now running out its string (well, nobody lives forever). "New York: It's Still a Hell of a Town!" read the ads in the subways, the newspapers and the phone booths—all over the place and in vain. A city that knows it's the biggest and best doesn't have to bolster its confidence by announcing the fact. What New York is really saying is, "It's a hell of a town—uh, isn't it?" while the convention bureau spreads the word that the city is not as dangerous as you've been led to believe, being behind Des Moines in mopery and Sioux Falls in jaywalking.

Too bad about the doubts and the visible decay, for in many ways it still *is* a hell of a town—at least from a distance and on high. If you're the kind of person who's impressed with rather than depressed by skylines, Manhattan's is the definitive one and San Francisco's can never be anything but second or third, no matter how hard its worst enemies try. The power and the glory continue to dwell in the penthouses, while the streets far below grow more sordid by the day. It used to be the place where you made it or else. Now it is enough to survive.

When can a city be said to be dying? For one thing, when its past far outshines its present and overwhelms the future, and New York is at that point. The giants have gone, along with the good days and easy nights.

I sit here in the Regency Hotel, looking down on Park Avenue, with its swirl of taxis and limousines, gorgeously uniformed doormen springing to open doors for people who are "wan with chic, arthritic with poise." All that is left of Manhattan's elegance is now concentrated in these few blocks of the Upper East Side, where the last of the greats live around the corner from each other, more for reassurance than friendship. A handsome street, with its luxuriant dividers and block after block of old apartment houses, their height strictly controlled. It is a vision of the way Rich New York looked in the golden days of the '20s and '30s but the high-rises are marching up the street from Grand Central, the older apartments are beginning to fray around the edges, just like their occupants, and the future is rapidly coming into view, gaunt and unsmiling.

"Manhattanization," an unwieldy word that keeps popping into the mind of a visiting San Franciscan for several reasons, many of them emotional and mystical, some of them confusing, all of them troubling. For New York is at once a symbol of what was gloriously exciting about great American cities, and a horrid example of dream becoming nightmare.

Despite their obvious differences, there are strong ties between New York and San Francisco. How many times we of a certain age used to hear "There are only two cities in this country" (them and us). There was a time when we took pride that our skyline, too, was impressive and instantly recognizable (unlike that flat city to the south). New York and San Francisco were both "great night life cities," world-famous ports, money centers, international-minded, reasonably cultured and "well dressed," whatever that means, and almost in the same league at slaking thirsts and appetites.

And how we glowed when a New Yorker would say over a well-turned martini on Montgomery Street: "Y'know, if I had to leave New York, this is the only city I could live in." Oh, days of innocence: how impressed we all were around here when somebody moved to Manhattan and didn't actually starve to death! In my own wretched phrase of the time, San Francisco was "this minimanhattan" (forgive me).

We live and we learn, or do we? The Giants moved to San Francisco and weren't nine feet tall, after all—it's just that we swallowed all the fables that came from the mysterious

159

and powerful East. We became more and more aware of New Yorkers moving here and others writing to say, "By the way, if you happen to hear of anything," and they'd even try to make do on $15,000 a year less. And yet in some perverse, childlike way we go on trying to emulate The Worst of Manhattan—piling building upon building, creating instant slums, blocking out the sky with smog, filling in a shrinking Bay (our most precious asset) and dividing people who once lived together in a fairly relaxed atmosphere.

"It's Still a Hell of a Town"—San Francisco more so than New York. The latter seems doomed but San Francisco can reclaim its soul if it will shake off its outmoded New Yorkiness and savor the uniqueness of wind and sky, view and fog. There is only one San Francisco—why bury it in a cemetery labeled "Manhattan West"?

A Tourist's Notebook

DATELINE: Somewhere in Europe: It was Corpus Christi Day in Rome. The lobby of the Hassler Hotel, an American lady, charm bracelets and cheeks aquiver, heard the awful news from the concierge. "Oh, Sam," she wailed across the lobby to her husband, "all the shops are closed—what are we going to *do* all day?" I don't mean to sound lofty, although it was a temptation to smirk along with the natives. While there are quite a few other things to see in Rome—like, for starters, the history of civilized man—you can get your fill of museums and other antiquities. Still, her quote was a good one—a possible three on a scale of ten—in the annals of tourism, and I scrambled to a neutral corner to jot it down.

The tourist in Europe is inescapably a comic figure. Back home, he may be a tycoon employing thousands, but when he has to pull out his currency converter in a restaurant, to see how big a tip to leave, he has lost the game. In a cab, he watches the meter with bulging eyes, hoping he has enough change; even when he pays half what he'd pay in the States, and undertips to boot, he is sure he is being cheated. He is continually exhausted from walking in wrong directions, and parades his inner shame by ordering prunes for breakfast. If he is the eternal sad sack, it's his own fault; he seldom bothers to learn the language or the customs of the countries he visits, and when he is treated with kindness—which is generally the case—he feels he's being patronized . . . But don't be too hard on him. He sent his laundry out last night and he's sure it will never come back.

The unbelievable tourists. In 1952, I flew to the coronation of Queen Elizabeth with a San Francisco group headed by then Mayor Elmer Robinson—and as we drove into London, we found banners proclaiming "ER" on the light standards. For "Elizabeth Regina," of course—but half the San Franciscans were fully convinced the "ER" was a welcome to Elmer Robinson . . . One afternoon during that visit, I was walking down Piccadilly with Lawyer Lawrence Livingston, a member of the Robinson group. We ran into a French friend of mine, and after we had chatted for a moment, he turned to Livingston and asked politely: "And are you a foreigner, too?" "What?" exploded Lawrence. "I'm not a foreigner, I'm an *American!*" Then, turning to me, he said hotly: "Imagine ME, Lawrence Livingston, being taken for a foreigner!"

Americans in Paris. The original joke, origins unknown, has an American lady saying: "I've been in Paris four days and I haven't been to the Louvre yet," to which her friend replied: "Neither have I—it must be the water." I have met Americans staying at the Plaza-Athénée Hotel who insist it's the "Plaza Anthony"; their friends are at "The George Cinq the Fifth" (the George V), and they dined the night before at "the Toujours d'Argent" (Tours d'Argent). Today they would be lunching at "Maximum's," having discovered to their astonishment that the Café de la Paix isn't on the Rue de la Paix at all, but on the Rue des Capucines. However, it was in a Copenhagen restaurant that we overheard a lady order a tournedos with sauce béarnaise as "One of those tornados with the Bernice sauce."

Linda Latz went on a tour of Europe with twenty other Americans and collected a few ten-pointers. In Copenhagen, one of her fellow travelers announced knowledgeably, "There's Hans Christian Andersen—you know, the guy who wrote Grimm's Fairy Tales." When they landed at Amsterdam, somebody else said, "Here we are in the Neverlands!" Driving past the Colosseum in Rome, one member of the group was moved to gasp, "My God, was all this bomb damage?" In Venice, the following conversation took place: "There's the home of Marco Polo." "Oh, really? I thought he was Chinese." In Sorrento, a plaque on a hotel proclaimed that Longfellow had written a poem there, inspiring the comment, "I'll be damned—I didn't know he was a Dago." In London, the tour guide pointed out Hyde Park and a laconic voice in the rear commented, "Oh yeah, President Roosevelt was born here."

Still and all, it's worth it, these mind-blowing, nerve-racking ventures abroad. It's good for the soul to get away from the regimented life: every hotel is a little different, even though the soap is still scarce and tiny and (old joke) when you turn the lights on it gets darker; as for the maids, they will still walk in without knocking to catch you naked. The Italians, unlike the French, love you for trying to speak their language; in Paris, they still spit at you, figuratively, if you don't speak French at least as well as Jean-Paul Sartre. *"Encore de café and du lait froid,"* I said to the waiter in a Parisian sidewalk cafe, rather proud of the sentence. "You needn't have put it that way," scolded the waiter. *" 'La même chose'* would have been sufficient, you know." Outside Harrod's in London, I was approached by a one-legged beggar to whom I said in all truth, "Sorry, I'm broke." Patting me on the shoulder, he said kindly, "Then good luck to you, mate." Yes, it's all worth it.

A Day in the Life

ROME: Here he is, your insipid correspondent on the loose in the Eternal City. He has given up the comforts of home and the forty-hour week to become a tourist. It is hard work —long hours and pay-pay-pay. But he is happy. It is a beautiful day in Rome as he picks his way down the Spanish Steps, trying to avoid stepping on zonked-out hippies. Well, he knows all about hippies. "Anybody here from San Francisco?" he calls out idiotically. They stare up at him, hot and sweaty. They think he is some kind of nut. They are right.

He walks across the cobbled plaza, with Fiats to the right of him, Fiats to the left, Fiats in front, Fiats on top of him. Breathing heavily, he makes the narrow sidewalks of the Via Condotti. Fiats come over the curb to nip at his ankles. He takes to walking backwards. If he is killed in Rome, he wants to see what got him. He steps into Gucci to buy the ritual pair of shoes and a Fiat tries to break down the door to get at him. When he walks out in the new shoes, it occurs to him that they are too tight, but he is already accustomed to these mild disappointments. Besides, they will probably stretch. If they don't he will cut off his big toes.

The smog, or whatever they call it, is terrible. There is no Italian word for smog, on the theory that, if you don't name it it doesn't exist. The closest phrase is *"miscuglia di gas velenosi"* (mixture of poisonous gases) or *"folata tossica"* (toxic gust). *"Molto smoggi,"* he says, shrugging. The traffic is the worst he has seen anywhere. If a country's progress can be measured in cars, Italy must be the most prosperous country in the world. On his first trip to Rome in 1949, a friend had said, "Don't tell me these people are poor—why, they're all driving foreign cars." He chuckles aloud at the recollection, looking idiotic again, but he doesn't care. He doesn't know anybody in Rome. Just then Mrs. B.W. of San Francisco and her bearded boy friend walk hand-in-hand out of a small hotel. They don't see him. He is relieved. So are they.

In his new Guccis, which are killing him, he is trying to

look Italian. *"Buona sera,"* he says to the Italians, who reply, "Good morning," which it is. How do they know he is American? By the International *Herald-Tribune* under his arm, the Instamatic over his shoulder and the new shoes which are too tight. Already he is either overtipping or undertipping but he likes the denominations. It does something for him to be able to say to himself, "I think I'll tip him a thousand lire" when five hundred would have been too much. *"Ciao!"* he says as he leaves. "Good-by, sir," says the waiter, beaming. "Come again, sir." Waiters don't respect people who overtip. They merely love them, the only love that money can buy.

It comes up twelve o'clock noon. Rome turns into one vast windup toy, a clock factory gone berserk. Ancient bells toll all over town, in clashing tones and rhythms. A cannon goes off, very loud. Sirens blow. In sun-swept squares, rusty figures emerge creakily from belfries, hammer on blackened gongs, then retreat with jerks and clanks. The swallows of Rome dart frantically about, emitting their shrill bat-like squeaks. (How can such a graceful bird make such an ugly sound?) Twelve o'clock noon is a great show. It should be held over till one at least, when nothing much happens.

At 1 P.M., Rome dies, to awaken again at 4. The shops close with a great rattling of grates, slamming of shutters. The sea of cars—*"mare di macchine"*—disappears by magic from the streets. The men go home to have lunch with their wives, or elsewhere to lunch with their lady friends. As Rome sleeps, or perhaps thrashes about (you never know what's going on behind those closed shutters), the tourist wends his weary way back to the Hassler Hotel. The Hassler is a lovely, staid, smallish hotel, beautifully run, incredibly quiet. In the cool inner courtyard, landscaped and serene, he lunches with his wife and son, Christopher, on one ton of pasta. In Italy you can eat one ton of pasta every day and never feel stuffed. It is light, even sort of fluffy. Why is American pasta so heavy, on the other hand? Perhaps our flour is too refined, but after three thousand years of history you'd think Italian flour would be refined as hell.

At 4 P.M., with pasta coming out of both ears, the tourist is ready to walk some more (in an old pair of shoes), with

Childe Christopher in tow. The sea of cars is again at the flood, but Rome is a great walking town if you don't mind a Fiat up your elbow. It is a small town, without secrets. You can peer into windows and courtyards. Washing hangs all over the place, in case you like to check undies—on thousand-year-old walls, from Renaissance balconies, on the decks of fancy penthouses. And amenities everywhere: there is always a bench to sink onto, always a sidewalk cafe for a Campari-soda, always a newsstand or a street-corner ice cream vendor. In the lush Borghese Gardens, Christopher immediately finds a bicycle for rent and tootles happily around with the Italian kids in the Stradale dei Bambini. His father sinks onto a bench with the other fathers. Not too glamorous, he reflects, but definitely folksy.

That night, he places the new Gucci shoes outside his hotel room door, hoping somebody will steal them. Nobody does. They are there the next morning, shining, bright and tight as ever.

The Old Family Album

ROME: CLICK! Here is a picture of the Piazza Navona, a beautiful stone square shaped like a race track. The American tourists flock to the Piazza Navona because it is closed to automobile traffic. Here they can walk around without worrying that they are about to be attacked from the rear or splayed against a wall. Snap! Those are the Americans. They are drinking Camparis and reading the international *Herald-Tribune*. They look at the stock market quotations, shake their heads and order another drink. Sound track: "Well, Myrtle, you can forget about that ring you liked at Bulgari's." "Oh, Alvin, you *promised*." "Look, Myrtle, my broker, *he* promised, too."

There are three huge fountains in the Piazza Navona. They are really worth looking at. Pft-pft-pft (am I going too fast?). As you just saw, they contain statues of a lot of naked full-grown men wrestling around with a lot of dolphins and other things that definitely aren't women, meanwhile spraying water in all directions. Well, as I always say, to each his own, right? Across the square—click!—is this big old beautiful church dating back to, oh, about the eleventh century. If they let cars into the Piazza Navona, the church would probably fall down and take the government with it. Snap. Here's a shot of the Government falling. Again.

ZOOM. Everybody knows what Hadrian's Tomb looks like, but this is a particularly striking shot with Christopher standing in front of it. He is not looking at the tomb because he never heard of Hadrian and vice versa. He is busy gazing at a bulldozer working on the banks of the Tiber. I think he's going to grow up to be a hardhat. Now here—zip—are the incomparable Bernini colonnades outside St. Peter's. If you stand on this marker, alongside the fountain, you get a trick effect: All the back columns disappear behind the outer row and the colonnades become one-dimensional. There are two markers because the first one was put in the wrong place. Italians are pretty relaxed about things like this.

SNAP! Here is Christopher with St. Peter's framed behind him. He is looking at a garbage truck. Pft-pft-pft: those are three Roman garbage trucks. I think Christopher is going to grow up to be a garbageman. Every time we see a garbage truck we have to stop because he is fascinated. They come in three models. One is like San Francisco's, one has a trolley that takes the garbage to the top and dumps it in; one has a hole that the garbage can fits into to be emptied. Here—click—is a great photo of three garbagemen pretending to throw Christopher into the truck. And here is a picture of me showing mixed emotions . . . I used to say that traveling with a child is like going third-class across Bulgaria. Make that Albania.

Interior shot with bad lighting. A long wall lined with portraits of Savoies, Windsors, Hohenzollerns, Hapsburgs, kings, queens, princes and princesses, in frames surmounted by crowns. Snap! That's one of our waiters, wearing velvet knee breeches, silk stockings and white gloves. Thanks to

166

Maria Clara of San Francisco, and her father, a Roman count, we are lunching in Rome's most exclusive club, the Circolo della Caccia—the Hunt Club. It is in a Borghese palace, an imposing sixteenth-century structure surrounding a vast courtyard. Click: the courtyard, crowded with cars. As Count Francesco Latini sighs: "Only in Rome are museums used for garages." Too many cars, too many antiquities —the story of Rome. The tragedy: the cars are destroying the antiquities.

Here is an underexposed shot of the Hunt Club's magnificent dining room, with its crystal chandeliers, its priceless frescoes, and all the waiters and footmen at attention, outnumbering the guests. Sound track: at the next table, a nobleman is saying to a group of visitors: "But Mussolini wasn't all bad, you know. His domestic policy was excellent. But his foreign policy—a disaster." Wherever you go in a certain circle, this nostalgia for Mussolini. A publisher from Milan: "Our fascism had some unpleasant aspects, of course, but you must remember we didn't throw people into ovens. Mussolini did so many *good* things for the public." The poor Duce, strung up by his heels outside a service station in Northern Italy, so close to Switzerland. An American with American cruelty: "Pretty rough way to treat a guy who lost his credit card" . . . Click! Here are the four big, permanent murals erected by Mussolini on a wall near the Colosseum. They show the growth of the Roman Empire under his rule. "You will notice," says a cynical nobleman, "that he left no room for a fifth mural. He must have known what it would show. But he wasn't all bad." And it's a little-known fact that Hitler was a good dancer.

Borgheses, Torlonias, Medicis, Orsinis, Colonnas—these are still the powerful people of Roman finance and society, living their charmed and charming lives in vast palazzi that, from the street, look anonymous, mysterious, impregnable. Click: this is an Orsini palace, with its modest entrance concealing floors of luxury. Snap: in this out-of-the-way corner of a dark, narrow, cobbled street live the Torlonias, a delightful couple. Regimes come and go, the tides of history sweep back and forth across the ancient city, but these old families survive, living perhaps a little in the past but still able to deal with the present. And, no doubt, the future, if any.

The Ski's the Limit

GSTAAD, Switzerland: Needless to say (so why say it?), the proper dress is of the utmost importance in a proper ski resort like this. That is, it's important to dress down, not up —inverse snobbery rides again! The better you ski, the tackier you dress, and the best skier I saw, a rather alcoholic Englishman, always looked as though he'd just been thrown out of a plane: tattered black sweater, frayed blue shirt, dirty Ascot worn with British flair, and disreputable pants. Not even a turtleneck sweater, which is absolutely *de rigueur* in these exalted climes.

Being the greenest of horns, as well as the nonnest of skiers, I arrived with a sumptuous wardrobe that turned out to be the envy of nobody. One of my suitcases contained nothing but turtleneck sweaters, an interesting exercise in self-delusion. Although I do resemble a turtle, I have no neck to speak of, so when I struggle into one of these dashing devices, the turtleneck comes up over my chin, of which I have several, releasing an avalanche of dewlaps. As Oscar Levant once said of David Susskind, I looked like a piece of salami dipped in chicken fat.

Add to this a bulky sweater from which I had forgotten to remove the price tag, a pair of aquamarine stretch pants, and fur booties, and you have a picture to turn to the wall. My first night on the scene, a nastily perceptive Dutch Provo named Jan squinted at me through his steel specs and said, "Is this your first visit to a ski place?" Examining his greasy corduroy suit and spotted tie, I retorted: "Is this your last?" but I knew it was no good; besides, he was a fantastic skier and fluent in five languages—definitely someone to hate.

However, the point penetrated my layers of cashmere:

nonskiers who wear ski clothes are no better than those miserable World War II desk jockies who affected Hotshot Charlie caps and wore jump boots. By the third day I had discarded my spurious finery and was down to an old gray sweater with holes in it, a blue shirt and knotted bandanna, and ancient slacks, which made me look so authentic that even ski instructors were asking, "Wasn't that you who came roaring past me up on the glacier today—near the ten-thousand-foot marker?" "Could be," I'd reply, fluttering my eyelashes. "Hit a bit of ice there, almost came a cropper, but managed to wedeln my way out." Actually, I did have a go at the children's slope, but as I lay there askew, with six-year-old American kids whizzing past and spouting torrents of flawless French, German and Italian, I knew it was back to the bar.

Fortunately for me and other phonies, the rains came, plus snow flurries, and there wasn't much skiing to be done for three days. So The Group sat around over Molly's Bull Shots at the Olden, thinking up party ideas. I should point out right here that Gstaad is one of the world's great party towns, even when there *is* good weather, and how these people can drink, ski and survive is a marvel, since a drunk on skis is even more dangerous than an Oriental in a Ferrari. It would also seem to be a happy hunting grounds for bachelors: women outnumber men 5–1, the perfect formula for martinis and piglets. I think even I could have scored, and if you've checked the scouting reports, you know I'm strictly good field, no hit.

Anyway, first there was a miniskirt party with an authentic rock 'n' roll group from Liverpool. Then somebody decided to give an Indian costume party. Not East Indian. American Indian. Ridiculous, no, up there in the snow? "Where do I get feathers?" I complained to a fetching Parisienne known as La Poupette. "Go pluck a duck," she suggested, showing a remarkable grasp of the idiom. Sure enough, from out of who knows where, headdresses and beads were produced, and the Indian party was a smasher. All too Iroqueer, my dear.

Teresa Chicheri, the Catalan beauty who reigns over the Eagle Club, elected to give a *Chinese* party in her chalet,

169

Frenchily named Plein Soleil, and damned if she didn't dredge up a chubby German boy who could cook Chinese food almost as well as Ming at Johnny Kan's. Where he got the ingredients I'll never know, but somewhere in Gstaad he found a hidden cache of bean sprouts, water chestnuts, noodles, almonds, fresh pineapple and lichees. In honor of the Red Guards, there were red paper bulletins plastered all over the walls and dangling from the ceiling, inscribed with gold ideographs that, upon closer examination, read "Peace" and "Love" and "Get Out of Asia."

Not to mention other obscenities.

FOOTNOTE: Parties in Gstaad are like parties in San Francisco. In spite of ten-foot snowbanks all around, everybody keeps running out of ice.

On one quiet afternoon, I strolled around the village, marveling at the foaming river that rushes through its heart, and the uncanny neatness of the buildings. In the heart of the town is the oldest structure—a peak-roofed wooden house inscribed 1632; it stands next to an almost identical building marked 1966 and looks every bit as sturdy and fresh. Here and there, three-man crews were sweeping the streets and gutters. I watched them for a while and it suddenly occurred to me that they were doing something that could only happen in Switzerland. They were cleaning up the clean.

How I Won the War

SOMEWHERE in Europe, Somehow: There have been a lot of them since, tragically enough, but the true and original D-Day took place June 6, 1944, on the beaches of Normandy—and the fact that I was even near the scene was all due to a pleasantly nutty light colonel from Florida. That's one story. How I fell into his clutches is another.

After Pearl Harbor, I tried to join the Marines but flunked

the eye test (they were still very particular at that time). The recruiting officer noticed that I was having trouble with the eye chart and tried whispering the letters into my bad ear. "Eh?" I kept saying, "Whazzat, Colonel?" "Christ," he spat, "you're not only blind, you're deaf."

He showed me the door—a very handsome one it was, too —and I went over to the Navy. After the physical, the doctor shook his head and announced: "Rejected. Tachycardia." Well, it's quite a shock to find out you have something you never heard of. "What's tachycardia?" I asked. "To put it in terms you might understand," he said unpleasantly: "your heart goes bumpety-bump instead of bump-bump-bump. The Navy will attempt to win this war without you." I've been a little cool about the Navy ever since.

However, the Army Air Force, which was in the process of building an empire and needed bodies, however rachitic, decided mine was just fine. As indoctrination, I was told to memorize three verses of "Off we go into the wild blue yonder" and then an officer asked me what I'd like to do. Since the derisive term "armchair commando," was already in vogue, I pleaded: "Anything but public relations!" "Okay," he said, riffling through my papers, "we'll make you a radio operator-mechanic."

Like so many of my contemporaries, I look back on World War II and wonder how we won it, so incredible were the waste and inefficiency ("The Germans must be even more screwed up than we are," we'd say to each other hopefully). I cite my own case only because it was typical. At Sheppard Field, Texas, I again narrowly escaped being plopped into public relations, and was shipped off to Chicago to learn the Morse code.

We were stationed for four months in the world's largest hotel, the Stevens (now the Conrad Hilton), which the Air Force had unaccountably taken over. You stick five thousand GIs into a luxury hotel and what you wind up with is the Sheraton Shambles. We were all supposed to become radio operator-gunners on bombers, but when I took the depth perception test, the sergeant squinted at the results and asked: "You putting me on?"

So naturally they decided to make an officer out of me. A

communications officer (the Air Force, already dreaming of becoming a separate service, wanted to get rid of the Signal Corps). I graduated from Yale as a second lieutenant and paid the traditional dollar to the first enlisted man to salute me. Singer Tony Martin. When he married the glamorous Cyd Charisse, I mailed him a dollar with a note reading: "Now you outrank everybody."

I was assigned to a squadron in Texas. We trained in the mud with the infantry in Louisiana. Just as we were about to be shipped to Burma, the squadron was unaccountably deactivated (I think they had found me out). "How the hell do I get overseas?" I lamented at a reassignment center in Birmingham. "Volunteer for Air Force Intelligence," I was told. Pronto: I took a crash course at Harrisburg, Pennsylvania, in aerial photo intelligence and next thing I knew I was one of fourteen thousand bodies aboard the converted luxury liner *Ile de France,* outracing German subs to England.

Here is where the nutty light colonel from Florida comes in. He was bucking for bird colonel and needed a larger empire, up there at Air Force headquarters near London. He recognized my name on a list, remembered I had worked for a newspaper, and grabbed me. After eighteen expensive months of training as a GI, a radio operator-mechanic, a communications officer and an aerial photo interpreter, I was right where I didn't want to be. In public relations. The fickle-finger award to that man.

As D-Day approached, my colonel got more and more restive. "Gotta be in on that," he kept muttering. "Why, sir?" we asked. "Hell," he groused, "don't you guys want a battle star on your ETO [European Theater of Operations] ribbon?" "Yes, sir," we chorused.

As a politician and string puller, he was not to be underestimated. On June 6, carbines and typewriters at the ready, our brave band was aboard an LST in the Channel, along with some true Second Division riflemen. The fact that we didn't get ashore till June 8 didn't bother our colonel one whit. "Lafayette, baby, we are here," he declaimed as we waded onto Omaha Beach, and off we went in search of the war, catching up with it infrequently.

Looking back on my military career, I know beyond doubt that we could discharge fifty thousand men from the Army immediately. I'm certain they're all in public relations, and, judging from the results, not doing a very good job of it, either.

Back to the Front

CAEN, Normandy, France: The first time Caen saw Caen was on June 12, 1944. The British were having a rough time there, having run into fierce and experienced Panzer opposition (the British made an easier landing than the Americans but then caught hell). Without orders, another nut named Mike Watson and I had crossed into the British sector at Bayeux and jeeped on toward Caen, since I was stupidly determined to have my picture taken alongside a road sign at the entrance to the city. An angry British MP turned us back short of target and it was just as well; a tremendous artillery duel was in progress and German patrols were all over the place. Caen (the city) was fast disappearing in smoke and flame, and the residents were dying by the hundreds.

The second time I came to Caen was in 1949. Although the rebuilding had begun, the city still lay largely in ruins. At night, the streets were dark and gloomy, and a good part of the population was living in cellars. As we kicked our way through the rubble, it seemed to us that Caen was dead.

But today, it is hard to believe that war had ever come this way.

The postwar buildings, which seemed so ugly when new, have already acquired a patina, and there are great shade trees everywhere. Caen is busy, bustling and obviously prosperous. The bell-bottomed young people, to whom the war isn't even a memory, gather in Le Drugstore, snapping their fingers to the latest pop records and staring without much interest at the sudden invasion of fading and faded old soldiers. So it goes.

For the twenty-fifth anniversary of D-Day we are headquartered at the Hôtel Malherbe along with some of the original cast. General of the Army Omar Bradley arrives, his nice homely face wreathed in smiles. I am amused to see he is wearing his nameplate—"Bradley" in white letters on black. "I'd have recognized you without it," I say. "I thought I'd better wear it," he says seriously. "You know, we've all changed a little in twenty-five years."

General "Lightning Joe" Collins is in civvies. "Lightning Joe" is now a white-haired man who wears a hearing aid. General Jake Devers in civvies, too, ramrod-straight and crew cut. The dashing ex-Air Force general, Elwood "Pete" Quesada, strides into the dining room. "What a tough old bird he was," recalls a former aide. "During the war I saw him break officers to enlisted men on the spot."

The management of the Hôtel Malherbe just can't believe that my name is Caen. All the messages and other communications in my box are carefully addressed to "Monsieur HERB."

The first night is one of rowdy camaraderie at the bar. The British, Canadian and French brass are wearing buckets of medals. They break up into loud-talking groups, discussing their various actions on D-Day, invoking the names of heroes long dead, units long disbanded. The comparison is unavoidable: they look like nothing so much as a bunch of old Stanford and Cal graduates, talking about the Big Games of yore. The only sour note is sounded by a U.S. colonel who glowers drunkenly at the correspondents: "You bastards really did me in in '44." Much later, he grabs a fire extinguisher and demands, "Which floor is the goddam press on? I'm gonna fill their rooms with CO_2." "Sixth floor," we tell him, and he charges out. The press is on the fourth. The generals are on the sixth. Fortunately, he never got there.

Next morning, we drove through the lush Norman countryside, looking for sights that would bring back memories, but peace had reclaimed the land. The hated hedgerows were once again just hedgerows, no longer places of concealment for German machine guns and tanks. The dead and

174

hideously bloated cows had been replaced by fat and apparently contented ones, chewing in their neat pastures. We drove along winding lanes and tried to visualize a Tiger or a Panther tank poking its ugly muzzle around the bend, and failed. The sickly-sweet unforgettable stench of death had long since disappeared from the fields. When a door slammed, it was just a door slamming—not a German 88. You can go home again a lot easier than you can find an old war.

At Carentan, I remembered how I had asked an old Frenchman in '44: *"Où est le lavabo?" "Où est le lavabo?"* he replied in surprise. *"Où est le lavabo? Mais, monsieur, toute la belle France!"* And at the Hôtel Lion d'Or in Bayeux, British press headquarters after the landing, a dear old lady came over to our table, shook my hand and said, "Thank you for what you did twenty-five years ago."

I felt like a hero without credentials.

☆　☆　☆

ST. LAURENT-SUR-MER, Normandy, France: "In Flanders fields the poppies blow between the crosses, row on row"—but no wild flowers mar the immaculately kept greenery of the American cemetery on the bluff overlooking Omaha Beach. Yankee know-how and dollars have created a lush, manicured park where, twenty-five years ago, there were blood, guts and carnage. The place has the depressing sterility of Forest Lawn. A reflecting pool mirrors a colonnade inscribed with sentiments that are pompous rather than eloquent, surrounding an unfortunate bronze statue of an upthrusting young man said to represent "The Spirit of Youth." On the emotion meter, it registers a flat zero.

But there is no mistaking the impact of the 9,386 white crosses marching in neat, perfectly spaced columns across the lawns opposite the colonnade. Men who died violently and messily, laid out at last in their regulation plots, by the numbers—the final tidying up of the unfortunate loose ends. A military cemetery tells you a little about war, but not much. Too many of us could remember the American bodies piled roughly into ditches by the Graves Registration boys, who cut off the dog tags and stuffed them into the mouths of their dead owners so they could be identified for burial. Now they are back in final formation.

Still, you feel something real at the first sight of those endless white crosses—a sudden sick feeling at the pit of the stomach, a fogging of the eyes. The age-old mystical questions race through the mind: why them and not me? Could anything ever be worth this silent parade of death? "Come on," CBS's Andy Rooney said brusquely, grabbing my arm. "The first thing you felt was probably honest, but don't start introspecting. Once you do that, you're thinking about yourself, not them. Let's get out of here." He was right. It did seem we could only pay tribute by turning away, still shaken by the first jolt. It is too easy, and self-serving, to become maudlin.

There were desultory ceremonies in the Army's traditional hurry-up-and-wait style. An Air Force unit marched up to the colonnade in the honored style of the Air Force—out of step and stumbling. An Air Force band was ranged nearby, a typical American mixture of the tall and the short and the fat. High-ranking officers came and went by helicopter. (The U.S. may be becoming increasingly militaristic, but the uniforms are still back in the Sad Sack era—floppy, baggy and two sizes too big. This may be a hopeful sign. If the Pentagon ever hires Bill Blass to design new uniforms, I say watch out.) A contingent of mean-looking French paratroopers stood nearby, being chewed out by an ugly noncom because their guns weren't lined up evenly. *"Merde de poulet,"* we whispered loudly, and a couple of troopers snickered, fortunately out of earshot of the masticating noncom. Amplified clichés—"They did not die in vain," "Last full measure of devotion"—floated out over the crosses and were blessedly lost in the Channel. The defenseless dead, assailed annually by platitudes.

Quiet and vaguely depressed, we made our way back to the Hôtel Malherbe in Caen, where the twenty-fifth anniversary of D-Day celebration was still in full swing. The town had a festival atmosphere: loudspeakers at every street corner blared waltzes, rock music, French songs and American, ceaselessly. The spirit of bonhomie was unmistakable. The Americans, the British, the Canadians and the French were all loving each other again in the warm feeling of a shared experience. The suspicion that the rapport was only temporary gave it a bittersweet quality.

"All junkets last one day too long," said Pan Am's Dick Barkle morosely as we took our customary station at the Malherbe's bar. Publisher William Randolph Hearst, Jr., sounded the battle cry—*"Encore de booze!"*—he had made famous during World War II. Cornelius Ryan looked gloomy. "Postpartum depression," he mumbled, reaching into his pocket for yet another Librium pill.

Conversation was sporadic, springing up and dying in bursts of clichés about vanished youth, the end of innocence and so on. Well, it had been the last "good" war, hadn't it? Everybody nodded somberly, perhaps thinking about the white crosses, row on row. Wouldn't have missed it for anything, right? Oh, right. I mean, there was a decent simplicity about it—the enemy was the personification of evil, not some pajama-clad peasant you ultimately felt sorry for. World War II was the last between Good and Evil, and we were the Good and we had prevailed. Hell, man, even the kids who protested against the war in Vietnam say they would have participated enthusiastically in World War II. All wars are lousy, but ours had some meaning to it . . .

"Encore de booze!" No thanks, Bill, I've had it.

We went to pack and Ryan growled: "I hope I never see this crowd again—the D-Day thing is finished, over, *kaput,* period." He left in search of a piece of chalk and was last seen scrawling "Yankee Go Home" on the war monument across the street. Operation Yesteryear had ended.

☆ ☆ ☆

CARTOONIST Charles "Peanuts" Schulz, resplendent in an out-of-date Nehru jacket, dined in the Sea Cliff home of cartoonist Marty "Bobby Sox" Links. "You should wear a medallion with that," said Marty, "and I've got the perfect one—I bought it in the Haight-Ashbury." She ran upstairs and reappeared with a heavy chain from which dangled a medallion reading "LOVE" in beautifully entwined letters. After fingering it for a few seconds, Schulz handed it back with a Charlie Brown smile. "It's just a little too much for me," he said. "Do you have one that says 'LIKE'?"

INSTEAD of Julius Caesar, Caesar's Palace in Las Vegas should have a statue of Charles Fey, a San Franciscan who died in 1944 at eighty-four. Back in 1888, in a loft at 406 Market Street, he invented the slot machine, the jackpot being three Liberty Bells in honor of the Philadelphia Centennial of 1876. Charlie Fey put Las Vegas in business and they never even heard of him. That's show biz?

Those Were the Days

THERE THEY WERE, the remnants of the Democratic Party in California, men who had known the power and the glory and the chauffeured limousines bought by the taxpayers. Shrewd old Irish, Italian and Jewish faces, the broken veins attesting to years of good scotch and bourbon, the paunches affirming the nutritious value of U. S. Government Prime, only the best beef for the beefy best. The anxious eyes still darting from face to face, begging to be recognized, to be remembered, perhaps to be feared a little even in these times of political adversity.

They were there in a private banquet room at the Fairmont, brought together in convivial conclave by the sixty-fifth birthday of the man they had helped to power and who had in turn given them power—former Governor Pat Brown. The names were like a call for volunteers in an old Warner Bros. war flick—Lynch and Swig, Shorenstein and

Alioto, Harris, Poole, Purchio, Malone, Feinstein, Rudden, Daly, Andros, Elkington, MacInnis, Coblentz. Judges, supervisors, regents, mayors, commissioners of this and that. The melting pot had churned them to the top for eight golden years, and now they talked of the past, daring not to think about the future.

At sixty-five, Pat Brown seemed younger than any of them, full of bounce, pink of cheek, "Golly" and "Gee whiz" still his speech marks, certainly one of the most likable men ever to go into politics. Now he has gray sideburns that grow down past the middle of the ear. The middle of the ear is the cutoff point between the straights and the not-so-straights, and Pat has made his choice. "I was growing a mustache, too," giggled this sixty-five-year-old man who can still giggle, "but Bernice made me shave it off. She said sideburns are sexy but mustaches aren't . . . ."

The wine was red and the beef was U. S. Govt. Prime as the festivities continued. The token Republican was former Mayor George Christopher, the bull-necked ex-dairyman. Ritual Republican-Democrat jokes with laughter to match. Then he told a longish baseball joke with a sly punch line that could be interpreted only one way: as governor, Pat Brown had messed things up so badly that even his successor (Mr. Reagan) couldn't play the position. Pat threw back his head and laughed, but as the point sank in, his eyes turned cold.

Bill Bennett arose to announce: "This is the first time I've had roast beef at the Fairmont without paying a hundred dollars a plate." Pat, nudging Ben Swig: "You may be premature." Then the ex-governor arose and began reminiscing about his campaign against Nixon in '62. "Golly," he said, "you just don't know what it's like to be in a race like that. You wake up in the morning and you don't know if you're in Berkeley or Fresno or Bakersfield." Interjected Cecil Poole: "I get the same feeling without ever leaving San Francisco." "Anyway," Pat went on, "I woke up one morning in a motel room somewhere, just feeling *awful,* and I glanced over at the next bed and there was a strange woman in it! 'That son-of-a-bitch Nixon is trying to frame me!' I said to myself. I started to dress to get out of there quick when she turned

179

over—and it was Bernice. My wife! Golly, I'd forgotten she'd joined me the night before." That was the evening's raciest story, mainly because there was a lone woman in the group, Madlyn Day. "You," George Christopher sighed to her, "are our Air-Wick."

"I remember the last day Pat Brown was in office," Cecil Poole said. "So do I," lamented Pat. "One minute you have everything at your beck and call—aides, secretaries, drivers, all the service in the world—and the next minute, *nothing*." Continued Poole: "I was with Pat that day, a cold, wintry day in Sacramento. We got into the back seat of the car and drove down Capitol Avenue to the river. As we crossed the bridge, I couldn't resist looking back at the capitol—one last look at the place where we'd worked for eight long years. But Pat, he never looked back. I think that's remarkable. I think it shows what kind of man he is." Brown picked up the story. "And a short time after that, I was driving in Palm Springs and I guess I was going too fast because a highway patrolman stopped me. He looked at me and said: 'Well, life is funny, Governor. Last year I was driving you. This year I'm giving you a ticket.'"

By midnight, the party was over. In a sense, it had been over for a long, long time. The present Governor of California, Pat Brown's son, doesn't like parties anyway.

SARTORIAL STUDY: Publisher John A. Vietor attended a party in Pacific Heights one Sunday night wearing a strawberry red seersucker jacket, button-down shirt, Yale tie, baggy gray slacks and 1940-ish white buck shoes. The first guest he ran into was art dealer Billy Pearson, attired in a black velvet suit lined with white satin, striped shirt, stiff white collar, string tie and gold watch chain across his vest. "Bill," said Vietor gravely, "one of us is wrong."

Mr. San Francisco???

EVERY TIME I put a mild knock on our town, which is seldom and always loving-mournful, I'm sure to get a few reproachful letters from Old Natives. (Old Natives are not to be confused with New Natives. Old Natives really *care* about the San Francisco of their dreams. New Natives don't care about anything, except maybe the parking problem.) What the Old Natives, bless their hurt feelings, have to say is along the lines of "How can you pick on our wonderful city, you who *dare* to call yourself Mr. San Francisco?"

Now this is something I've been meaning to straighten out for years. Believe me, friends, I've never thought of myself as Mr. San Francisco or Mr. Anything Else. I'm not that presumptuous, daring or, I hope, corny.

For the record, I will admit that I used to write columns headed "Mr. San Francisco," but these were not meant to be autobiographical. In the language of the creative writing classes (may they all go fallow), I was trying in those columns to *project* myself into the life of San Franciscans playing various roles: running cable cars, picking up girls in Montgomery Street bars, walking on the beach, taking their kids to the zoo, necking at Coit Tower, drinking after hours at Joe's Wine Cellar, and so on. Nothing personal, but the title was catchy. It stuck, and against my will, I found myself stuck with it.

So I stopped writing columns headed "Mr. San Francisco."

Nevertheless, to this day I find myself being introduced in various places as "Mr. San Francisco," an appellation that makes me fall to the floor, foam at the mouth and sob a little. It is such a dated concept: what it brings to mind is Jimmy Walker, his fedora turned up on one side and his smile turned down on the other, leading the St. Patrick's Day Parade. Or Jimmy Rolph, wearing his gold-heeled cowboy boots and that thin little phony smile under that thin little toothbrush mustache, roaring at the people of North Beach, "I am a son of California, I am a son of San Francisco and I am a son of this beach!" (Cheers.)

Don't get me wrong. In my salad days (as in green and mixed up) I had a picture of a "Mr. San Francisco," and he didn't resemble me in the slightest. Maybe there even was such a guy. In my poor blind purblindness, I suppose I saw him as a man who wore a homburg with dash and English clothes with style. He was a sort of Mr. First Nighter, getting the best table at the Bal Tabarin and the best seats at the Curran with just a snap of the fingers and a quietly proffered ten-dollar bill, folded. At Jack's or Amelio's, he ordered French dinners in French, Italian dinners in Italian, as his mistress, decked out in all her Shrevery, gazed up at him admiringly. He kept her in high style—penthouse on Nob Hill, car and driver, open account at Magnin's (nobody knows how to keep a mistress properly these days). If such a character exists today, we couldn't call him Mr. San Francisco. More like the Big B-o-r-e.

On radio or TV programs, when I strenuously object to being called "Mr. San Francisco," the interviewer usually presses: "Well, who *would* you call Mr. San Francisco?" Lefty O'Doul sometimes came to mind, but he doesn't count because he couldn't have cared less. When given a chance to think a little longer, I invariably settle on August Rinaldo "Gus" Oliva.

Gloomy Gus, Poor Gus, Good Old Gus—here is a man who would have loved the title of Mr. San Francisco. In the easy days of Prohibition and stock margins, he amassed a fortune of over $4 million and he spent it. On five wives. On a fabulous Russian Hill apartment that rivaled that of his illustrious neighbor, Templeton Crocker—$100,000 worth of furnishing from France ("I prefer Dago, myself," Gus said at the time, "but my decorator says French is the thing"). Gus fixed everybody's traffic tags, picked up everybody's dinner checks and got the keys to the city from Jimmy Rolph and Angelo Rossi.

And on Easter Sunday, he would hide seven thousand eggs in Golden Gate Park and the whole town would turn out, because there'd be a hundred-dollar bill in some of the eggs, fifty dollars in others and prizes for everybody. Gus Oliva's Sundays in the park were legendary—the "Gus-Ins" of yesterday were bigger, and infinitely more profitable, than

182

the "Be-Ins" of recent vintage. I remember him as a man who lived as high and wide as the headlines that heralded his exploits and heartaches, a man who would never hesitate to do a favor for somebody above him. To me, he will always be Mr. San Francisco—a title out of the world that no longer exists. Or did it ever?

A Little Mood Music

THE SEASON: spring. The time: dusk. The day: Thursday . . .

We all live by different rhythms, pulled forward and swept back by tides more mysterious than the oceans'. Days of manic joy, nights of deep depression, or sometimes the other way round as we gaze out upon the cityscape, drink in hand, eyes on the present, heart in the past, wondering at the inner turmoil.

But even if you are a winter person, there is no denying the sweet, soft grip of spring, another beginning in a life of false starts and stops on the road to dead ends. Again, a chance to be young. Dreams of salt spray rising over a prow headed toward the Golden Gate and out into trackless adventure, fantasies of roads winding through fields of poppies toward mountains even more purple than this prose . . .

Have you noticed there are no longer fields of poppies? The California flower, like the American eagle is endangered, fading toward extinction, dying under tract houses and "mobile homes" going nowhere, while the eagle, so fierce of profile, is all too vulnerable to the slings and arrows clutched in its symbolic claws.

A Thursday dusk in spring, the perfect time to be alive, in San Francisco. Wind rising fresh from the Pacific, washing away the smog. The commuters, the auslanders, the Elsewhereans, are heading for the bridges and Bayshore, fleeing the city, leaving it to those who love it best.

As the slow shadows grow, San Francisco reverts to the San Franciscans. Walls of light shining in The New Downtown. Impressive, no doubt, even though those cubicles high in the sky were built to house the people now rushing out of town as fast as their wheels will carry them, back to the doubtful safeties and doubtless dullnesses of San This and Terra That and La Plastic the Other.

At the gentle dusk in Newtown, even the Transamerica pyramid takes on a glamorous thrust. In the daytime, it resembles a gawky big-eared kid who's about to say: "Aw shucks." Awash with lights, its ego becomes more assertive.

Thursday, a good day. Maligned Monday is okay, too; it streaks past in a flurry of postparty *tristesse*. Tuesday you play catch-up and even get something done. The week peaks on Wednesday, all systems go, and Friday is too obvious, Saturday special and Sunday bittersweet. As you pause to consider the weekend, you curl your hand around the drink you now feel is your due (alcohol, grass, partner, whatever makes your hand curl).

America's two great drinking towns are San Francisco and New York. The tradition is studiously observed. "Scotch and water—make that J & B." "Right." You lay your money on the bar. In San Francisco, you pay by the drink. In New York, you can run a check. The difference is you can leave your change on the bar in San Francisco and nobody will steal it.

Alone and yet not alone, you look out toward the Bay as the Ferry Building's lights come on. Silently you toast the building and the memories and the pretty girls grown old.

A cable car rattles emptily down the Chinatown hill and coasts to Market, the crew lounging. So relaxed and relaxing, the financial district after the penthouse windows no longer reflect the final sun blaze. Pagodas perched on rooftops overlooking pillared old piles, stirrings in the alleys, smells of cooking drifting upward. Inside the glass walls of Newtown, old San Francisco still struggles. At the cocktail hour, it comes to full life—briefly—as it always has over the long, hilly years.

It's true that some of the great bars have gone. One misses the original Lower Bar at the Mark, where so many adventures were hatched at dusk (Reed Funsten and Jake Ehrlich, Jr., battling, Bill Saroyan fishing greasy shrimp out of his jacket. Oil mogul Al Marsten flattening a very young columnist). El Prado was one of the good ones (women in flowered hats over silver foxtails, showing much leg, tooth and zeal). Millionaire George Lewis, silver champagne bucket at left elbow, ravishing keptive at right, presiding over his sycophantic circle at the old Templebar.

Still, it's hard to find a bad bar in San Francisco, where there is so much to drink to and think on, where a man can sit alone, staring at himself in the mirror, discounting the evidence as unreliable, and say to himself that tonight may be the night . . . Women don't understand about men and bars.

Thursday dusk in April, chefs in their white toques taking a breather outside the restaurants, pretty Japanese girls in kimonos sliding town the hills toward the tempura temples, ice tinkling in that first drink as the lights come on to make us all young again.

Then and Now

DURING THE great depression, nobody had any money and everybody seemed to be having a lot of fun. Today, a lot of people have money and nobody is having any fun at all, and why is that, Doc? Kindly explain.

These perishable thoughts occurred to me as I lunched with Agostino (Bimbo) Giuntoli, who has had a lot to do with what passes for fun in this town. At seventy or so, he is a handsome man, his hair thick and only slightly gray. He sports a neatly trimmed mustache of the type fancied by movie heroes of the thirties—say, Antonio Moreno. A diamond-studded "365" sparkles in his well-tailored lapel (with hand-picked edges). When he rounds out the picture with homburg at a jaunty angle, cashmere overcoat and gray spats, he is the embodiment of an American picture long faded: the immigrant boy who came here to look for gold in the streets, and found it.

Like millions before him, Agostino came here alone from his native village in Italy a half century ago. He entered the San Francisco scene on the ground floor: janitor at the Palace Hotel. Then he graduated to cook for the character named Monk Young in a speakeasy nearby on Market (Monk couldn't pronounce "Agostino" and dubbed him "Bimbo"). In 1931, the redoubtable team of Monk and Bimbo took over an upstairs loft at 365 Market and opened the 365 Club. Monk is long gone, and now, years later, the rich man named Agostino Giuntoli—rich in family, friends, honors and money—is almost ready to call it quits. His pride and joy, the "new" 365 on Columbus Avenue, is open now only for private parties.

Well, so what? Night clubs come and go; don't they? True, but the cliché "end of an era" was never truer, for the 365 is/was a true night club in a style we will never see again. Chorus girls! The first local live nudie—"The Girl in the Fishbowl." Jugglers, dance teams, standup comics, crooners, chantootsies, stage door Johns, a proper band in uniforms and a leader with a baton long enough for the symphony. Multicourse dinners, Red Cap Sparkling Burgundy in the silver bucket, and a nice-bucketed lady in a silver fox stole garnished with a gardenia bought from the "pro" in the men's room. All over, done for. You may be dry-eyed but Bimbo, who talks like Henry Armetta and has a laugh that crackles like a shortwave radio, is crying. Of all the big clubs that once flourished in this city of long nights, only the 365 survived this long, and it hurts.

Looking back, it's hard to believe. During the Depression, hardly anybody had two four-bits pieces to rub together, yet the town was jumping. Name bands in all the hotels. Griff Williams and Jimmy Walsh at the Edgewater Beach, at the edge of the Pacific. At Topsy's Roost, you entered by sliding down a wooden chute to dance to Ellis Kimball. Joe Merello's Club Moderne, Papa Riccomi's Music Box, the Embassy at the Wharf, the lavish three-story Deauville on O'Farrell (the dance team of Chaney & Fox, Eddie Fitzpatrick's band) and a dozen joints with shows that ran all night. Upstairs at O'Farrell and Stockton, a full-fledged gambling palace. When Hildegarde opened in the Mark's Peacock Court, it was bigger than first night at the opera. Same for Sophie Tucker at Gerun & Martinelli's Bal Tabarin, now Bimbo's. Every other apartment house downtown had girls for hire, two dollars and up; Sally, Dolly and Jew Ida. The cops ran the town and, in retrospect, they ran it well. Bookies, pinballs and slot machines were everywhere. The buck was scarce but somehow everybody made one.

Even in this setting, the old 365 on Market was special. You rode upstairs in a rickety elevator and stepped out into a big square bar, the best kind. The showroom ran as late as the traffic would bear; a full show at 3 A.M. was not unusual. In a heavily curtained back room that stayed open till dawn, pretty girls presided over high-dice tables, and that's where Bimbo made a good chunk of his fortune. "The house took all ties," he cackles. "That's all I needed, that little edge."

Three things finally beat Bimbo. "Jet planes, Las Vegas and TV," he enumerated as we fork-and-spooned the spaghetti at Julius' Castle. "In the old days, who had time to go anywhere? Now you get on a plane, boom, you're in Las Vega in a few minutes. You see Frank Sinatra. At my joint, you see Joe Schlock. How can I fight those Vegas salaries? I don't blame people. I got a family place. I put in big acts, I gotta raise prices and my customers say: 'Bimbo, you can't do this to me, I'm part of the *family*.' Then there's TV. It ain't so good but it's free.

"I've been beating my head against the wall till I got a headache. I don't mind throwing good money after bad, but now it's like throwing it off the Golden Gate Bridge. I don't wanna die broke. I know too many guys, they die and people say what a great fellow—when he had it, he spent it. Hell, I had it and I spent it and I'm quitting while I still have a little left."

Then he smiles his sunny smile. Turning to his son-in-law, Graziano Cerchiai, he said, beaming: "But the old days, kid, they were really something. Too bad you missed it." "Why?" said Graziano, "If I'd been there, now I'd be as old as you are." So much for sentiment. It's deader than the night club business.

187

POINT OF VIEW: Robert Cameron, who put together the book of dazzling aerial photos titled *Above San Francisco,* tested some of his special camera equipment on the roof of Bank of America's World Headquarters. "By the way," Cameron said to banker Bill Lewis on the rooftop, "what happens to this building in case of an earthquake?" "Not a thing," replied Lewis. "It has been designed to withstand a shock one and a half times greater than the strongest quake ever recorded." "But," persisted Cameron, "what if there's a quake twice as strong as that one?" "Then," said Lewis, grinning, "instead of having the tallest building in town, we'll have the longest!"

☆ ☆ ☆

JOE PICCININI squeezed his car between two others in a Safeway lot, inched his way out, and came back to find a note on his windshield: "I hope one of these days *you* get pregnant and someone parks that close to you!"

Half-Past Summer

OLD BAGHDAD-BY-THE-BAY: the population is decreasing but the traffic gets worse all the time, an unhealthy sign. By day, the great city looks richly powerful; at night it empties, topless towers silent, and in the morning, the radio station helicopters hover to flash the latest traffic disaster. Now at last we know what we have become: tourist town and commuter city, pockmarked with ghettoes, milked by outsiders. The famous piers stand empty (buoys and gulls crying in the night) and there is much talk about Victorian Villages, cable car centennials and Lola Montez Carnivals on the waterfront—the slick taking up the slack. Once the

188

city sneered at tourists, but now we love them, one and all, and will spend millions to get them here. Please?

But don't get me wrong, we're a long way from Disneyland North, thanks to cocky scavengers, salty firemen, the best-looking women anywhere, Victorian houses that come to life at a touch of paint, and of course the incredible weather. Three and a half hot days and then the fog nosing around like a familiar busybody, blotting out the emptiness of the great Bay, and bringing a satisfied smile to the True Believers. "What terrible weather!" grumps the visiting goose-pimpled seersucker (camera-crested) you're meeting at the St. Francis. "Yes, isn't it wonderful?" you reply, meaning every word.

Bay area summer, nothing like it anywhere: steaming days and cool nights in Sonoma, where the bouquet of grapes is always in the air, and even steamier days in Napa, perspiration trickling. There is little to lure you south and east in the world of July, so you inevitably head north, to the enchantment of redwood heights, cool inlets and brooks that sing between pine-needled banks. Despite their proximity, the Peninsula and the East Bay have never seemed joined to San Francisco, philosophically or emotionally, one being too "Southern," the other Midwestern. One of the sensations of which I never tire is the four-wheeled plunge into a fog-shrouded Golden Gate Bridge, all windshield-wipered wetness, and the sudden emergence into sun-swept Marin, with its delicious summer smells and promise of secret groves. Nowhere else in the world can the transition from concrete jungle to pastoral retreat be made so swiftly and dramatically. Savor it.

Indeed Marvelous Marin: turn right (or wrong) to San Quentin and left (or right) to the rich profusion of a town named Ross. A few scant yards off a busy boulevard, this hushed *faubourg* of small children and big dogs, old streets (no sidewalks) lined with towering elms, shady byways more beautiful than France's. Clip-clop, clip-clop. A uniformed nanny leads a child on a pony, slowly backward through time. On a grassy hillside outside a Maybeck house, a lovely girl in a romantic dress and picture hat swings back and forth, given a lazy push now and then by a man in a white suit (F. Scott? Dick Diver?). A magnum of champagne is cooling in the silver bucket at his feet . . .

Inside Midsummer Marin, the barbecues and the jugs of Louis Martini's Mountain Red and White, and the Pool Sweeps going on automatically at 6 A.M. to begin their strange Martian-like prowling across chlorinated waters. Topics of conversation: where are you going to school in the fall, need more ice, do you suppose those electronic mosquito-dispellers really work? In the pool, the long-legged girl with the even tan does a perfect crawl, back and forth, barely splashing. She gets out, every good bone wetly outlined. How you envy her, you who splotch and burn and thrash and bellyflop . . .

A great new breed, these kids. No matter how much junk they eat, and they eat tons, they stay thin, tall and beautiful, their gaze steady and direct. All those lessons: no wonder they ride, play tennis and dive so well. Sprawled carelessly at poolside, Sony tuned to KTIM, innocent and indolent and graceful, the last best hope of our civilization—but not to get heavy about it, for they are young and it is midsummer. For the moment, it is enough to be warm and alive, with somebody to grease your back. Another winter will come soon enough.

Please Call It Frisco?

A FEW of us were sitting around, discussing our third favorite subject, after sex and the weather, and Rex Adkins came up with a truly original thought. "San Francisco," he ventured over the Mountain Red, "is a city that wishes people would call her Frisco again," a remark that caused the rest of us to nod with sad half-smiles. Only a few years ago, Adkins' aphorism wouldn't have crossed his mind, and it occurred to me later that I no longer hear people say either "Frisco" or, in automatic reproof, "Don't call it Frisco." An ominous sign, but any old portent in a storm.

It was the sailors who first called this port "Frisco," as they called San Diego "Dago," San Pedro "Pedro" and Oakland by several unprintable epithets (that has changed, too). They also thought of this city as the best liberty this side of Port Said, by which they meant they could get screwed and tattooed and maybe even shanghaied but never bored. Why, on Kearny, pronounced "Carney" in old Frisco, you could raise a crew to sail for the Galápagos in the course of one block and lose every man jack of them in the next. Frisco was a place for heroic hangovers, prodigious deeds and herculean lies, all printed immediately by fuzz-cheeked reporters, and only the pompous asses of Nob Hill insisted on "San Francisco, sir, if you please."

There's no doubt that it's San Francisco today. They're selling health food sandwiches at the Cliff House, out there where you could once dance all night and sleep all day, with a different belle for each shift, and Playland has disappeared into two big holes surrounded by rickety fences. If the sea gulls seem to be crying as they wheel over the breakers, and the sea lions sound more mournful than foghorns at midnight, there's reason enough and blame for all. For in spite of the brave young beards, the faded jeans and the mucho macho boots, the city has gone straight and its soul belongs to innkeepers and snake-oil salesmen selling corn and porn.

It's San Francisco now, a matchless harbor crowded with the ghosts of ships that have gone elsewhere while a superannuated Port Commission tries to make up its mind about something. Anything. It's San Francisco, with black blockbuster buildings and pointy-headed novelties and plastic towers that house commuters who don't call it "Frisco" because they never heard of the word and wouldn't know what it represents anyway. Good-by, Frisco, good-by, and hello, San Francisco, where a onetime giant of the waterfront, Harry Bridges, a man who once fought fascists, scoffs at those who would save what's left as "hard-nosed environmentalists," surely one of the great phrases of the decade. If the nose grows hard, consider the smell.

There's a pun there somewhere—does the smell of the past evoke nosetalgia?—but it's hard to make even feeble jokes as a beloved city wanders off in all directions, having

191

lost its way. "Don't call it Frisco," was the battle cry of The Respectables, and they appear to have won. The city of legends is being carved up by thieves in the night, and the money grubbers grow fatter (and grubbier) in the high-rising market places. This is no place for dreamers. Weavers of spells, come not here, to paraphrase the Bohemian Club motto. Jack London would look around and retreat to the First and Last Chance Saloon. The shade of George Sterling stands askance at his despoiled, vandalized monument on Russian Hill. Saroyan stays in Fresno.

Frisco. Surely something of it persists, for there is an unquenchable spirit here, as Saroyan is unquenchable. We feel it stirring on foggy mornings, when the mind's ear catches the far-off chunk-chunk of ferry paddles and the blasts of the *Lark*'s hooters at Third and Townsend. In the old streets, steam rises from a thousand underground pipes, the hot breath of a city whose pulse still beats in cable slots. On Telegraph Hill, once Tellygraft, Tom Cara reminds us that Mother Nature continues to fight "progress": after each heavy rain, Italian parsley sprouts from the street curbings in Edgardo Place. And on the rooftops above tawdry North Beach, a glass-roofed garret here and there where a young artist lives, even today, *la vie bohème.*

At Fisherman's Wharf, a little Frisco lives in the form of sea gulls on pilings and the "helldiver" grebes disappearing soundlessly into the murky waters after a quarry only they can see. Sunset brings the brave figure of mustachioed William May at the wheel of his faded fishing boat, the *Belle of Dixie,* with five dogs yapping on the afterdeck. Lovely old William, one of the last of the great fisherfolk, who squints up at the Russian Hill skyline and says, "Been livin' sixty-eight years here in Frisco—pardon me, San Francisco." No, William. Pardon us.

THE PEOPLE saddled with the thankless task of planning the city's bicentennial celebration may commission a grand opera based on the life of a celebrated San Francisco figure, and could and will do worse than command one based on the life and times of the Reverend Isaac Kalloch.

Before you say, "Isaac Who?" consider that this mustachioed worthy, elected in 1879, not only ran the city from the Palace Hotel bar, he was the only Baptist minister ever to serve as mayor, and what a term! The victim of an assassination attempt during the campaign, he survived to triumph as defendant in a criminal adultery trial and was later impeached but not convicted.

The Reverend Kalloch had red hair, and his amatory powers were such that he was known as "The Sorrel Stallion." Hereto all the way, one hastens to add. So strong is the Kalloch mystique that the Isaac Kalloch Centennial Society, boasting forty-eight members, meets regularly at the Little Shamrock bar at Ninth Avenue and Lincoln Way to bandy tales about the great man and lay plans for the hundredth anniversary of his benign reign.

The fact that the Reverend died in 1930 in Oakland is rarely mentioned but provides the opportunity for a properly tragic ending to the opera.

IN LOS GATOS, Carolyn Finn took her eight-year-old Patrick to Magoo's Pizza Parlor and immediately he had to go to the toilet. Almost immediately he was back with a problem: "Mommy, am I a Beauty or a Beast?"

HONORA MOORE, musing honorably away: "If we continue to drive later and later through traffic lights that have turned red, won't there come a time when green will mean stop and red go?" Dear Person, the time may be now.

GOOD OLD Charlie Bittman of Los Altos Hills is just back from Hawaii, "where," he reports good-naturedly, "it is

193

easier to find a bar mitzvah than a luau, $11 a day rent-a-cars come with $20 an hour rent-a-girls, the practice of pacifying volcanoes by throwing virgins into a crater has been abandoned but not for want of volcanoes, and grandmothers from Kansas line up for lunch at the Dunes, to be served by naked waiters. A San Franciscan who ran out of money tried to earn the price of a ticket home by working as a waiter but quit the first day, when a leather-voiced granny bellowed: 'Bring us another round, Shorty!' "

☆　☆　☆

TILT: Phil Gros, the resident genius who dreams up new ice cream flavors at Raskin-Flakker's on Hayes, shows a slight Communist slant in his latest creations. Reading from left to left: Marxist-Lemonist, The Party Lime and Critique of Pure Raisin.

☆　☆　☆

"HOW DO YOU expect to get into heaven?" Marquerite Antonucci snapped at her young son Raymond, who was acting pesty around their El Cerrito home. "Well," fidgeted Raymond after some thought, "I'll run in and out and keep slamming the door till they say: 'Come in or stay out' and then I'll go in."

I Like This Place

"CITY WITHOUT PITY," some melodramatist has called it, but pfaw! To the rest of us, even the pigeon haters, it will always conjure up St. Francis as Birdbath, white stains on his cowl but smiling through, Assisiwise and uzzerwise. San Francisco, old Frisco, stars barely glimpsed above the misty spars of ships fresh in from Cathay.

That's the thing about the city, ghosts and legends on the prowl through hard new streets between soulless new buildings, wondering where everybody and everything went. But here and there the traces remain, if it matters; perhaps ghosts and other spooks don't need reassurance in the first place. The rest of us do, though, which is why we squint a bit on foggy nights at the *Balclutha,* imagining a masted forest on the waterfront, homesick Cantonese girls drowning themselves in Chinatown wells, dray horses breaking legs and getting shot on the spot as they slid helplessly down the slick cobbles of Nob Hill.

At the top, Mrs. Mark Hopkins is entertaining, it reads in the *Daily Chronicle,* to which a rival hostess sniffs, "She may be giving a party, but entertaining she isn't, nor has she ever been." Across the street in the Flood mansion, firelight reflected in snifters of noble brandy, and much gossip of Tessie Fair, a woman destined to go places and be miserable.

What a great town! Think of it: years without leadership in City Hall, a library system that's a "disgrace," an "embarrassing" and bankrupt school system, falling-down transit, museums that make the experts strain for euphemisms to keep from being downright insulting, incredible smugness at the top based on the accomplishments of mythmakers long gone, dark and dangerous streets, traffic be damned and public be jammed, and yet though nothing works, everything works, and the city goes on being a good place to live if you're not killed and fun to play in if you don't have to make a living at it. The endless carnival. Beads, bangles, banjos and bells. Somewhere in San Francisco, bells are forever ringing, some in alarm, some in joy, some because the system is falling apart and so what?

"Perfectly mad people," Kipling called us, and we called him square, preferring Browning, browning, boozing and bitching. And yet he was right, ruddy old empire-building Rudyard, for it is still a good town to go crazy in, as many a statistic will show. The Giants are always having a lousy season but in the VD league we are breaking records. This is no longer the home of world champions—once we had the great fighters, the heavy sluggers, the best swimmers—but

195

the swan dives off the Golden Gate Bridge are beautiful and awful to behold.

San Francisco, the uninhibited isle, its Crusoe forever the Caruso who fled in '06, our finest hour, and Friday is when you thank God and head for the bars. No World Series for us, but a world of cirrhosis, a lousy way to live and no way to die.

Meanwhile, live, laugh and indulge yourself, my friend. Navigate the Lombard curlicue on a pogo stick. The Mason Street hill, down from California, is a true test of your skill on the unicycle. Sneak into the Fairmont Tower and move a couple of those lamps centered so perfectly in each window. Doesn't it drive you bananas that not one goddam lamp is off-center? So much to do, so little time: turn ex-hooker Margo St. James loose in the Pacific Union Club, unleash a thousand spiders in the Bohemian Club ("Weaving spiders come not here"), streak the Francisca Club, hijack a cable car.

Town where nothing is happening, and everything. No great writers, artists, poets, in the long view of history, but terrific bartenders, fabulous waiters and pretty girls all in a row, bare midriffs on display in the new "Slow March" from the Wharf to the Cannery to Ghirardelli via the BeeVee. In the old days, the beauties in their fitted suits, Cape jasmine gardenias at the throat, strolled the "Cocktail Route" of Market, Kearny, Sutter, but nothing lasts forever and the faded gardenias are cloying. The old men in derbies are long dead. The heavy watch chains survive but now they are camp when they're not kitsch.

Can a town that has sour-dough bread and honey butter muffins be all bad? Not on your life! The crab may be frozen but it's fresh frozen, and the Swan Oyster Depot is more redolent of oysters than swans and everything is fresh there, especially the paisans. The cheap white wine smells like a wet collie, so hold your nose delicately 'twixt thumb and forefinger and drink, for tomorrow, keed, we die.

I keep telling you, it's a great town. You've got to be crazy to think so and crazier not to. Stay off the cable cars and out of the health food stores and you'll outlive us all.

You Are What You Read

AUTHOR MARK HARRIS, a onetime eccentric professor at San Francisco State, sullied the Sunday pages of the New York *Times* recently with a piece titled "The Last Article" in which he advised his readers to stop constipating their minds by reading newspapers, a habit I gather he has abandoned. One might well wonder why Harris would have to employ the pages of a newspaper to spread this message, or even why a newspaper would bother to print it, but where Harris is concerned, ours not to reason why. (I'll confess I admired some of Harris's books, especially the baseball ones, but that's because I'm big-minded whereas he's small-minded.)

As I recall, Harris's point, if any, is that if anything of importance happens in the world he'll hear about it anyway, eventually, from his friends, if any, but how these friends acquired the news, he doesn't say. My guess would be that they read it in a newspaper or heard it over the airwaves. Where he dwells, I don't think they have jungle telegraphs, bwana, and you don't have to start worrying till the drums stop beating.

It's difficult, even after forty-odd years in "the newspaper game," which it once was, to decide what is essential news, or even news. When you have to churn out a thousand words a day, a ridiculous exercise on the face of it, the question is doubly troubling. I never walk the streets, ride the busses, climb the hills and look at the San Francisco faces without wondering: "What do these people like to read about? What would they like to read that they're not getting? What do *they* consider news? Is Mark Harris right?"

Obviously, what's news in Hunters Point isn't the same thing as what's news in Sea Cliff. If there's a common denominator, anything that immediately affects the lives of the city's people qualifies as news, I suppose, but the reader does not live by facts alone. He also wants to be moved, amused, confused—and given glimpses of a world and a life other than his own. At least, that's the theory.

I walk through the Emporium, listening to the voices of the Deep Missionites who shop there in great numbers. I know nothing of their world, they know nothing of mine. I think about what I have written in the next day's column and I feel frustrated and not a little sad: certainly they don't give a damn about Truman Capote's crack to Whitney Warren, Birgit Nilsson they never heard of, Alioto is a far-off figure under a big dome, they'll never go to Trader Vic's, and the cost of a ferryboat running to Marin must be Z-minus on their list of priorities. I don't even know *if* they read a newspaper. My only halfhearted consolation is that if I wrote the kind of column that might interest them, it would bore the residents of Russian Hill, say, so it's back to Square One.

"News," we used to say with fine arrogance back in the 1930s, "is what gets printed." In a sense, that is still true: the world has changed but the "stories" are still very much the same as they were forty years ago—what this politician said, what the one didn't say, the murders, accidents and "human interest stories" right off the police beat, the only concession to the times being a shallow overlay of slick stuff about "new life styles" that aren't new or particularly stylish. There may be too many old gaffers, like me, making these decisions, but I don't see any youngsters coming along who can do better, nor can I imagine why they'd want to try. The daily deadline is a killer and the "romance" of newspapering is dying out with my generation.

But we still believe in trying to get out the news, even if the news is something so utterly trivial as a good one-liner or a bum joke or a paragraph about Old San Francisco (nostalgia will always be news here). Stashed away behind typewriters in fortresses, we try to put it all together, our link with the outside world being teletypes, telephones and mail. The time for personal contact is minimal, so we can only guess at what people are really thinking and talking about. If the mail means anything, the principal concerns are dirty streets and sidewalks, our crummy administration, our crummier athletic teams, "things ain't what they used to be," Remember The Maine and Old San Francisco, and whatever happened to the seventy-five-cent meal in North Beach? "Don't pay any attention to the mail," a really cynical old-timer keeps advising me. "Only a nut would write to a newspaper in the first place."

I don't believe that and never will. Only a nut would write *for* a newspaper, perhaps, and that makes Mark Harris just as nutty as the rest of us who can't imagine a world without newspapers.

The Walking Caen

WHEN A NUN at the wheel of a Volkswagen ran the light at Post and Franklin and almost clobbered me, I knew it waren't a fit day for man, beast or columnist, which may be redundant, so I parked my Kleenex Mark VIII in a throwaway zone and began walking. As the old cruisers who dread naught are always saying: "San Francisco is a great walking town," and a good thing, too, for there is never a cab around when you want one, the Muni busses stop and start with a jerk, in some cases at the wheel, and driving a car is definitely hazardous to your wealth . . . Still, I do wish you'd seen that nun, in black habit, hunched over the wheel of her Volksie, scattering pedestrians like quail. A truly original sight in a society that is becoming more and more stereotyped, even here in Only in San Francisco West, Ltd.

"Life is just a bowl of clichés" is a refrain I find myself humming quite often, not that I resent your platitude, or anybody else's. On Upper Grant in Nord Beach, I don't even look once any longer at the strung-out hippies yelling obscenities at city-deaf passers-by. Tough, but I've seen his dirty, pathetic ilk too often. "Any spare change?" Another

199

cliché. What's spare change? If you have to make a phone call, quick, and you gave away your last dime, was it a spare one? Around Fifth and Mission, always the classic scene: the passed-out, grizzled drunk alongside the empty wine bottle. A cliché tragedy that has lost its power to evoke compassion.

Passing parade of quadraphony stereotypes, scruffy kids playing nickel flutes on corners (isn't the scruffy look a bit passé?), executive honchos in their fifties wearing with-it sideburns down to their jowls and driving macho cars that are now an obscenity, right-on blacks carrying radios blaring soul-rock so loud the distortion is distorted and muttering: "Cool, man." Is it still cool to say "cool"? Well, maybe so, since some of the terms from my hep, not hip, childhood, like "truckin' " and "boogie," have made a comeback. Our cool and hip, not hep, symphony conductor, Maestro Ozawa, might even consider having his shoulder-length hair bobbed a bit. Long hair no longer proves anything.

"Follow your nose," the friendly neighborhood philosopher once said. Since my roamin' nose wanders all over my face, that isn't easy, but walking the streets of San Francisco is rewarding in any direction and much safer than driving in the path of flying nuns. At "Nut Corner"—Powell and Market —two sidewalk preachers, a white man and a black woman, were shouting of love and looking at each other with hate. Three Muni men went back-to-back against a Powell cable, swinging it around on the turntable in the dearest San Francisco cliché of all. The latest in a line of small boys who have watched this scene in wonder for a hundred years watched this scene in wonder.

I walked where I always walk when I have no place in particular to walk to. Into the Tenderloin. It may be too strong to say I love the Tenderloin, but I dig it. Every city should have one. Going a step further, any city that doesn't have a Tenderloin isn't a city at all, but more likely seven shopping centers in search of a tradition a little more exciting than freeway markers reading "Next 10 Exits." The manic-progressives keep trying to knock and knock down our Tenderloin but so far they haven't made it. Their heavy handiwork is, however, painfully visible South o' Market, which now resembles London during the blitz and is likely to stay that way for a long time if we're damn lucky.

The Tenderloin—breakfast all day, moving shadows behind drawn curtains all night. Leather-clad beauties whose wardrobes are a misdemeanor and whose chrome pimp-mobiles are a felony. Foot cops looking warily at hookers who look back wearily. Faded old 110 Eddy, once the open-all-night headquarters of a dynasty presided over by Dutch White. Restaurants with flyspecked windows and greasy menus on which the prices have been changed once too often. Chinese, Greek, Armenian, roadside American, babble of a dozen tongues and smells of a dozen cultures mixing with the musty mélange of age, urine, poverty, dogs; hopelessness with its collar turned up and a hole in its shoes.

The Tenderloin—so what's to like? Rundown blocks, rundown people, rundown apartment houses between the big and sterile Federal Building on one side (is that what we really want?) and the Hilton Schmilton on the other. What's to like is the action, the struggle to survive on one's own terms, the togetherness of losers and loners . . . Hands in raincoat pocket, head down, I walk among the poor, the sad and the ugly, one of them. It would be sentimental and nice to say that they all have hearts of gold, but I wouldn't count on it.

Once More, with Feeling

"TAKE ME out to the ball game, take me out to the park . . ."

The late Albert Von Tilzer wrote that, and it is certainly one of the great American songs, right up there with George M.'s "Yankee Doodle Dandy." A song filled with sunny innocence and the bounciness of a brash country that was still young enough to enjoy a child's game played by overgrown children.

"Buy me some peanuts and Cracker Jack, I don't care if I ever get back!"

Peanuts a nickel, hot dogs a dime, and so what if they *were* made of puppy dogs' tails? The country had strong stomachs to go with the strong backs that, ran the wisdom of the day, accompany weak minds. A hot dog should have mustard on top of it and a ball game behind it, otherwise what's the pernt? . . . "I don't care if I ever get back"—what a fine carefree line. Today the complaint is that baseball is too slow, but back then a game simply couldn't go on too long. Besides, what was there at home? No radio, no TV. A windup phonograph or a player piano, if you were lucky, grinding out "Roses of Picardy" on a stifling summer night.

"Root-root-root for the home team, if they don't win it's a shame . . ."

It really was a home team. The kids you went to school with, suddenly almost grown up, chaw of tobacco in cheek, wearing the spangles and performing before the home town crowd. No mercenaries then, no teams changing names and uniforms at the drop of a franchise. As the double domes would put it today, you could *identify,* and when the kid went up to the Bigs, the Majors, the Land of Titans to the East, you felt proud and awed . . . (To those who maintain that winning is everything and a matter of life and death, I would like to point out the wisdom of the late Albert Von Tilzer. If the home team loses, it's only a "shame," no big deal.)

"So it's one-two-three strikes you're out at the old ball game!"

Moreing Field, the Coast League park in Sacramento, was where I fell in love with the old ball game that no longer exists. For a dime you could sit in the bleachers and get splinters and a sunburn and a great view of the left fielder, a beer barrel on legs named Merlin Kopp, who had deceptive speed. The grass was greener than any grass before or since. The players wore real flannel uniforms, cotton sweat shirts and woolen socks that must have been hot as hell. On opening day, the uniforms were as pristine and beautiful as

Gatsby's shirts. The first time a player slud and got his pants dirty, we all said: "Awww."

(These days the grass, the uniforms, most of the parks and quite a few of the players are strictly synthetic. Also, except for a respectable few, they wear ridiculous socks that show too much of the white "sanitaries." Every team looks like the White Sox.)

When I didn't have a dime, I stood around outside Moreing Field, waiting for a foul or a home run. If you brought the ball back, you got in free. One day, before the game, the clubhouse door opened and a god named Wilbur Davis, the Sacs' first baseman, said, "Hey, kid, run across the street and get me a hamburger and a beer, willya?" When I came back, he let me into the clubhouse for my first sniff of liniment, my first look at supermen suiting up, spitting, swearing and other "s" words.

A fop at ten, I was wearing plus fours and shoes with floppy leather fringes, a character out of a Fitzgerald novel yet to be written. "You gonna be a golfer, kid?" asked Davis. "Gosh, no, Mr. Davis," I said. "I want to be just like you." He shook his head and belched.

Remembrance of Flings Past

PAUL ROBESON, singer, actor, all-American football player, and very black, walks up to the bar of the Mark's Peacock Court and says smiling: "Scotch and soda, please." The bartender sets the drink before him and says icily: "That'll be ten dollars." Still smiling, Robeson lays a twenty-dollar bill on the bar and purrs. "Won't you join me in a drink?" . . . Later, Robeson goes to Vanessi's for dinner, is refused a table, and files suit—perhaps the first suit of this nature ever undertaken in San Francisco. Joe Vanessi looks hurt. "Why don't he tell me who he is?" he complained to

203

me. "If he tell me he's Jackie Robinson, I let him have a table any time!"

Nostalgia is a thing of the past. The dread San Francisco disease. But as I move around the old town, every corner, every crook and nanny, produces memories that are still surprisingly sharp. The incidents described in the first paragraph happened three decades ago and could not happen today, in this enlightened age (only slight sarcasm there), but whenever I go into the Mark, I think of Robeson's classy gesture, and at Vanessi's, I remember his anger.

The Mark, a Gatsby hotel of the Fitzgerald era. When Prohibition ended, owner George D. Smith rolled the first barrel of beer through the lobby and into the Lower Bar, only it wasn't called Lower then because the Top had yet to be built. I don't remember what they called it, but a lot went on there, under its glass ceiling. On bandleader Skinnay Ennis's opening night in Peacock Court, a suicide leaped from an inside window and landed on that glass, one arm dangling gruesomely over the first-nighters below.

"I hate crashers," mumbled Skinnay, downing a double and looking faint. Then he stumbled inside to play his theme song, "Got a Date with an Angel," as an ambulance sirened up to remove the man who'd kept his date with death . . . A few years later, George Vanderbilt jumped to his death from an outside window of the Mark, landing on the Mason Street hill. The village idiot witnessed the tragedy from across the street and couldn't wait to phone George Smith's son, Hart, then running the hotel. "Hey, Hart," said the idiot, "your scion fell down."

Windmills of the mind, revolving backwards. I walk past the old City of Paris, whose walls will tumble soon. How many remember that Station KFRC used to have its studios there, its call letters shining from a rooftop antenna—and what did those letters stand for? "Keep Freely Radiating Cheer." Wow! . . . Anybody remember the handsome mounted cop who used to patrol around Union Square? I mean handsome. Mounted more than his horse, he did, and once too often; he finally left The Force under a cloud of kisses. Anyway he had dash and color and never forgot to remove his spurs in the clinch.

The St. Francis on Big Game Night the Cal and Stanford bands marching through a lobby from which every stick of furniture, every carpet, everything breakable had been removed . . . Across the street, the Golden Pheasant, with its delicious confection, Small Blacks, and its tall windows opening on the sights of the then simple city. Up the block, wraiths in chiffon swayed to "Blue Skies" at the tea dansant in Marquard's, satin draperies and crystal chandeliers bugging the eyes of a kid from Sacramento.

Nostalgia, a lousy way to live but a great way to die, suffocated in mauve velvet and dusty sentimentality.

Bill Hewitt had the town sized up: "Small enough so you think you know everybody and big enough so you don't." A neat town, everybody and everything in its place. The cops were the mob, ran the wisdom of the day, and the bag men carried real bags. When an outside hood tried to muscle in, two inspectors took him to Third and Townsend and put him on a train with a one-way ticket . . . I stroll past Third and Market and think of the *Examiner*'s Bill Wren, who ran the town. One recent day in North Beach, I saw the police towing away an *Examiner* truck. That couldn't have happened in Bill Wren's day. If it had, there'd have been a new Chief the next morning . . .

"How come we don't have as many laughs as we used to?" the old-timers mope. I don't know. Maybe we used them up.

Destruction Derby

I STOOD AT Fourth and Mission and watched the saber-toothed bulldozer strutting about with a pile of debris in its mouth, like a retriever with a pheasant. Crunch, chomp, splat . . . In the holy name of Redevelopment, another corner of oldish San Francisco was being chewed to bits, and once again, I was boggled at how fast a landmark—even an eyescore of a landmark—can be made to disappear.

In what seemed like the twinkling of an eyebeam, the doomed area was flat as a Henny Youngman joke. I tried to remember what had been there just a few hours before—for at least fifty years—but out of sight, etc. Certainly there had been a saloon, featuring watery beer and wheyfaced old-timers who never took their hats off. At least one bookie joint, which had its front light on when it was safe to enter. A skinny shoeshine stand, one door wide, run by a clean old man who was careful not to get polish on your socks.

Gone, like that. Fwoosh. Nothing for the landmarks people to get excited about, obviously, but still a slice of the city, a place where a few score people gathered every day and, in the horrid term, "related" to each other in a semblance of life.

Across the street, a steel ball, known in trade as a "headache tablet," was being swung with devastating results against the tired brick walls of the Milner Hotel, "Coast-to-Coast," as the sign proclaimed. The Milner was the hotbed of the revolt against Yerba Buena Convention Center, and now it was getting its comeuppance or pulldownance. Whack. Whap. Gaping holes appeared in the hoary walls, which, if they could talk, would have sad tales to tell of mothers' sons gone astray, golden girls laid low by fate's fickle finger. Windows shattered, frames flew through the air, curtains flapped for the last time.

And so the way has been paved at last for Yerba Buena Center, just a glimmer in Downtown's eye twenty years ago and not much more than a glimmer now. But when something promises to cost around $250 million, it has to be built. Like the *Titanic*. I mean, we're not playing with kids around here. Not when insanity is available.

Back on the "right" side of Market, the street life continues to be as lively (i.e., freaky) as you'll find anywhere west of New York, but we could use a few street-corner vending stands. Now and then, wouldn't you rather have a hot soft pretzel than a cold hard chorus on a conga drum? Union Square is beginning to look like a plaza in a small Mexican town, not that this is all bad. The wrong people sit in the sun, stripped to the waist, looking either fat and ugly or thin and ugly. On the Geary Street sidewalk, peddlers and their wares, with white-shod tourists clucking around to be plucked of their chicken feed.

A busy scene, to be sure, but light years away from the time when Union Square, like Fifth Avenue or Boul' Mich', was a synonym for something called "smartness," meaning proper dark clothes and Minnie Mouse white gloves, I guess. Looking over these motleys, listening to the pitches and the cons and the crummy music, I had to laugh at the way Stanley Marcus is being made to toe the line, hat in hand, in his efforts to build a Neiman-Marcus store across the street. Hasn't it occurred to anyone that we're lucky to get him?

Of course, he's lucky to get us, too, us with the egg on our face, flower in thinning hair.

Drove along Washington by Lafayette Square, admiring the mansions of the mighty: McGinnis of the Southern Pacific, Magowan of Safeway, Spreckels of the sugar. Big discreet apartment houses with doormen to match and houseboys walking dogs along enchanted paths. City dogs, ugh, turning our parks and streets into comfort stations and our sidewalks into minefields . . . But we shall get through, never fear, Gridley, and I'll meet you later at the Milner for a nightcap, okay?

☆　☆　☆

IN THE WAKE of the Patty Hearst case, I discovered that the music library at UC-Berkeley is so up to date that its files even contain the score and libretto of an opera with the following plot: "A beautiful young woman is kidnapped by an organization which has ambitions to change the world. At first, she pleads to be rescued, but finally decides to denounce her family and remain with her abductors."

You knew all the time it was Mozart's *Magic Flute,* didn't you?"

VALIANT if clunky pun inspired by the sight of Senator Thurmond slurping chowder at Fisherman's Wharf: "Is this the clam before the Strom?"

JULIAN GROW'S wisdom: "Ours seem to be the only nation on earth that asks its teen-agers what to do about world affairs and tells its golden-agers to go out and play."

☆ ☆ ☆

WORDS OF one syllable (big sign in the city of Oakland's summer camp, up near Quincy): "Sick Call After Every Meal."

☆ ☆ ☆

LIST OF ITEMS available at a garage sale in San Clemente, occasioned by a suddenly canceled lease: One Quaker Bible, never used; a set of worry beads, worn; large used suitcase, laundered; one copy, "How to Speak Chinese in One Easy Lesson"; unused portion Washington-San Clemente-Washington plane ticket; pumpkin, hollow, very old; copy of General Motors invoice for one white Eldorado Cadillac delivered to Moscow; two dozen no deposit-no return milk bottles; one copy, "How to Fight Inflation," unused pages uncut; Disneyland "Jungle Ride" blazer with initials "R.Z." (may be withdrawn); 432 deleted expletives; one woman's good cloth coat, faded on one side due to flash bulbs; foot-operated tape-erasing switch, used only once by Little Old Lady; used car which owner has been unable to sell.

☆ ☆ ☆

STEWART HAMILTON, browsing TWA's Skyliner mag, came across another prime piece of nostalgia—these instructions to the airline's first stewardesses on May 15, 1930: "Before each flight, clean cabin, sweep floor, dust seats, window sills, etc. Make sure all seats are securely fastened to floor. Warn passengers against throwing cigars and cigarettes out the windows. Carry a railroad timetable in case plane is grounded. Keep an eye on passengers when they go to the

208

lavatory to be sure they don't mistakenly go out the emergency exit" . . . All that and "Coffee, tea or parachute?" too.

☆ ☆ ☆

WHILE MUSING alongside the wishing well fountain outside the de Young Museum, Berkeley's Randall H. Alfred composed the following notice to be posted there, in keeping with the times:

"Effective this date, pennies will no longer be accepted for the processing of wishes. Coins of denominations of five cents and upwards will continue to be accepted as before. We sincerely regret this step, which has been necessitated by the drastically rising costs of supplies, labor and overhead.

"This in no way alters our previous plan to convert to electronic data processing of wishes on Jan. 1, 1976. Subsequent to that date, as per our previous notification, all applications for wish-fulfillment should be mailed on the appropriate form to Educational Testing Service in Berkeley."

Faded Summer Love

THE CAMPERS, two-legged and four-wheeled, are heading home from all over the West. Back packers struggle out of their gear and the obligatory sawed-off jeans, sink into a hot tub, anybody's, murmuring, "Oh, my aching" (fill in blank). Swarming down from the mountaintops and lake fronts, the giant American station wagons, jammed with bratty kids (theirs) and wonderful young people (ours and our friends'). Everywhere, hitchhikers taking their lives in their thumbs: it is as dangerous to be picked up as it is to do the picking up . . . On Interstate 80, kids seeking that last precious infusion of sunburn were sticking their fine legs out of car windows. Is it worth the chance of becoming Instant

209

Toulouse-Lautrec to achieve the most golden tan on the block? Obviously and apparently and let us hope not tragically so.

Vacation is over, the highways and freeways a sight to be labeled with Norman Rockwellian brilliance, "America on the Move!" There you were, trying to hold the speedometer needle at a steady fifty-five (and failing), surrounded by every kind of pleasure-loving gear known to this pleasure-loving nation: cars with four racing bikes stacked upside down on rooftops (good show, ecological soundness), cars with trail bikes lashed to the rear (bad, polluters, disturbers of the peace), cars towing Chris-Crafts fishtailing dangerously from lane to lane, cars teetering under overloads of rubber rafts, surfboards and motorcycles . . . And the new breed of superpatriot: the man, generally in a gas-guzzling Cadillac, who hogs what formerly was known as "the fast lane" with his windows up, air-conditioner on and his cruise control set at fifty-five. If anyone passes him in the former middling to slow lanes, he honks his horn, scowls, gives the "V" sign, sometimes with only one finger, and points at his American Flag decal. He is absolutely right and absolutely self-righteous and probably politically to the right, which may have nothing or everything to do with it.

Recently I recorded that S.F.'s Hunt Conrad, at a party in La Jolla, had remarked that he was going to "the Grove" the following weekend, inspiring a Southern Californian to explode, *"The* Grove, *The* City, *The* Bay—you San Franciscans are really incredible. Don't you think there are any other groves, cities and bays in this state?" To that list might be added *"The* Lake" (the answer to the Southern Californian's question, by the way, is no).

The Lake can only be Tahoe, which either Mark Twain or Edward (Bud) Scott dubbed "The Blue Pearl of the High Sierra," and blue it still is, as blue as those who plunge into its icy waters. For San Franciscans of a certain habit-bound class, Pebble Beach, Carmel Valley, Sonoma and Napa, and even Yosemite are very much within vacation range, but Tahoe, northern end thereof, remains the logical high altitude extension of Nob Hill, Pacific Heights and the Peninsula.

It should be added that for another kind of San Franciscan, the kind who prefers Las Vegas, Palm Springs and the Nevada side of the Lake, and is a secret white shoes freak, Tahoe's northern end remains irrevocably Nowhere, strictly for the birds and bores, a feeling that is warmly reciprocated.

Tahoe, the continuing fight to preserve the old and familiar, the endless if unarticulated battle between the First Familes and the last to arrive, the clash between styles and cultures. As presumably, "the views belong to everyone" in San Francisco, yet seem to be owned mainly by the powerful, so an "unspoiled Tahoe," theoretically, is everyone's to use as he sees fit, but some ideas are fitter than others, and in the eyes of the First Families, highrises, supermarkets, and more casinos are the least fitting of all.

"Those rich people," a Nevada entrepreneur says bitterly, "think they own the lake." The rich people, old sport, own everything, whether they're in the Social or the Cash Register.

Old Tahoe, with its smell of dusty pine, its skinny piers, its lake-front houses set back among the trees, is infinitely the best of what is left, as it always has been. Status symbols: two-boat boathouses with an overflow boat or two, a sailboat, a "compound" of comfortable (never chic) houses, whose population includes at least three generations of the same family.

Tahoe in pink dusk: talk about your purple-mountain'd majesty, rimming a blue lake now shading into green, and a smog-free full moon, probably owned by Bill Harrah, rising out of Nevada to spill creamlight over the swells—those on the lake as well as in the fancy houses. Around midnight, in the silence at lake as well as in the fancy houses. Around midnight, in the silence at lake center, with the cruiser idling, you can almost imagine you hear Dick Jurgens' band floating out from Globin's . . . "A Faded Summer Love" . . . "Leaves come tumbling down, 'round my head, some of them are brown, some are red . . ."

Ye gods, that was back in '31 or '32, but some things remain evergreen at *the* lake, especially summer loves.

☆ ☆ ☆

THIS PAST SUMMER, the bee-busy Delancey Streeters somehow found time to take fifty kids a day, from "disadvantaged" neighborhoods, on tours to Alcatraz. One day, the guide pointed out a solitary confinement cell—"Just this tiny room, with a toilet and a bed"—at which an incredulous voice from the ghetto piped up to inquire, "You mean he had a whole room to himself?"

☆ ☆ ☆

MERRILL LYNCH may be "bullish on America" but one of its officials is a bit bearish about the New York Stock Exchange adding thirty minutes daily to its trading time in an attempt to increase business. Observes Bob Farrell, a Merrill Lynch vice-president in New York, in a message received here by broker Lou Bartolini: "If everyone was having a good time, it would add to the fun to ask the band to play an extra half hour. Until the party gets more congenial, however, the crowd is hardly likely to dance any faster."

☆ ☆ ☆

BOB ORBEN, President Ford's gag writer, may lose his job for this: "I don't know if we're in a recession or a depression but I just saw a pawn shop with an express lane."

☆ ☆ ☆

A TOAST: "Here's to Ronald Reagan's performance as governor," salutes Walter Jacobs. "I don't know whether it was well done but it certainly got Brown on both sides."

☆ ☆ ☆

UNANSWERED QUESTION: Oakland's Esther and Mike Preston, visiting Yellowstone Park, listened attentively to a ranger lecturing on what he called "The Little Fellers." Advised the ranger in conclusion: "Go into the forest and sit

212

very quietly. Pretty soon the little fellers will come out where you can watch them. It will be a wonderful experience, which you will always treasure." "Uh," interrupted Mike, "what if you're sitting there very quietly, waiting for the little fellers, and a big feller comes along?"

UNLIMITED RISIBILITY: S.F.'s Jim Tishler, visiting Kyoto, Japan, was stopped by a giggling bevy of uniformed schoolgirls, one of whom said, "Trying out English—what's your name?" When Jim told them, they dissolved in shrieks of laughter. Most mystifying, till one girl gasped to another: "I told you—they *all* named Jim or Bill!"

☆ ☆ ☆

AMAZED VISITOR to Dan Bunker: "How come there's so much traffic here on Sunday mornings?" "Early Mass transit," replied Dan.

☆ ☆ ☆

MEMBERS OF the San Francisco Pro Musica orchestra returned from a tour of Alaska, where they had to buy a plane seat for their biggest instrument. Since Alaska Airlines' computers are programmed to reject any seat holder without a name, researchers will someday discover that in November 1974, a Ms. Harp C. Chord flew from Wrangell to Anchorage . . . This information will undoubtedly find its way into the column of some future Alaskan three-dot columnist, poor soul.

Passing Parade

IT WAS A beautiful Sunday morning and then the phone rang. Ben Wright, on the horn from New York, said in a choked voice, "Make yourself a drink, old cockeroo, and drink a toast—Connie died last night."

I lifted a glass and looked through it toward the past, to the days and nights that had been enlivened by the rollicking presence of Cornelius (Connie) Ryan, journalist, courageous adventurer, good guy in good times and bad. "Born with the gift of laughter," as Sabatini wrote about someone else, "and a sense that the world was mad."

It was sadly ironic that Ben Wright had phoned at that moment because I had just been scanning the weekly bestseller list and there was Ryan's book, *A Bridge Too Far,* in second place and undoubtedly on its way to the top. As I was imagining how pleased he must have been feeling, he was already dead.

Only a month earlier, he had phoned in exultation. "Old cockeroo," he said in his favorite term for aging friends, "it looks like a winner—a million one hundred thousand in hard cover. But you'll never know what it took out of me just to finish the damn thing."

Of course we all knew, and so did he. Cancer was killing Connie Ryan but he was determined to meet what he called "the last deadline before the last deadline." A year or so ago he was at Stanford Medical Center, "very much off the record, kid—it makes people nervous when they think you're dying and then if you don't die they get sore at you."

In and out of great pain, he kept working away at his book "because two books do not a trilogy make" and he was determined to memorialize World War II, his war, in three volumes. The first, *The Longest Day,* was a brilliant success and made him a hero, even among his fellow war correspondents, who needled him lovingly as "The Man Who Invented D-Day." His second book, *The Last Battle,* covered the fall of Berlin, and his latest and last, *A Bridge Too Far,* covers a battle that obsessed him, the Allied airborne disaster in Arnhem, Holland, thirty years ago.

In September, anniversary of the debacle, he and Ben Wright and a handful of survivors went back to Arnhem, to be greeted by his old friend, Prince Bernhard. It was a perfect launching for Connie's book, and the Prince laid on a great show. Connie had invited me to join the thinning crowd—"It'll be the last reunion, you know"—but I begged off with lame excuses, like "Who wants to celebrate a defeat?" and now I am sorry, for he sounded hurt.

Connie Ryan, dead at fifty-four, a wild and even rather wild-eyed Irishman, a helluva newspaperman, an Olympian drinker and talker, one war correspondent to whom the term "dashing" actually applied. He never stopped dashing, trench-coat collar up, eyes ablaze with the fever of great events. In the company of the most sterling group of reporters ever assembled, he was a standout.

Some of the names and faces are beginning to fade. Was it Ed Kennedy of the AP who broke the release date on the signing of the German surrender? Who cares any longer? If Ryan was the man who invented D-Day, Walter Cronkite was the man who invented the air war, flying more missions in bombers than most flight crews, and at United Press's niggardly wages, too. Charles Collingwood was a young CBS reporter—imagine trying to cover a war with a microphone. Bob Cromie of the Chicago *Tribune,* now a mild-mannered book critic, was "Task Force Cromie" then, jeeping ahead of the combat patrols. Hemingway took the bows, Cromie took the chances.

Joe Willicombe, John Thompson, Bob Capa, Collie Small —and Connie Ryan. The Last Man's Club is nearing the last meeting.

Cornelius Ryan died on the hundredth anniversary of the birth of one of his heroes, Winston Churchill. That very morning, the *Examiner* had seen fit to comment editorially on these ill-chosen words from *Rolling Stone* magazine, which had described Sir Winston as "an egotistical, reactionary, bombastic, blundering, drunken show-off."

A hundred years from now, who will remember *Rolling Stone,* but meanwhile, this publication might eke out a little respect for a man who helped make its existence possible (how *do* you say Rolling Stone in German?). Its editor, of course, is too young to remember when England stood alone, rallied only by this "drunken show-off's" ability to mobilize the English language in the name of honor and gallantry.

In honor of Connie Ryan and the British bulldog, I went

to Grace Cathedral for the evensong observing the centenary of Sir Winston's birth. Both men would have loved it: trumpets and banners, dignity and solemnity, the great cathedral echoing to the slow step of old men and young. The Black Raven Pipers Band marched off to "Amazing Grace," there in amazing Grace, with organist John Fenstermaker adding pedal tones that shook Nob Hill.

"The shining stars marked their shining deeds," sang the gifted chorus, clear voices of the boy sopranos shining, too. Tears glistened on cheeks, and in the context, words like "liberty" and "democracy" seemed newly minted. "A rejoicing is necessary to the human spirit," Churchill once said, and let us rejoice that men like Sir Winston and Connie Ryan walked this earth.

The Cars That Were

CADILLAC, "American Standard For The World," may be making a mistake in its slick and glossy magazine ads. In the foreground we see the latest models, looking for all the world, give or take a chrome strip or two, like the '74, the '73, and the '72. (We've come to a pretty pass when all Cadillacs look alike, but there's the pass, and isn't it pretty?) In the background is displayed a Cadillac from the early 1930s, representing a phenomenon impossible to explain satisfactorily. Why, in the depths of this country's worst depression, were the truly classic U.S. cars being produced? The Pierce-Arrows, Duesenbergs, twelve-cylinder Packards, Lincolns and Cadillacs of that era were marvels of elegance and luxury at a time when 15 million Americans were unemployed.

The "old" Cadillac shown in the latest ad is a 1931 phaeton whose spirited and rakish style puts to shame the "new" Cads, which simply appear lumpish, oversized and lacking in imagination. The '31 is long and lean, its aristocratic profile set off by a graceful, flying radiator ornament. With its side-mounted wire wheels, its great chrome lamps, the luggage rack and true white sidewalls, this car is alive, even now, with romance, the lure of the open road, the promise of adventure.

It exemplifies what the experience called "motoring," as opposed to just getting there, was all about. Built at a time when most people couldn't afford even a used Model T, these great automobiles represented Detroit's finest hour. They were a shining goal to strive for "when our ship comes in" and the "bad times" were over. Americans still believed prosperity was just around the corner, in the dazzling form of that '31 Cadillac phaeton.

Cadillac: pinnacle of the American dream (since subject to change) and symbol of having Made It, whatever "it" was. A very recently barefoot boy with cheek from Sacramento, I found myself buying my first Cadillac, much to my amazement, in 1941.

Oh, unforgettable day: I was driving up Van Ness in my used '40 Buick when I saw the Dream Car in the window of Don Lee, then the Cadillac distributor here—a bottle green convertible with a vast tan top, green leather upholstery, a proud chrome prow topped by a full-breasted chrome lady, hair streaming in the wind. I parked (parking was easy in those days) and walked inside to admire this unattainable perfection at closer quarters. The price tag: $2,250.

Don Lee's chief, Fred Pabst, strolled through the showroom just then. "Why don't you buy it, kid?" he grinned. "Can't afford it," I sighed. "What're you driving now?" he asked. When I pointed to the faded Buick, he said, "I gotta be crazy but I'll give you $1,250 for it. Do you have $1,000?" I nodded dumbly (actually, I had $1,037). "Okay," said Fred, "write me a check for $1,000 and you can drive out of here in this Cadillac right now."

I did so. All this and thirty-seven dollars too!

No car since has given me such a boot. I drove straight to the Marina Green, where I parked and got out to study this incredible work of art. I sprawled on the grass, gazing at its multifaceted perfection. I walked across the street to admire it from afar. It was love. "It's perfect," I said to myself. "I will keep it forever. Nothing could possibly be better than this one. I will never change it." Since then I have said the same thing about wives, friends, houses and other cars, meaning it sincerely every time.

My generation may have been the last star-struck one where cars are concerned, or do I mean car-struck? The annual auto shows of the late 1920s and 1930s were great events, with elaborate shows headlining Paul Whiteman, Jack Benny, Bob Hope, Chevalier, Cantor. Incredible as it seems now, the models changed every year—completely. We could hardly wait to see how the '29 Chrysler compared with the '28, how different the '32 Buick would be from the '31, what new tricks they would come up with at Franklin, Graham-Paige and Marmon.

The decline and fall of car-as-symbol has been particularly traumatic for most of our crowd. In our salad days, there was no television, radio was in its infancy, and only the car and the movies symbolized glamor and excitement. In our dreams, the top was always down on the raciest car ever built, and we were behind the wheel, the cigarette dangling insouciantly from our lips, Constance Bennett (or Clara Bow or Laura La Plante) snuggling at our side.

The dream dies hard. The car today is more enemy than friend, even though we are still addicted. Worse, they all look alike. The cigarette is a killer. Constance Bennett turned out to be fickle, and the world is running out of resources. And yet—we are still being urged to buy Cadillacs. I can resist. After all, I had the best, back there in 1941.

On Caring

"IT'S EASY to criticize," scold the critics of the critics, but it isn't, not if you love a city. You want it to be perfect, pink-purple and poetic, the way it appeared in the old E. H. Suydam drawings, all graceful building casting soft shadows over god-like people, a few of whom were allowed to be Oriental. In that idealized San Francisco of the 1920s, blacks lived elsewhere and nobody was poor.

I was musing on Mr. Suydam's sketches, and the innocent prose of Charles Caldwell Dobie, as I walked along Fifth toward the New Market Street. When they were producing their glowing books about San Francisco, there must have been a seamy side to the city, too, yet somehow they managed to be seen on sidewalks, no blind beggars bumped into legless ones, the streets were never torn up, and the skies were of a Maxfield Parrish perfection.

Were these earlier chroniclers as blind as the beggars, or simply able, in their Bohemian Club style, to look upon the bright side exclusively? If so, I envied them, even though their portrait of the city must have been overblown. Or maybe the city really was more pleasant when the dread words "traffic jam" hadn't been invented. Well, an exercise in futility. We'll never know, so we must take the city as it is today, the bitter with the better . . .

Between the Pickwick and Lankershim hotels, this grizzled old drunk was passed out, his head flat on the sidewalk next to a planter filled with guck. Passers-by were going to great lengths to avoid looking at him, some stepping across his body while gazing heavenward. Drunks are part of the San Francisco story, aren't they? I stared just long enough to make sure he wasn't one of my old city editors, then dialed the police. We have a million of 'em and the sight is always depressing.

Market and Powell, crossroads of our world, the air made foul by the constant machine gunning of pneumatic drills. A black in wide-brimmed hat, long flared coat and platform shoes bumped into me and muttered a highly favored twelve-letter word, but his heart wasn't in it. An automatic. An old white guy was playing "Red River Valley" badly on an accordion, so I gave him a quarter. He had paid his dues. When I failed to favor a conga drummer, too young to have paid any dues, he gave me the twelve-letter word. "Up yours," I said with a thumb and a smile.

219

I gazed down into Hallidie Plaza, a frozen expanse of prison-gray stone with a few scrawny trees planted here and there. Even on a sunny noonday it made you shiver, this centennial tribute to the inventor of the cable car. If you like the yard at San Quentin you'll love Hallidie Plaza, but when the trees are in leaf and street musicians are playing it will look less like a bear pit.

One hopes so. It's not easy to criticize. You have to care.

When I get down about the city I drive to Potrero Hill, with its eternal verities (civilized Bohemia, simplicity, good talk over cheap wine) and around Buena Vista Park for its tree-framed views of church and bridge towers (yes, it IS the most beautiful of American cities) and past the great old houses of the rich, each time noticing a rare one you hadn't seen before, or a winding street leading to a walled and secret garden.

And then to the rarest treasure, Golden Gate Park on a car-free Sunday morning, the air wet and clean, the meadows green with the promise of spring. Not a single automobile: the silence is deafening, you can actually hear the branches dripping moisture, squirrels scrambling through the underbrush—and the birds! Hundreds of redbreasted robins bobbing across the lawns, now that there are no cars to frighten them. On Stanyan, the families are renting bikes and heading into the winding trails.

Slowly it dawns on them that they can use the main drive and the roads! For once the world does not belong to the automobile. The bicycle is king again and the rider may go where fancy dictates, without looking nervously over his shoulder. You are even allowed, for a few unrealistic minutes, to reflect on how pleasant life would be if the car were banned in San Francisco.

Slowly, peacefully, pedaling down the middle of the main drive on this wet and wonderful morning, tires humming pleasantly, wire wheels singing. A time-warp sets in and you are soon traveling into the past. The old statue of the baseball pitcher comes to life and pumps a ball in the direction of Uncle John McLaren, standing gruffly amid his flower beds. John Philip Sousa is playing in the bandstand, a horse clip-clops in the distance, a carriage full of laughing young people careens past in a blur of boas and blazers, heading for Tait's at the Beach . . .

There it is, the wonderful and awful thing about San Francisco, the ease with which it can lead you into fantasies about a city that may or may not have existed. But one can't dwell forever on the ugly reality of old drunks passed out on Fifth Street sidewalks, not when there is a convention of robins in the park.

Pavane for a Dead Princess

GRAY AND GLOOMY, a day to reflect on the remarkable death of Ann London Scott, daughter of Claire and the late Dan ("Mr. St. Francis") London. Ann, dead of cancer at forty-five—is the whole world dying of cancer, do we all have an appointment in Samarra to meet the Turk?

Few people faced death more resolutely than Ann. Nobody beats Old Bony, of course, but she tried by the expedient of discussing her terminal condition openly, talking about her reactions on radio and TV, helping a New York *Times* reporter write her obituary, selecting her favorite photo for the newspapers. Maybe it all sounds a little weird but it wasn't, because Ann wasn't pretending to be "brave." She was undoubtedly scared as hell but she felt death, like life, was an experience one should plumb to its very literal depths.

Ann left a touching souvenir, a poem she translated from the Spanish and sent to all her friends shortly before she died. Titled *"Mística,"* it was written by Salvador Díaz Mirón (1853–1928), and this is her version, a solace and a sadness:

If in your garden, when I die,
when I die, a flower appears;
If in a cloud-rumpled sky you see a star,
you see a star no one has ever seen;

221

and a bird comes close and murmurs to you,
murmurs to you with a sweet sound,
opening his beak along your lips
saying the things I have said to you;
that broken sky, and that flower—
they will be my life: changed,
all changed, according to god's law.

They will be my substance under another face—
wing and corrolla, coal and mist;
they will be my thoughts transformed—
odor and air, song and sun.
I am a body—when will they bury me?
I am a traveller—when do I go?
I am a larva, transmuting itself—
when will god's law come to pass
and O my white girl I become
sky and bird, flower and star?

ANN LONDON, 45, vital statistic, dead. Rains fall on the city where we are all dying. At the Golden Gate, foghorns commiserate like old crones. The incoming tide crashes against the sea wall, setting the boats to rocking in Yacht Harbor, chewing away at the stones with foamy power. In Union Square, huddles of wet pigeons press against Mr. Dewey's monument, celebrating a famous victory, as the people scurry-flurry along the pathways, headless under funeral umbrellas.

Across the way, the gray St. Francis, where Ann and her sister played as children, and Dan, most elegant and suave of hotelmen, greeted the MacArthurs and the Eisenhowers and other immortals long dead. Across the street, the late Lefty O'Doul swings his mighty bat on a sign outside his restaurant, flailing base hit after base hit. Even dead, he is hitting. Shortly before he died he said, "If they'd let somebody run for me, I could sit at home plate in a wheel chair and still hit over .300."

☆ ☆ ☆

THE GOOD DIE young at heart, the others get elected to high office, and cancer is now something we can talk about, even eating away at Presidencies, as John Dean said. Is there a cancer of the spirit, too? Can it be willed? All these deaths, all the people we know who are dying: one is almost tempted to sink into foolish mysticism and conjecture that it's nature's revenge, and yet I suppose the statistics show no sudden Everests. They all laughed at the punchy fighter when he observed, "There are people dying today who never died before," but the line ran deeper than he suspected.

Beautiful, lively San Francisco, a city with a tempestuous past and violence in its veins, but never before a city of hate. At midnight, sirens are screeching their hateful songs in George Sterling's cool gray city of love, but George, like Ann and Dan and Lefty and all the others, is dead too.

On a night too cold and lonely for love, he killed himself, becoming sky and bird, flower and star, one with all the Anns of the world. In Golden Gate Park, the magnolias are beginning to bloom and there may be another spring.

Mister Nice Guy

IF THERE'S one thing you can say about me without risking a libel suit, it's that I have terrific manners. As Bill Saroyan wrote one time in the California *Pelican*, "He drives you crazy, he's so polite, jumping up and down every minute, shaking everybody's hand, saying 'Gladda knowya,' 'Nice tuv metcha,' 'thanxamillion' and so on."

All true. It's my Sacramento upbringing. Manners were very large in Sacramento when I was a kid, and my old German mother, the sweet singer of the Saar, was a strict disciplinarian and straightforward: "Look, you're not handsome and you don't have much talent so you had better be polite." "Thank you, Mama," I would say, getting ready to duck.

Along with being straightforward, she had a mean and effective left hook. Also a mezzo-soprano that rattled windows for blocks around the old neighborhood of Twenty-sixth and Q Streets.

Today she could do Memorex commercials. A wonderful mother, wife, musician, cook and belter.

I'll tell you how polite I am. After I dial "POPCORN" and get the time, I say, "Thank you." When I get the recorded announcement that "The number you have reached is not in service at this time," I say, "Gosh, sorry." I have never sent a bottle of wine back for fear of hurting the feelings of someone with purple feet. When I order a hamburger rare and it comes well done and the waiter says, "Howzit?" I say, "Well done." At table, I keep my left hand in my lap or somebody's.

I always jump to my feet when a lady enters the room, usually knocking over the drinks. I jump to my feet when women enter the room, too, and also transvestites. Well, not all transvestites. Only those wearing women's clothes. The other kind are women who wear their vests inside out.

I'm everything a real nonsexist person shouldn't be these days: a chair-pusher, an elbow-holder, a door-opener. The last time I grabbed the elbow of a liberated woman, attempting to help her up the stairs, she turned on me like a vixen, flashing her fangs and snapping, "You some kinda queer? You got an elbow fetish or what? I'm not a cripple." If it weren't for my being so polite and all, she would have become one right then.

In elevators, I always remove my hat, even if I'm the only passenger. If I'm not wearing a hat, I remove my head and hold it under my arm. And to expedite egress, I let those who are going out first, a sentence that may boggle you at first. I was first boggled by it during World War II, when I saw this sign over a cafeteria door: "Kindly Let Those Who Are Going Out First," a difficult sentence to punctuate.

There are many rewards for being polite, most of them in heaven. As I walked into Livingston's department store the other day, which is like stepping back thirty years, I held the door open for a dear elderly person, wearing hat and gloves, who beamed in motherly fashion and said, "Thank God there are still a few gentlemen left in the world." This so embarrassed me that I let go of the door an instant too soon and it hit her square in the rump, knocking her into Notions & Sundries. Of course I was also slightly embarrassed that she was wearing only hat and gloves. Quite well set up for her age, by the way.

As you may have noticed, this is not the golden age of good manners. Here we have these $900 museum-quality trash containers on Market Street, and people keep throwing their debris on the streets or around those dear sycamore trees fighting for life. "Pigs! Pigs! Pigs!" I want to shout at these palpable pigs, but I'm too polite. Also chicken. Some of these pigs are large and probably mean.

Pedestrians bump into you without so much as a "Parmee." Shaggy kids say, "Any spare change?" and when you give them some, do they say, "Thanks"? Of course not. Even though they have yet to pay their dues, like the old winos, they take it for granted. Full marks for honesty, at least, to the young mendicant on Powell who was flashing an Ashleigh Brilliant card showing an outstretched hand and the inscription, "Give Me Some Money To Help Support My Fight Against Materialism."

On crowded busses, equality among the sexes has been achieved: it has been years since I've seen anybody besides me arise to give his seat to a person of the female persuasion. At the Powell cable turntable, the clawing and kicking for a seat grew so fierce that now we all have to stand in line. The motorists, of course, are the worst—a red-eyed crisis at every intersection, blood boiling, gorges rising, fists flailing.

It's all so unnecessary, he said in his calm, well-modulated voice. What gaineth it a man if he jumps a red light and clobbers a pedestrian? It is no way to make friends. In the old days, Yellow Cabs had this message on the windshield, facing the driver, "Wave 'Em Through and Watch 'Em Smile!," something I haven't seen a cabdriver do in years. It's worth a try, though, if you'll pardon the rude suggestion.

San Franciscana

OH, IT'S A CITY, all right. Idle statistic: San Francisco has some eight hundred buildings over seven stories tall, more than the rest of California combined. Places like San Jose, Sacramento and possibly Cucamonga have a tendency to grow out, rather than up, into a series of shopping centers, featuring fast-food outlets with heartburn to match. At last count, San Francisco's chefs could cook in forty-seven languages, all of them lying drippingly on the tongue, and more Vietnamese cooks are arriving every hour on the hour.

The view from Kite Hill, one of the northern flank of Diamond Heights. Off to the right, Potrero Hill floating above a Bay studded with empty oil tankers, riding high. Bernal Heights, a name almost as old as the city itself, staring down at the site of the old Union Iron Works, where ornate battleships once came to life. The peak-roofed flatlands of the old Mission: what was there about this area that once produced major leaguers and world champion fighters and then suddenly went fallow?

Downtown, Newtown, forest of high-rises, anonymous square-tops all in a row. From Kite Hill, you get the proper juxtaposition of Transamerica Pyramid and Bank of America World Headquarters (the latter title is impossible to say without hearing the sound of distant trumpets). At sunset, glittering white point up against black mass, an urban blockbuster.

A city, yes, but the scale is still possible. The hills of Marin and everybody's favorite mountain, Tamalpais, are visible across the dispiriting roof tops. In between, a luminosity: the fog is crawling in, catching the last rays, creating a definitely Japanese aura. The most beautiful bridge in the world hunches one shoulder out of the oriental mist.

A good town, the sycamores now green along Market, over the brick sidewalks that will spew Irish confetti in all directions when the next Big One strikes. Tourists with double-knit faces buying orchid corsages from sidewalk stands thick with carnations and daisies and irises; so who needs orchids? Old Number One, the newest cable car on the Powell line, leaves the turntable, kids pelting themselves against its sides. Knock the Muni all you want, but dedicated craftmen built this blue, white and maroon beauty from scratch —without much scratch to work with, as usual.

Cherry blossoms in Japan-town, where ugly new buildings, not at all Japanese, are replacing irreplaceable Victorians. Sukiyaki palaces next to chop suey lunch counters. In Chinatown, chop suey has all but disappeared, but now the aroma of hot dogs and coffee floats through the streets that once sniffed only jasmine tea and dried fish. On Stockton, in "New Hong Kong," old women squat on the sidewalk, selling snails and clams, while in the nearby gutter, frogs strain hopelessly to escape from their wire prisons. The fat man selling them looks like a frog no kiss will ever turn into a prince.

The serendipity that brightens the eye of a city stroller: The Francisca Club's impeccable doors, always gleaming white paint, polished brass fittings. In Stevenson Street far downtown, the editorial offices of the *California Farmer,* topped with an imperial eagle atop a bronze globe, very early Hearstian. Mammy Pleasant's own stand of eucalyptuses, waving in the zephyrs at Octavia and Bush, where her dark mansion once stood (her grave in Napa is cracked and falling apart, covered with poison ivy).

In the midtown supermarkets, more and more genteel impoverished oldsters are buying dog food for the pets they don't own, so you know they are eating it themselves. At the same time, more and more people are letting their dogs go because they can't afford to feed them. Does this mean that killer packs of starving dogs will soon range the city streets, or am I having nightmares again?

Near-naked bodies turning brown on the Union Square greens, Thomas Starr King's tomb at First Unitarian, an oasis of tranquillity alongside the race-track rush of Franklin and Geary, the Montgomery Streeters in their time-warped 1950s uniforms (narrow-brimmed brown hats, baggy three-piece suits with the pants flapping around the ankles over gunboat cordovan brogans—campy now!), the last of the old-time bootblacks stand whose "boys" still snap their rags and whisk-broom your shoulders, the foreign newspapers outside Harold's, next to David's on Geary, and David standing outside of Harold's and . . . Oh, it's a city, all right, up one day, down the next, but moving, always moving.

In a Mist

MEMORIAL DAY. Lift a glass to the city that was, to Cape Horn clippers careening through a bridgeless Gate, Matson's great white *Malolo* heading out to the Sandwich Isles under a canopy of screaming sea gulls, sea lions barking in fright as a city burns, filigreed ferries inching into the Hyde Street slip with a great creaking of pilings, clang of metal gangplank being dropped, high-topped cars with wooden wheels and skinny tires lurching out, one after the other, to struggle up Russian Hill . . . Out at Ocean Beach, proper young ladies shrieking as the Big Dipper plunges straight down to certain destruction, only to rise again, and the Shoot-the-Chutes gondola hits the water with a mighty slap, salt spray ruining many a permanent wave and causing that Bull Pupp enchilada to bark in your innards. Nearby, the merry-go-round spins to mournful melodies, sticky fingers reaching for brass rings that are never there.

A day to remember the dead, even dead cities buried just below the hard surface of Here and Now. A toast to cable cars fallen in the line of duty, marvelous Victorians, destroyed in the line of beauty, "iron monster" streetcars that had leather and wicker seats and match-scratchers of real brass and cowcatchers for cows that were seldom seen on Geary Street. A salute to proper gripmen, motormen and conductors in their honest, shiny black uniforms with leather trimmings, fine peaked caps squared away above fine square faces. They cared, they really cared. They were proud of being part of the finest nickel ride in the world, right here in the most terrific city in the best country ever invented, and let's go have a beer.

Death takes a holiday, and the streets are alive again with ghosts venturing out of the shadows. Doorman Joe "Shreve" Foreman bowing to the ladies (and ladies they were) at Post and Grant, Templeton Crocker at the helm of his long black *Zaca* off Yacht Harbor, Alma de Bretteville Spreckels purring over her pitcher of martinis in her sugar palace on Washington, Little Bill Johnston racing after a lob on the Golden Gate Park tennis courts, Smead Jolley slamming one a mile at Recreation Park, and out at the beach, the first of the great black boxers, Jack Johnson, training with a punching bag and at the end of the session knocking it right out of the socket and into the crowd with one mighty blow.

Rest in peace, Papa Coppa, Mimi Imperato, Silvio Zorzi (better known as Joe Vanessi), Tessie Wall and Frankie Daroux. Toll a bell for Fat Tiny Armstrong bustling around Union Square, chirping away on his bird whistle, ringing up his handouts on a toy cash register. He didn't ask for "spare change"; you gave it to him because he paid his dues, he made you laugh, he got himself up in a goofy costume—and, with his bum ticker, was dying before your very eyes. A moment's silence for Barney Ferguson, butt of every banker's joke, eating millionaires' leftovers at Jack's, and uncover for Felix Hoffman, who hung around the Golden Gate Theater, a lugubrious moocher amid the hootchy-kootchers.

A day dedicated to the death of kings, soldiers, ways of life, and style. A day to remember Lucius Beebe and T-Bone Towser ("How do you like your Rolls-Royce, Mr. Beebe?" "Which one?"), and the Palace's great chef (Lucien Heyraud, all truffles and *foie gras*), and that neat little eating place at Geary and Mason called the Kit Carson (with an invaluable back bar mural by Maynard Dixon), and Izzy Gomez asking Newsman Neil Hitt, "Hey, Neil, you think if I threw some sawdust on the floor I could turn this dump into a joint?" and Steelmogul Bill Gilmore presiding every night at the bar in John's Rendezvous, "The drinks are on me, fill more with Gilmore!"

The Memorial Day Parade: Jake Ehrlich lunching day in and day out in the No. 1 back booth at Fred Solari's on Maiden Lane, Dashiell Hammett writing for peanuts in the Tenderloin, Jack London drinking himself to distraction in search of inspiration, Harry Richman pounding the piano for Sid Grauman at the 1925 fair, Papa Alfred Hertz sitting side-saddle on a stool to conduct the symphony at Civic Auditorium, a quake-frightened Enrico Caruso leaving town with his two most precious possessions intact—his golden voice and his silver-framed autographed photo of the man he admired most, Teddy Roosevelt.

Where are they now, the long, the short and the tall, the *News* and the *Call,* the *Bulletin* and *Post,* Corny Vanderbilt's tabloid and the old newsmen's saloons where they knocked back drinks between editions and gorged on Bay shrimp served free in water tumblers? The shrimp, the crab, the Monterey sardine—they'd last forever, and nobody would ever forget Fremont Older or Gertrude Atherton or Kathleen Norris or John Francis Neyland or Art Hickman or all those kids who marched off to die at Belleau Wood and Kasserine Pass, Inchon and Pleiku . . . but life and memories are short. Remember that today of all days, if only for a long moment.

Play It Again, Sam

THAT'S RIGHT, Sam, you dig: the September song of San Francisco, oratorio for massed foghorns, lament in E flat for outgoing ocean liners (basso profundo), pizzicato polka on a theme of cable car bells, double concerto for double-parked trucks, all of it in counterpoint to a nicely sentimental old song for the midnight hours, perhaps Johnny Green's "Body and Soul."

Play it again, man, for a faded summer love. Fall is rising and the city is the place to be—this city, San Francisco, where you can never be older than middle-aged, and to be young is to be blessed. So much to see, feel, smell, hold. All the wildly corny beauty: great bank of white mist side-stepping into the Bay, white sailboats (like gentle dorsal fins) dancing around a freighter, the Golden Gate Bridge disappearing into the fog as though it had never been completed.

City with a smell all its own—indefinable but undeniable.

Bottle it and make a fortune, this blend of (what's your guess?) sea spray and salt, coffee and whiskey, soy sauce, popcorn and chili beans, a frying hamburger, sweaty perfume in a crowded room and a eucalyptus leaf crushed underfoot. Oh, and the carbon monoxide, never forget the Muni's carbarn monoxide.

Play it again, Sam, something chicly maudlin by Rodgers & Hart—you know, that one with the line that goes "And now I even have to scratch my back myself." That's right. "It Never Entered My Mind," good song for this wasteful, wanton, romantic city perched at the tip of a spit of land, a little ingrowing world far from the great world, here in September, the best month to fall in love with people, places, things.

In love with a city? Maybe it never entered your mind, but in September all things are possible in (Frank Norris's bitter words) "the city that never thinks." In a way, he was right. Don't think, simply sink into the sensations: slice of sunshine between two great slabs of fog-near-the-coast, Bank of America losing its head in (yes) a high-flying deposit overdrawn (oh no) at the fog bank, the mock-medieval tower of St. Dominic's skimming past and in the dappled distance the greenery of Buena Vista Park . . .

Polyglottal city of soaring spires and screeching tires, sirens in the night, jukeboxes in churches and sermons in saloons.

No, Sam, forget "I Left My Heart in San Francisco." That's not a song, that's a travel poster and just as one-dimensional. Little cable cars don't climb halfway to the stars, man. They keep breaking down and even when they don't you're lucky to find one and luckier to get aboard. The song is schlŏck, San Francisco isn't.

What it is is muck and guck and memories, views that take your breath away at the top of hills that take your breath away, tuberculars in Chinatown and tuberoses at Podesta Baldocchi, Black Panthers in the Fillmore and black leopard coats at Roberts Brothers, another glittering season at the Opera House and a lot of out-of-season people eating alone in cafeterias and staring out at a world that doesn't stare back.

Love makes this town go around, Sam, love and hate, pot and booze, despair and buckets of black coffee, most of it stale. But when the wind is fresh off the sea and you're walking in the sunshine with the foghorns already blowing way out there by the Gate, you know this is where you want to be, loving what you see, hating it only for not being what it could be.

"They Can't Take That Away from Me?" Yeah, that's a good song, Sam. Gershwin? Right. "Funny Valentine," "Can't Get Started" and what was that old speakeasy song— "Drunk with Love"? Those are San Francisco songs even if they aren't: slick and sophisticated but still a little tough-sentimental. Something slightly illicit about certain songs with their hints of silk sheets and drawn blinds, champagne at 4 A.M. and breakfast at a place like the Cliff House. Too bad about the Cliff House. It must have been something— once—but weren't we all when those songs were new?

The perfect imperfect city, the blemishes as important (and worthy of love) as the beauty part. The perfectionists are at work again—bury those wires, tear down those billboards, get rid of those signs—but they don't stand a chance and it's just as well. The streets are dirty, clean up the streets! Don't they know that people are slobs, every one of us, sloblike, dreamlike and fine?

The downtown buildings get taller and uglier (from Bauhaus to the bowwows), the old houses in the neighborhood grow gracefully lovelier (our most precious possessions) and the streets teem with hippies and harlots, panjandrums and panhandlers, girls with great legs and beggars with none—a daily passing parade in which even Emperor Norton would not draw a second look. To realize how wonderful this is, you have only to walk the streets of some of the antiseptic suburbs around us . . .

Play it again, Sam—something about San Francisco being alive and well, or even alive and sick. I don't care as long as you put a little heart into it.